Lord o

CheckPoint Press

LORD OF THE DANCE

A True Story About Life With Sai Baba

a novel by

Ishtar

Lord of the Dance
Published through CheckPoint Press

ISBN: 978-1-906628-03-1

All rights reserved
Copyright © 2009 by Ishtar

Cover design by CheckPoint Press. Nataraja image courtesy of Exotic India www.exoticindiaart.com

Interior Book Design and Layout by www.integrativeink.com

No part of this publication may be reproduced, stored in a retrieval system, or transmitted in any form or by any means electronic, mechanical, photocopying, recording, or otherwise, without the written permission of the author or publisher.

CheckPoint Press

CHECKPOINT PRESS, DOOAGH, ACHILL ISLAND, CO. MAYO,
REPUBLIC OF IRELAND
TEL: 098 43779   International: 00353 9843779
email: EDITOR@CHECKPOINTPRESS.COM
WWW.CHECKPOINTPRESS.COM

This book is dedicated to Bhagavan Sri Sathya Sai Baba

*Because You love the Burning-ground,
I have made a Burning-ground of my heart.
Day and night blazes the funeral pyre
That You, Dark One, hunter of the Burning-ground,
May Dance Your eternal Dance.*

Contents

CHAPTER 1 THE DANCE OF KRISHNA 1
CHAPTER 2 THE DANCE MASTER 13
CHAPTER 3 THE DANCE OF THE ENCHANTRESS 29
CHAPTER 4 ON WITH THE DANCE! 41
CHAPTER 5 NATARAJA, THE DIVINE DANCER 53
CHAPTER 6 *LILA*, DIVINE SPORT 69
CHAPTER 7 THE WISH-FULFILMENT TREE 85
CHAPTER 8 THE LOTUS FEET OF THE LORD 107
CHAPTER 9 PADNAMASKAR 121
CHAPTER 10 THE SUMMER OF BLISS 129
CHAPTER 11 THE TASTE OF LOVE 139
CHAPTER 12 THE YOGA OF ACTION 151
CHAPTER 13 WHERE TWO WORLDS TOUCH 163
CHAPTER 14 WHERE TWO WORLDS COLLIDE 175
CHAPTER 15 MOHINI STARTS HER DANCE 189
CHAPTER 16 THE THOUSAND NAMES OF GOD 201
CHAPTER 17 THE LAST DANCE 215
CHAPTER 18 POSTSCRIPT – CHRISTMAS DAY, 2005 227

Chapter 1
The Dance of Krishna

I first danced with the Krishna, the all-pervading Godhead, one autumn evening about seven years ago. I was, I confess, a little drunk at the time. But only a little. In fact, I hadn't drunk enough. I was on the verge of starting yet another pointless, vacuous relationship and I usually had to be very drunk to do that. I only mention this in case you thought that I might have been hallucinating. I wasn't. Having, in the past, taken just about every mind-bending drug known to man—or at least, The Man—I can assure you that two glasses of cheap Chardonnay were barely enough to blur the edges, which, as I said, was my dilemma.

My problem, that evening, was Jamie, a young man with the looks of an angel, who was lounging next to me on my sofa. He was starting to run his arm along the back of it, and his normally soft grey eyes were beginning to harden with calculations about how best (and how soon) he could decently get me into the bedroom.

It was all I could do not to let out a sigh.

Here we go again, I thought. *First we'll have the initial protestations of undying devotion. Then the inevitable fumbled coupling. And following immediately on will come the interminable justifications about how right we are for one another until finally, one of us, probably me, will be forced to admit, well... actually, no.... this wasn't such a good idea after all.*

So I stood up and went to poke the fire. When I sat back down, it was in the straight-backed armchair facing him.

But why so jaded? Well, I was in my mid-40s by now, with two failed marriages and countless other relationships, liaisons and one-night stands behind me. I'd always had to be in love, you see. I was like a love junkie, continually needing the next fix from Cupid's arrow.

It wasn't my fault, though. I was just like anyone brought up in the Western world of the Fifties. Conditioned by Doris Day films and songs about love and marriage going together like a horse and carriage, I was convinced that, somewhere out there, was my Mr Right.

However, the Sixties came and went, and so did several men. I duly learned to Love the One I'm With and lose my Fear of Flying. Yet still I believed that my perfect other half, my soul mate, was probably just around the corner. So I kept searching, despite the fact that each such encounter was becoming increasingly more desperate—and each candidate, less likely.

The truth was, I couldn't survive without thinking that each man I was with was potentially my next husband. I couldn't even get out of bed in the morning without at least kidding myself that I was in love with someone and that he was in love with me. It worked well enough too, for a good long time.

Otherwise, the days would be unbearable. I would feel as if I was standing in a vast dark cave, alone and shivering with the cold. In my hand, I'd be holding an unlit candle, just waiting, until some other similarly lonely soul came along with a light. Then the deal would be struck, along with the match. And we'd both huddle over the candle together, for the warmth and the light ... until it finally spluttered out. It always did in the end.

Sometimes the candle was one of those huge church ones. It would burn passionately for days, weeks, months, and even years. At other times, it was a tiny nightlight that barely made it through until morning. But however long it took for the candle to burn out, it was always the same, whichever of us finally extinguished it. The cold and dark would accentuate the emptiness of loss, and the only way to bring back the light and warmth was to strike up another match. So I just kept going, candle after candle. The supply appeared to be endless.

It was easy, you see. I'd always been able to use my looks to get what I wanted. It wasn't even a conscious act anymore. It was written into my DNA. I couldn't remember a time when men didn't wolf whistle at me in the street, or do a double take as I walked into a bar. By the age of 13, I'd developed a full-grown bosom and my huge green eyes, fringed with thick dark lashes, were a virtual Venus mantrap. This meant that I could get pretty well whoever I fancied, within reason. Most men (or the ones I got to meet, at least) were really not that discriminating, anyway. As long as you looked fairly okay and had all the right bits going in the right directions, you could easily get them to tell you that they loved you. Some of them probably even thought they meant it, at the time—they really did.

But I was gradually beginning to see through this lie. I was starting to see that this 'love' was highly dependent upon certain visual criteria. Criteria that I would one day fall well short of. Already, the writing was on the wall and in an increasingly deepening scrawl all over my face. Bits of my body that were supposed to stay up were sinking fast, while the bits that were supposed to stay down were steadily crinkling skywards. As if that wasn't bad enough, the gentle dusting of white on my head was now migrating to my eyebrows—as well as to other parts of my body where they had no business to be at all.

On top of that, my love fixes seemed to be getting younger and younger. Again, it wasn't my fault. I blame the magazine writers. Those who'd once taught me the "ten top ways to get him to propose" were now finding that their own advice had failed as a blueprint for marital happiness. So they were also now out again in the singles market and instructing me not to bother with,

"... the older man, because they can't seem to leave their baggage from their previous marriage at your front door. Or even worse, he may never have been married at all, for which there's usually a very good reason! So you'd be far better off getting yourself a younger man..."

I'd tried that. But I found that being with a young man had its drawbacks too, especially for someone who enjoys good conversation. There was the time, for instance, when I'd made a brilliant joke to my then young amour, Freddie, and the punch line alluded to the Profumo affair of the Sixties.

It was completely wasted on him. At 16 years my junior, he hadn't even been born then. So he just stared at me blankly.

That relationship, like most of them, had held such promise in the beginning. He had looked like Tom Hanks (well, Tom Hanks in *Big*, anyway). He was gorgeous—half Italian—had tons of energy, was great in bed and he used to make me laugh, which was all you could ask for really.

Freddie reckoned he was one of those young entrepreneurs. But as far as I could see, he just did a bit of this and bit of that, with always half an eye out for the main chance. This suited me fine because I worked from home. So he would often just turn up in the middle of the day. Love in the afternoon always seemed so much more thrilling than having to wait until bedtime.

It was exciting. With Freddie, you never knew what he was going to do next. There was that time when, after one of our afternoon sessions, he leant back against the pillows and lit a cigarette. Then he handed me the packet, asking, "What do you think of that design—I mean the colours?"

"Well, hmm ... yes, I like it," I finally decided. "You wouldn't expect blue, gold and green to go together so well."

"Good then," said Freddie. "Because those are the colours I'm going to use to do up your flat."

My flat hadn't been decorated for years. The walls and ceilings had great cracks like the cobwebs of an enormous prehistoric spider. The tiles in the bathroom were either broken, missing or chipped. The carpets were worn through in several patches and the paintwork was scuffed and marked. So I could hardly refuse.

We immediately set about clearing all the furniture from the bedroom into the living room, so that he could make a start there. Then he spent the whole of the next week working on my flat. He knocked down all the old plaster and put up new tiles in the bathroom. Then he re-plastered and painted the walls in dove blue, sea green and pale gold, and finally laid a new gold soft pile carpet. When he'd finished, it looked so fantastic that I crowned the whole look off with a new dark blue sofa.

But then the problem was that Freddie seemed to have moved in—and so had his dog, which would spread itself across the nice new sofa and drop hairs everywhere.

At first, I didn't mind too much as I was starting to get used to having him around. Freddie, I mean. I never could get used to the dog. But it only took a few weeks for my red-hot Latin lover to undergo a personality change. Now that the dynamic had altered, and we were in this husband-and-wife situation, it had brought out the other side of his Italian genes.

As a journalist, I would often be invited to parties and drinks functions where he would have felt out of place. Personally, I couldn't bear those occasions. I only went to them to network and would leave as early as I could. But I'd often arrive home to find him sitting brooding by the fire, and the first question would invariably be:

"Did you meet any men?"

I would try to lighten the atmosphere with:

"Yes, hundreds! But none so gorgeous as you!"

But it didn't really work.

Another time, I was interviewing a well-known celebrity over lunch in Soho. I'd arranged to meet Freddie in the bar of the restaurant afterwards. But Freddie turned up early. Unknown to me, he had stood glowering at us from the bar as I was blithely plying my quarry with alcohol and then employing every weapon in my flirting toolkit to try to get him to admit to an affair with his young co-star.

Freddie was disgusted:

"How can you behave like that?" he yelled at me afterwards, as he stomped down Wardour Street in the pouring rain. "That guy must have really thought you fancied him!"

"He was supposed to," I gasped, trying to keep up with his furious step so that I could stay under his umbrella, as well as avoid bumping into the pimps and prostitutes.

"How else could I get him to open up? Look Freddie, I promise you, there's nothing to be jealous about. It's just my job."

Then he stopped and turned on his heel, so that I could see his face. I was surprised how boyish he looked when he was hurt.

"Well, maybe I am jealous," he said. "But how would you feel if I met a younger woman and was attracted to her? Wouldn't you be jealous and fight to keep me?"

For someone who'd never bothered to fight to keep a man because there'd always been another waiting backstage—if not actually straining his head around the wings—that question was easy. But there was more to it than that.

I put my hand on his arm.

"Look, it's only natural," I said. "One day, you will realise that you want to have children. Obviously, I can't give them to you. So no, if a younger woman comes along, I won't stand in your way. And I hope that I would be gracious enough to send you off with my blessings."

I wasn't absolutely sure about that last bit. It was more about who I aspired to be than who I really was. But anyway, it turned out to be the wrong answer.

In the following days, I noticed that there was a slight, but definite, chill in the air, like there is when summer is just turning into autumn. Freddie seemed no longer interested in instigating any exciting afternoon trysts, and he would turn his back to me in bed at night. In the evenings, he would lie on the sofa stroking his dog when he was supposed to be stroking me. Then he started to complain about never being able to find a clean, ironed shirt, or dinner not being ready on time, or the wine being tasteless.

The honeymoon was definitely over.

One day, while I was washing up the dinner plates as he lay on the sofa watching football, I thought to myself, *Hey-ho, I've been here before. Now, how did that happen?*

And once I'd made that realisation, the relationship headed south quite rapidly. When the last trumpet sounded, I got to yell the immortal line:

"Just get out, and take that stinking dog with you!"

But he had just turned to me slowly and, with the traces of a cruel smile hovering around his thick Italian lips, had replied, "Why, you're just a sad, middle-aged old bag!"

I was so hurt. I didn't leave my flat for three days. Then when I finally did venture out into the town, I would stare into all the shop windows to see if he was right.

So I hope you can see why I wasn't too anxious to enter into yet another of these *danses macabre*. I just couldn't summon the energy.

But Jamie Marsden (double first from Oxford, management consultant, looking about 16) was still waiting expectantly.

"Aren't you going to join me then?" he said, smiling seductively and indicating the space next to him.

"Just give me a minute," I replied, and got up from the armchair.

Stroking his hair as I walked past, I went out into the dove blue hallway. Then I disappeared into the sea green bathroom.

THE DANCE OF KRISHNA

I sat down on the loo seat and put my head in my hands. Within seconds the black dog of despair was clawing at the pit of my stomach.

How cruel is this? I wondered to myself. *Which sadistic god is salivating over this gladiatorial sport?*

Suddenly, I couldn't remember what on earth had motivated me to get out of bed that morning, or any morning, as I ruminated on 'the human condition'.

All we ever want is love, my thoughts rumbled on. *Yet whenever we think we've found it, it's snatched away from us. Or even if we do manage to keep it alive for a whole lifetime, we lose each other anyway at the point of death. So what's the point of it all? We're just bonded slaves to a god of materialism. He allows us to fall in love just long enough to form an economic unit and breed more clones.*

For the first time ever, I felt the true pain of what it was to be a human being. Of course, it wasn't a new idea. It was more a culmination of thoughts that I'd been trying to keep at bay with sex, drink and drugs for most of my adult life. It had been the elephant in the room for some time. Now it was standing on its hind legs and trumpeting.

We need eternal love, I carried on, *the kind that doesn't splutter out on you. But we're just not designed that way. It seems to me that everything on earth is subject to decay, including us and our experiences.*

Just then, something sparked in my head. Gradually, a memory was beginning to form. It was based on something I'd read long ago in a book about Lord Krishna.

I expect you've heard of Krishna because he's quite famous really. Or maybe you've seen pictures of this beautiful, blue-skinned god in Indian shops among the joss sticks and the incense burners. He's usually wearing a peacock feather in his hair and carrying a flute. Anyway, according to this book, he was born in India over 5,000 years ago, as an incarnation of God. It's said that he had given such a wonderful experience of divine, eternal love to all his dairymaid devotees that they would dance around their milk churns in ecstasy.

That's it, I finally realised, letting out a long sigh. *What I need is divine love, everlasting love.*

Now I did know that those stories about Krishna were supposed to be just myths and legends, the origins of which were lost in the mists of time. But it was then that I decided that if they weren't true, it was about time someone made them so.

So, mainly out of sheer exhaustion and desperation over the whole sorry business, I closed my eyes and started to pray. It went something like this:

"Lord Krishna, if you really are there, please help me. The stories say that you are omnipresent—not limited by time and space—and that you come to desperate people when they're suffering and need you. So why don't you come to me? Can't you see that my heart is dying? If you really are God, if you really are the incarnation of God, then please come now and give me some of that lovely divine love!"

Then I opened my eyes. But the bathroom still looked exactly the same, with Freddie's new blue tiles stuck neatly in place where the blue-skinned god should have been.

So I tried again:

"Because, I have to tell you, I really cannot stand another go-round-the-houses on this trashy piece of imitation crystal we here, on earth, call 'love'. This tainted love. It's like a mirrored ball in a dance hall. It bathes everything in magical hues and shadows just long enough to get us all hooked. Hooked into the illusion that it's divine, it's magic, it's bigger than both of us. Then when we wake up, it's the morning after the night before.

"I just can't do it again. Really I can't. And if you don't come and help me, I reckon I've had it this time. I really do."

Still nothing ... just the sound of the dripping tap that Freddie had always meant to fix.

But you may be wondering why I should have even been reading a book about Krishna. Well, my life had always seemed like a schizophrenic smorgasbord of the sacred and the profane. Running alongside my ongoing hunt for my physical Mr Right, there had been another, more subterranean, search going on, this time for my spiritual Mr Right. Not 'right' in the sense of being 'a good fit'. But right ... well, just because he's right—because he knows the truth about God.

Ever since the Seventies, I'd practised meditation and undergone all sorts of austerities in spiritual retreats of varying religions. I'd had a *guru* (spiritual teacher) and I would rummage through loads of scriptures and accounts of quests for spiritual enlightenment, like *The Ramayana*, *The Mahabharata*, the *Bhagavad-Gita*, *The Life of Ramakrishna* and *Autobiography of a Yogi*.

All these writers had said there was a realisation of God that you could have. Not a belief or a faith, but an actual practical experience that felt like utter bliss, or being wrapped up in a cotton wool blanket of love, or something like that anyway. It wasn't, they said, to do with dogma or belief and you didn't have to be in any particular religion to experience it. So I'd been hunting high and low ever since for someone to teach me how to reach it.

I'd learned hatha yoga at a retreat on Paradise Island in the Caribbean. I'd spent days, weeks and months in various spiritual workshops, sometimes in England, and other times in more exotic locations, like the Greek islands. I'd sung Gregorian chant with the Benedictine nuns on the Isle of Wight. I was a Reiki Master. I'd dowsed, I'd rolfed. I'd also practised a Polynesian type of deep spiritual healing called *huna kane*. I knew about the *chakras* (the spiritual energy centres in the body) *prana* (spiritual energy) and *devas* (don't ask!).

In other words, I'd trodden the well-worn path of the spiritual seeker. Yet despite reading reams and reams on the subject, and praying and meditating every day, I'd never met a single person who could lead me to this other Mr Right. Many said they could. But you could just tell from how they acted that it was all just deluded ego. In fact, it became almost a rule of thumb that the closer they claimed to be, the further away from it they truly were.

However, and with the odds diminishing as fast as they were in my other search, I still had a deep-seated, inner compulsion to find my spiritual other half. It was like a feeling in the gut that flew in the face of experience. But at least it had been getting me out of bed in the morning—until now, that is. Because just as I was having to admit that my hunt for my worldly Mr Right seemed to be ending in failure, my search for the spiritual one was also running into the Slough of Despond.

Anyway, I tried to shake myself free of these depressing thoughts and forced myself to get up from the loo. I checked my eye make-up in the bathroom mirror. Then I set my chin to rejoin the next candidate in the living room for another spin on the not so merry-go-round.

But as I walked through the living room door, I could see that I'd been granted a reprieve. Jamie was sprawled across the sofa and fast asleep. His mouth was slightly open. A little silver filigree of saliva was rolling down to his chin. There was even a suggestion of a snore. With his blond curls all tousled now, he looked so childlike, so first soprano choirboy, that any staggering survivors from my shipwrecked libido were immediately swamped by a tsunami of maternal instinct.

I leant over him, and ruffled his curls to wake him. His eyes shot open in alarm. Then he leapt to his feet, smoothed down his hair, and muttered something apologetically about an early morning breakfast meeting the next day.

"Sure, that's fine," I smiled, and handed him his jacket.

Within seconds, he was gone—and I was breathing a huge sigh of relief.

Then I started to laugh. It was erupting up from somewhere deep inside me, great rolling waves of pure, joyous gut laughter. I didn't understand what was happening because I'd never really laughed like that before. Then suddenly, I realised that he was in the room. Krishna, that is.

I couldn't see him. But the air was thick and nectar-like with his merry, tinkling laughter and I found myself being whirled around in a giddying dance by a partner that I couldn't see or feel. It was as if I'd broken through to another dimension. Or perhaps more accurately, as if he had broken through to me. I couldn't stop laughing, and my body wouldn't stop moving in a dance I'd never known before. I was whirling like a dervish. It was ecstatic. It was bliss. It was complete joy.

I could sense the young, boyish charm in my partner, the playfulness of him. But I could also feel that he was ageless and eternal. It wasn't sexual or romantic. But neither was it completely platonic. I couldn't understand it. It didn't fit into any of my mental templates. So in the end, I stopped trying to analyse it and surrendered myself to the pure enjoyment.

Afterwards, when I tried to put words to the experience, I would say that it was as if Love had taken a body, a physical form, and dropped in to dance with me—just for the play of it, just because I had asked—and that he'd seemed vastly amused at his own joke or game.

THE DANCE OF KRISHNA

But I can't tell you how long this dancing went on because time seemed not to exist. I suppose it could have been about half-an-hour. Then it stopped almost as abruptly as it had begun, and I'd fallen into bed, barely able to undress and, quite quickly, dropped into a very deep sleep.

Days later, I would wonder if it had just been an hallucination, or a dream. Then I'd think that I couldn't possibly have been capable of imagining such divine ecstasy. But even if I had, I would reason to myself, the feeling that it had generated was so intoxicating, and so overwhelming, that it couldn't have come from any normal earthly source.

So I was forever churning it over in my mind.

Did Krishna really answer my cry for help? I kept asking myself. *Could it really be that, in all the long decades of boyfriends, husbands, partners, dates and one-night-stands, this finally might be it? Was it divine love? Was it God? Or was it complete madness?*

In the end, though, I realised that I didn't care what they called it, so long as I could find a way to get it on tap.

As I'm sure you can guess, I had a long and extraordinary journey ahead of me.

CHAPTER 2
THE DANCE MASTER

A few months later, I found myself standing in the cold and the dark on a mountain in India along with hundreds of other women in brightly coloured *saris*. Whirls of white steam were wafting cardamom, ginger, cinnamon and cloves from a huge pot on the handlebars of the *chai* boy's old black bike as he pushed it along the snaking queue. Then, as the dawn sun finally began to redden the sky, a young Indian girl came along plying her wares.

"Glass Ganesh," she called out, thrusting the glass ornament of the elephant-headed god of good fortune towards me. "Glass Ganesh. Very cheap."

"Typical," I said to my daughter, Miranda. "If you wanted a glass Ganesh, you'd never be able to find one. But stand in a place where you've absolutely no use for a glass Ganesh, and you get one thrust in your face."

But perhaps I should start from the beginning.

Miranda and I had recently arrived in this hill station town in southern India called Kodaikanal (pronounced 'Koe-dye-kanal'). Well, they called it a hill. I'd have said it was a mountain, with its snow-capped peaks and steep-sided valleys. Suffice to say that, at more than 2,000 metres above sea level, the air was a blissfully refreshing ten degrees cooler than down on the blistering plains only an hour's perilous drive below.

We'd arrived in Kodaikanal the previous evening. We'd gone there to see an Indian *guru* called Sai Baba. He was quite famous in that part of India and we'd heard, through the grapevine, that he might have some answers for us.

So we'd found ourselves a quaint little hotel just on the outskirts of the town.

Our room was large with high ceilings and white-framed French windows leading to a wooden veranda. We dumped our rucksacks and rushed out to have a look. Leaning over the railings, we looked down on to woolly white clouds that were veiling a fjord-like waterfall that was crashing into the steep, pine green valley below.

Inside, there was an enormous double bed covered in a dark green and gold embroidered silk bedspread. So we tipped out the contents of our rucksacks on to it. Then, feeling much too excited to bother about putting away our clothes in the mahogany tall boys, we rushed out to explore the town.

It wasn't long, though, before we saw our first rotting carcass—of a cat. A few yards further along, and we came across the festering corpses of two mangy looking street dogs. They had obviously been lying on the pavement for days and were surrounded by swarms of flies. On another road, a foul-smelling tramp sat in the filthy gutter while streams of insects buzzed around his greasy-haired head. Then, as if to complete the parasite motif, we were orbited by a swarm of beggars whose knack for getting under our feet while keeping up a low, passive whining tone eventually caused us to capitulate and give them some rupees, if only to get rid of them.

All the shopkeepers were out on the pavements too, trying to entice us in to see their wares.

The streets were wider than I expected for an old Indian town, although they were still jam-packed with hooting cars and motorised rickshaws. The odd bedraggled-looking cow would stray into the middle of it all from time to time. But there was a reason for the wide roads, we discovered. It turned out that Kodaikanal had been a favourite resort of the British in colonial times. Apparently, during the pre-*monsoon* periods, when the heat would descend like a suffocating blanket, the *memsahibs* used to retreat to this tiny summit settlement arranged around a cool, glistening lake. They eventually turned it into a small town that wouldn't have looked out of place in Surrey.

In fact, in terms of its architecture, Kodaikanal didn't seem very Indian at all. It certainly didn't look to be the sort of place where you'd expect to find an authentic Indian guru. But at least

Miranda, who was never very good in the heat, could cool off here for a few days.

Perhaps, at this stage, I should tell you some more about Miranda as she figures a lot in this part of the story. She was probably what you'd call a true child of the Sixties. Mark, her father, and I had been a couple of wandering hippies with pretensions to the philosophies of Dr Timothy Leary, and Ken Kesey's Merry Pranksters. Just before Miranda was born, we had temporarily fetched up in an enormous, white Georgian house overlooking Blackheath Common in London.

It belonged to our friend, Harry, who we'd originally met at art college in Canterbury. Or rather, it belonged to his parents. But they worked for the British Council and had been posted to Uganda for the duration. Before leaving, they'd encouraged him to invite his friends to keep him company there. I don't think they'd ever met any of us.

In the end, there was a whole crowd of us—maybe 10 or 12 living there at any one time. We transformed the decor to suit our own psychedelic tastes. We painted the grand, sweeping staircase with the colours of the rainbow and the wall over the Nash fireplace, in the main room of the house, a giant black-and-gold dragon whose jaws encased the fire.

Miranda's cot was in this room. So she was usually lulled off to sleep each night to the strains of Santana, Bob Dylan, George Harrison and Ravi Shankar.

We were all street dancers and musicians and most of us were pretty well travelled. Between us, we'd managed to build up quite a collection of just about every form of percussion imaginable. There were Indian tablas, big African drums, conga drums, bongo drums and Jamaican talking drums, to name a few.

Miranda's father, Mark, had an Indian music teacher, Sri Srinivas, who taught him to play the tablas. We used to take little Miranda to visit him in his tiny, cramped room above what must have been one of the first Indian takeaways in London, off Tottenham Court Road. As a result, I've never since been able to separate the lilting trills of the sitar from the aroma of deep frying vegetable samosas and the sound of the big, red buses trundling past.

Anyway, one day while Miranda and I were waiting for Mark to finish his tabla lesson, Sri Srinivas beckoned me to approach.

Wearing what looked like white pyjamas, he was sitting cross-legged on the floor and holding an enormous polished teak sitar.

"Come here, my dear," he said. "Don't be shy. I have something for you."

He turned around and behind him, under a shelf, I could see an enormous dark red leather-bound book that was embossed with silver lettering. He hauled it out and then carefully passed it to me.

I handled it gingerly and then put my nose to the spine. It smelt of Indian joss sticks. Then, turning it over, I saw that the silver letters spelled out the words: 'Srimad Bhagavatam' ('shree-mad baga-vatam'). I opened it up. The leaves were almost as fragile as rice paper and the writing looked like spiders crawling across the page. I just about recognised it as Sanskrit.

"Do you read Sanskrit, dear?" he asked.

"Well, just a little. I've just started studying it," I replied.

"Then this is for you. It contains all the great spiritual knowledge of my country, mother India, and you will also find in it the life story of our dear Lord Krishna."

"I couldn't possibly accept such a precious gift ..." I tried to say.

"No, no my dear," he insisted firmly. "I brought it with me when I first came to this country, and I've been waiting for the right person to give it to. It's part of a wider body of spiritual literature called the *Vedas* ('vay-das'). But this book, the *Srimad Bhagavatam*, was written especially for married people, like yourselves. So you must take it."

I couldn't refuse.

We carried the enormous tome back to the house at Blackheath. It made an excellent doorstop for Miranda's bedroom door, so I could hear when ever she was crying at night. But over the months, as my Sanskrit lessons progressed, so did my understanding of the contents of this book, which turned out to be full of stories about Krishna and his games with the cowherds and milkmaids.

One of the stories was about a dance. It was called the *rasa lila* ('rah-sa leel-la'). In this dance, Krishna cloned himself as many times as was necessary to provide himself as a partner to all the milkmaids. Then they all danced in a circle, on the banks of the river Yamuna. Here's a small excerpt:

Then Krishna created many identical versions of his physical form so that each milkmaid could have him as her partner. He then put his arms around them and held them so close to him that each thought that she alone was dancing with Krishna.

The milkmaids sang in ecstasy in praise of their handsome Lord Krishna, and as their delicate feet danced, their elegant hands gestured and their eyebrows rose up and down with their smiles. With their long silver earrings swinging on their cheeks, and fragrant pink lotus flowers behind their ears, Lord Krishna's young dance partners gleamed like streaks of lightning in a rain darkening sky and swarms of bees sang in accompaniment.

At the time, I interpreted the *rasa lila* as an erotic allegory. I could hardly have done otherwise in the Seventies. By then, sex was so in our faces, we could no longer see how it was distorting everything. So it was difficult to get my head around this pure divine and unconditional love that Krishna apparently had for these milkmaids. But, according to this book, he had been with them, and in love with them, lifetime after lifetime, and this dance was just one expression of that divine love.

Then one day something extraordinary happened that allowed me a small glimpse into that ancient Vedic world.

It was during a dance rehearsal in the room with the dragon fireplace.

We were dancing in a circle, twisting and twirling individually as the circle revolved. Then something in the atmosphere changed, something magnetic or electrical. It built up gradually at first. Looking into the faces of the others, I could see that they were in various stages of becoming aware of it too. Then suddenly, in just the space of time it would take for someone to click their fingers, we no longer existed as separate people but became one unit, and one small component of a vast, cosmic dance.

After that, we carried this dance out into the streets, the parks and even the more run-down inner city schools. Miranda was also a part of the performance, banging the tray of her high chair that we'd painted red and decorated with glittering gold stars.

None of us really understood this dance that we'd tuned into. But we all felt it was pretty 'cosmic'. That was as much as we knew about spiritual matters. We thought smoking marijuana was pretty 'cosmic' too.

So this was Miranda's background and, like any child, she was conditioned by her upbringing. We also taught her, as she grew older, to think for herself, to accept nothing on face value and to ask questions. So, eighteen years later, she asked the big one.

It was about a decade after her father and I had parted. Not many relationships survived in those creatively charged days of the mid-Sixties and early Seventies. Mark and I had been slow to learn that there was no such thing as 'free love' and that, on the contrary, everybody had to pay. The cost, in our case, was our marriage.

Miranda and I moved back to my birthplace, the old Kent town of Sevenoaks. And shortly after that, on one fine autumn afternoon, we were walking down the London Road next to the bus station when she turned to me and asked:

"Mum. What is the meaning of life?"

"To realise God," I quickly replied.

I had all the certainty of someone who knew the theory backwards, but little about the practical reality.

"So do you mean that we don't have any choice in the matter?" she asked.

"Oh yes, we do have choice. We have free will. But eventually, as we reincarnate over hundreds of lifetimes, all the things we choose with our free will come to seem worthless to us, and so then we use our free will to start to search for something more meaningful…"

"No, Mum," she interrupted, frowning. "I mean, don't we have any choice about having to go through this whole process—lifetime after lifetime of being deluded by *maya* until finally getting it right and finding enlightenment and *mukta*? Why can't we just stay in God consciousness? Then there'd be no need for all this suffering."

"I don't really know," I had to admit.

I also hadn't realised until then that she'd been going through my books. The language she was using was straight out of *Autobiography of a Yogi* by Paramahansa Yogananda.

"Because if that's the case," she went on with a note of anger entering her normally tranquil voice, "he must be a pretty cruel God to put us through all this pain."

That was the deciding point for Miranda. Over the coming weeks and months, we talked about this subject more and more. Eventually she decided that she simply could not take another step without finding out more about God. So her next port of call was that well-worn resort for spiritual travellers, the study of religion.

She spent three years at Magdalen College, Oxford, learning about Hinduism, Islam and Buddhism. The course also had a bit of a New Age flavour to it, and so they also did mysticism and all that pagan goddess stuff.

It was towards the end of her university course that I'd had the experience of dancing with Krishna. It had had a massive effect on me. I knew I would never be happy again until I found the source of this experience. It seemed corny. Friends joked about "going to India to find yourself". But I didn't know where else to go.

So I went to visit Miranda in her campus bed-sit to tell her about my planned trip. Afterwards, we decided to go for a walk.

It was a mid-winter's day—freezing, but bright and sunny. Wrapping ourselves up in coats, hats, scarves and gloves and taking a full thermos flask, and some Scottish shortbread left over from Christmas, we went out across the frost-covered lawns of her college. We found ourselves a slatted wooden bench overlooking the River Cherwell and we sat there, surrounded by tiny yellow aconites and white snowdrops that were barely plucking up the courage to push their noses up into the biting, icy air.

Miranda got out the flask.

"So how are your studies going?" I asked.

There was a bit of a silence, then:

"I've come to the conclusion," she said, as she poured steaming hot chocolate into a plastic mug, "that God doesn't exist."

"Really?"

"Or if he does," she continued, "it's highly unlikely that he could be found through any religion. In my opinion, they're just political and cultural groupings that exist solely for the subjugation of the people, particularly women."

"Well, I reckon that's been three years well spent then," I laughed, and she passed the steaming mug into my hand.

So there was nothing else for it. We were both at the end of the line.

"Why don't you come to India with me?" I said, surprising myself. I hadn't even thought of her coming until then.

"Mum, don't be silly," she replied, looking at me disapprovingly. "I can't. I've got to be sensible and find a job. I've got to start paying off my student loan."

"Oh, Miranda, for heaven's sake!" I said. "Don't be so boring and come to India."

So that is how, a few months later, we found ourselves landing in a stinking and fetid Mumbai.

The nauseating smell of the shanty part of Mumbai hits you like a wave as you walk down the steps of the aircraft. We decided to leave immediately. We'd been discussing spending a couple of weeks in the Goa sun, to acclimatise ourselves to India. So we took the first hydrofoil out that night, arriving in Goa the following morning. Then it was just a short rickshaw ride along tree-lined roads to a hotel we'd found in our *Rough Guide to India*.

It wasn't exactly rough. In fact, for two whole weeks we barely felt like moving from our luxury hotel. It was on an idyllic beachfront among tall, swaying coconut palms. So in vivid contrast to our frostbitten Oxford conversations about God, we could now resume them amid the jasmine-entwined latticework of our private veranda while slowly sipping iced mango *lassi* as we gazed out over gardens of exotic orchids and birds of paradise, and then on to the deep sparkling blue of the Indian Ocean.

We had already decided, back in England, that we should first go to see Sai Baba, as a few people we knew had been impressed by him. Then one day, in a bookshop near the hotel, I came across a couple of books about him. I couldn't wait to start reading them. So I rushed back to the idyll of our veranda and quickly ensconced myself on the sun lounger next to Miranda.

But within just a few pages, I started to become quite disheartened. I tried to plough on, but the feeling of disappointment was slowly turning into one of disbelief and dismay. It finally overwhelmed me to such an extent that I ended up throwing the book across the floor.

"What's up?" asked Miranda from behind her biography of Marianne Faithful.

THE DANCE MASTER

"This Sai Baba's not going to work for me," I muttered darkly, and picked up the suntan lotion and proceeded to rub it vigorously into my thighs.

"Why not?"

"Well, for one thing, he seems to be living in another age."

"How do you mean?" said Miranda, putting down her own book now.

"It isn't that what he's saying doesn't ring true, or even that I don't agree with it. It's just that he's talking about living in such a way that people like us would find totally impossible."

"Give me an example," said Miranda calmly, as she took the suntan lotion from me and poured some into her hands.

"Well, for one thing, he talks about loving everyone, and always helping others and putting their needs first. He's obviously never travelled on the London Tube in the rush hour!" I snorted. "Then he has these nifty little sayings like 'Love All, Serve All' and 'Help Ever, Hurt Never'. It's cute. But doesn't he know that we tried all that thirty years ago? How many of us from those days are now living in an earthly nirvana?"

"Maybe we shouldn't go to see him then," said Miranda tentatively.

This was not what I wanted to hear. I immediately started to panic. There I was, in a strange land and, all of a sudden, not knowing which direction to take.

"I don't know where else to start, really, then ..." I ventured.

"Well perhaps we could just use his place as a base while we make other plans," she said. "It's supposed to have good facilities—and also Western food."

Western food was a big plus factor in Miranda's calculations as her stomach was constantly having disagreements with all the spices and chillies. However, it wasn't why we were in India.

"Yes, but we could have got good food back home. We haven't come all this way just for our stomachs," was my instant response.

"No, but it will give us space to think and reassess," said Miranda.

"Hmmm, possibly," I said, beginning to wonder why I'd chosen to go to see Sai Baba at all.

For the past year or so, I'd been working as a freelance journalist and specialising in 'new age', environmental and complementary health stories. One day, I received a phone call from a PR woman. It turned out that she'd recently taken on an Indian yoga teacher as a client, and that he had just escorted a minor royal to India to see a certain Sai Baba. So was I interested in doing the story?

"I'm trying to get the Daily Mail on board," she said "and the idea is, we'll fly you out there and you can check out this Sai Baba for yourself, see what he's like. Sound okay?"

"Sure," I said. "Let's see how it goes."

Two days later, she rang with the news. She couldn't get the Daily Mail interested, and neither was anyone else. However, that very afternoon, I went to see an acupuncturist that I was doing a story about. As I sat down in his therapy room, there, on his desk, was a picture of Sai Baba. The following morning, I had to interview a homeopath. Amazingly, the same picture was on her desk.

"I don't believe it!" I said. "I'd never heard of this guru until a few days ago. Now he's cropped up three times!"

She laughed.

"It's always like that when Sai Baba comes into a person's life," she said. "He just keeps popping up all over the place. He must be calling you."

Somehow, now, I was beginning to doubt that. I got up slowly to retrieve the book from the other side of the veranda. I tried to carry on reading it. But my heart was no longer in it. I may have been in a worldly paradise, but suddenly it didn't seem so wonderful. I knew that it was wasted on me if I couldn't find the real paradise, the one I was looking for.

Miranda went back behind her book and we didn't really talk about it again. We just continued on the unspoken assumption that we were still going to visit Sai Baba, if only as a temporary measure.

So by the time our holiday part of the trip was over, and we were ready to leave for some real travelling, I felt quite empty and confused. Then once we'd left Goa and hit the real India, what I saw was so depressing, I couldn't believe that I'd put my life on hold to spend time in such an awful country.

Until then, my opinions about the British Raj in India had been formed by the likes of Graham Greene, E.M. Forster and David Lean. In other words, a quite unsympathetic and caricatured view of the uptight, arrogant, intolerant British. But on actually experiencing India first-hand, two things really surprised me. The first one was how much the Indians still, and despite everything, absolutely love the British. Secondly, I was amazed at how completely different Indian people are to us, on every level.

Coming from the West, there is so much one takes for granted about how life works and it isn't until these assumptions are confronted that one realises it. The trouble with India, especially when you first arrive, is that everything you ever thought was true about life is being challenged at every second. It's gruelling, shocking, exhausting and depressing all at the same time.

For instance, the towns were insufferably noisy, dusty and crowded. The transport services were unreliable, to say the least. Railway timetables were a work of fiction. Trains promised to be leaving in 'just five minutes' could depart anything up to an hour-and-a-half late, with no word of apology or explanation.

Going by road was no better. We would regularly pass a bus or lorry that had come to grief and fully expected to die at every other second. And everywhere, everywhere we went, people asked us for money. It was an unremitting assault on our inner humanity and we could never escape it. On the streets, taxi drivers, bus drivers, people starting up conversations with us on trains—even when we thought we'd made a new friend, they'd soon ask us for 20 rupees. It wasn't the money. To us, 20 rupees were just a few pence. It was just that we began to feel that whenever anyone looked at us, all they could see was a walking cash machine.

None of this should have been too much trouble for a couple of travellers such as ourselves. It wasn't as if we had a business, or an empire to run. So if it was getting to us, I would muse to myself, imagine how it must have been for the British of those colonial days, trying to keep it together in the unforgiving heat, with their buttoned-up starched collars, frock coats and rigid conventions about always being on time for dinner.

After being buffeted around on the wooden seats of buses and trains for a couple of days, the dust seemed to enter our souls. We felt dirty and exhausted with all the new ways of living that we were having to deal with. On top of that, Miranda was starting to suffer from heat exhaustion. So after getting as near to Kodaikanal as we could by train, we got off at a small industrial-looking town called Salem. Then dropping all pretensions to roughing it, we hired a taxi.

From there it was a further 10-hour-drive across relentlessly flat, parched plains with the sun beating down on us. With the warm pre-monsoon winds coming through the window, the car soon became impossibly hot and, after a while, I started to get quite worried about Miranda. She wilts quite quickly, even in the heat of an English summer. Now she was practically unconscious on the back seat and just occasionally surfacing to gesture that she needed the water bottle.

At one point we stopped in a tiny village, outside a local eatery. There were long trestle tables set out, full of gossiping villagers who were eating with their hands and using huge banana leaves as plates. As we walked in, everyone stopped eating and chattering to stare at us. It seemed incredible to us that there were such places left—apart from, say, in the depths of the African jungle. But I honestly don't think they'd ever seen white people before. So they looked at us and we looked at them, and for a moment there was complete silence.

Neither of us felt like eating. So we just sat opposite our driver, who immediately began to pile rice, vegetables and chapattis into his mouth with his big workman's hands, and slowly sipped our water. Then he licked his banana leaf clean and we were up and off again.

Within an hour or so, we'd reached the mountain road that coiled its way upwards to Kodaikanal. It turned out that our driver thought nothing of speeding around some quite terrifying steep drops. But at least the coolness of the air started to revive Miranda. So by the time we finally reached the top, and found our hotel, she'd actually become quite chirpy and was just as excited as me to explore our new surroundings.

We'd wandered around the busy streets for hours, trying to find Sai Baba. We could find no sign of him, and evening was now starting to pinken the sky. Not having eaten any lunch, our stomachs were rumbling. So we headed back towards the town square where we found a small restaurant, and took a table on the upstairs balcony.

THE DANCE MASTER

We had a delicious meal there of rice and curried vegetables in coconut with pickles, yoghurt and naan bread. Then, just as we were finishing our ice cream dessert, we saw that several Western-looking women dressed in Indian *saris* had appeared on the square. Guessing that they must be devotees of Sai Baba, we quickly paid our bill and went down to speak to them.

As we walked towards them, a cheery looking, buxom blonde woman in a bright pink *sari* turned and smiled at me. I immediately felt encouraged. So I asked her if she knew where Sai Baba lived.

"We've just come from there," she replied in an English accent, her eyes shining. "It was wonderful! He was leading us in *bhajans*."

It sounded like Budgens, and I wondered why Sai Baba would want to lead his devotees around a supermarket.

"What's *bhajans*?" I asked.

"It's devotional singing to God," she said. "It's very beautiful because the words and musical notes of the *bhajans* carry a special healing vibration. So it's a wonderful experience."

"Oh, I'd like to have heard that," I said.

"Don't worry," she said, putting a friendly plump hand on my arm. "He leads the *bhajans* every afternoon. So you can go tomorrow!"

"So we'll have to wait until tomorrow afternoon to see him?"

"Well, he does also see his devotees in the mornings too," she replied. "He has these sessions called *darshan*," she said.

It was pronounced as it looks, 'dar-shan'.

"What's *darshan*?" I enquired.

"It's when he circulates among the devotees, talking to them, answering questions, taking letters, that sort of thing. Sometimes, he'll give a discourse on spiritual matters. Other times, but more rarely, he performs healings. But you do have to get there really early, to be sure to get in."

You actually had to be there at the crack of dawn. So the next day, Miranda, who was still recovering from the journey, decided to have a lie-in while I went alone.

It was still dark when I arrived outside the gates of this quite suburban-looking bungalow in Lake View Road. I was the only one there. It was so cold, I huddled next to the gate pillar, shivering. Eventually, though, a few more people began to arrive.

Then there were about a hundred there and, by the time the sun started to rise, several hundred, all shivering and rubbing their hands. So the sound of the chai boy's bicycle bell was very welcoming as he came along with his hot, spiced Indian tea. Then gradually more and more people started to fill the tiny tree-lined lane until there must have been more than a thousand.

They all looked so pure and holy, compared to me, that I began to feel quite out of place. I must have looked as if I'd just fallen out of a nightclub, with my tight green silk sarong and top revealing every curve of my figure. One kind-faced Japanese woman suggested that I borrow her shawl, explaining that it was correct, in India, to keep the shoulders covered to blur the outline of the bust. I gratefully took it, but it didn't make much difference. My hair was swaying around my shoulders instead of the regulation 'tied back', I was wearing glossy red lipstick and very dark sunglasses. I was dying for a cigarette. In short, I looked as I felt—wrecked and washed up with no place to go.

Eventually though, the line did start to move through the gates and into the compound of Sai Baba's bungalow. It turned out that being the first to arrive was no criteria for actually getting in. They had a complicated queuing system, which I won't bore you with here, except to say it was probably the only fair way of doing it. So I ended up being one of the last to get in.

I found myself sitting on the cold, hard ground (you were supposed to bring a cushion) right at the back. I couldn't see a thing.

Never mind, I thought. *Perhaps I will have better luck this afternoon. After all, I've only just arrived. I'm sure there are far more deserving people that he would prefer to see.*

Despite the discomfort, it was a pleasure to be in such a contented and happy atmosphere. The courtyard was beautifully decorated, as if for a fiesta. There were strings of multi-coloured bunting, silver foil decorations and a few jaunty red paper lanterns bobbing in the dawn breeze.

Then I noticed that an Indian woman, who looked like one of those in charge, was signalling to me. She beckoned to me, saying,

"I have just two places."

I didn't know what that meant. But the woman to my right, a grey-haired Australian woman, did. She quickly grabbed my elbow and pushed me up. Then the Indian woman led us forward to a spot about two rows from the front.

"Quick, quick," she said, pushing us down as she nervously eyed the porch of the bungalow.

I soon saw the reason why. We were barely in place before Sai Baba appeared on it. He came out to the front of the porch. Then he came down the steps and started walking towards us and, I have to say, it was like the sun coming up. It was like the sun coming up in my heart and all over the world—and I completely forgot the cold, hard concrete in the enchantment of the most heart-rendingly beautiful sight that I had ever seen.

CHAPTER 3
THE DANCE OF THE ENCHANTRESS

As I watched Sai Baba in his orange robe gliding around the courtyard and going from one devotee to another with a word here, a pat on the shoulder there, taking a letter from one and blessing another, he seemed like a gardener tending to his plants and they, in turn, were looking up at him so lovingly, like exotic flowers turning up their faces to meet the sun.

The air was thick with the scent of the creamy jasmine flowers that the women were wearing in their hair. A silence had fallen like a heavy curtain, and the birds and the very air itself was still, seemingly poised on tenterhooks.

The sheer tenderness of the scene was so alien to my own hard living, cynical world that I probably wouldn't have been able to comprehend it if it hadn't been for the fact that I'd once had a *guru* too. So my mind started to wander back to that time.

This Indian guru had come to England in the early Seventies. His name was Guru Vedananda and I'd eventually become one of his foremost devotees. I'd spoken on the stages of large assembly halls to huge crowds, encouraging them to join his movement. I used to have such amazing experiences in meditation, of which I'd assumed that he was the source. I became so completely devoted to him that, by the early Eighties, I'd given up everything to dedicate myself to his mission, which, he'd declared, was to bring world peace.

I'd lived in one of his London ashrams. *(Ashram* is the Indian word for monastery, or nunnery.) So at the women's ashram, opposite Hammersmith tube station, we observed the rules of chastity and poverty. We would rise early every morning to meditate. In fact, meditation took up much of the day, unless we were involved in collecting clothes for one of the many jumble sales, to raise funds.

It was quite an austere lifestyle. Those of us who worked donated their whole salary to the running of the ashram. We never had any money of our own. However, while we were dressing ourselves from jumble sale cast-offs, living on brown rice and vegetables and sleeping six to a room, we gradually began to realise that our guru was immersing himself in *la dolce vita*.

This was brought home to me with a vengeance one fine May day when I went to visit some followers who were looking after one of Vedanada's many homes around the world. By now, our guru was mainly based in California, and just visited the UK once or twice a year.

I was picked up from the railway station by a blue limited edition Aston Martin. It was being driven by a chirpy young man named Johnny. On the drive to the guru's house, Johnny told me that he was a car mechanic by trade. He said that his job was to service Vedananda's cars, of which this was one.

"But you shouldn't have collected me in such an expensive car," I said as we turned into Vedananda's long, gravelled driveway, the trees on either side bursting into full cherry blossom. "Wouldn't it have been more economical to come in something a bit more practical?"

"Not really," he replied, as he drove us into an enormous garage under the spreading boughs of a cypress tree and parked next to a gleaming Mercedes. "My job here mainly consists of taking each of these cars out for a run everyday. I have to keep them ticking over while Guru Vedananda's away. Today, it was the Aston Martin's turn."

As I stepped out of the car, I saw that the garage housed about eight cars; there were three Mercedes, a Rolls Royce, a Jaguar, a Ferrari and two Porches.

Then, as we came out, I noticed that there was another garage next door.

"We had to build this one recently, because we were running out of room," said Johnny, as if it was the most normal thing in the world.

This garage contained a Bristol, a Maserati, another more sporty Mercedes, a Rover and two BMWs.

"But he only visits England a couple of times a year," I said, "and even then, he only stays for a few weeks. How on earth does he even find the time to drive all these?"

Johnny just grinned and shrugged.

That evening, when I got back to the Hammersmith ashram, I found Rob, the head of the guru's UK organisation, lounging against the windowsill in the huge open plan kitchen. A number of devotees were sitting and chatting around the large oblong-shaped pine kitchen table. Another was chopping carrots for that evening's vegetarian dinner.

"How's it going?" Rob asked as I entered the room.

"Well, okay," I said, a little uncertainly, picking up a water jug on the table and pouring myself a glass. "I've just been over to Guru Vedananda's house. I was picked up in a really swish Aston Martin. You should see how many cars he's got over there."

One of the girls around the table giggled, and Rob nervously cleared his throat as I headed towards the fridge at the other end of the room to get some ice cubes.

"Actually, that's why I'm here," he said, and he started to shift from one foot to the other.

"What do you mean?" I replied, heading towards the fridge for some ice.

"Well, as you know, it's Guru Vedananda's 30th birthday next month," Rob went on. "So I came over to let you know what we've decided to get him."

I was just opening the fridge door when I heard him say:

"We're buying him the latest Mercedes." Another clearing of the throat and then, "It's what he's asked for."

As I stared into the depths of the ice-making compartment, I felt my blood run cold.

That's it, I thought. *It's over,* and my heart sank with a thud as the realisation hit home.

I'd given my heart and soul to this man and he'd turned out to be a complete charlatan. The pain of yet another lost love seared through me, and this time I didn't know how I would get back from it.

Within a few weeks, I'd left. But my departure from that spiritual world into a much more material one had felt so brutal, and so painful, that it had taken me many years to recover and find a way to cope. And it had come at a price. As one of my friends later put it:

"After you left, you hit normality. But then you just kept on going."

She was right.

The pain of the rupture with Vedananda was worse than the divorce with my husband. But as a journalist, it was really easy to anaesthetise myself against it. Being an alcoholic was almost part of the job description. And as I could no longer remain in a pure spiritual environment, I decided to throw myself into the worst excesses that the material world had to offer. I was bent on self-destruction.

My working day would start around mid-morning with a press conference, and champagne or wine would be offered on arrival. Then lunch, usually with a celebrity or PR contact, would last for two or three hours—and as many bottles of wine.

I'd somehow make it back to the office halfway through the afternoon and then start to work on a story. But within a very short time, my blood sugar level had plummeted, making it well nigh impossible to resist the invitations of my colleagues to go with them for 'just a quick one'. Needless to say, I rarely made it back to my desk after that.

Sitting in Sai Baba's courtyard that morning, I began to realise, for the first time, the extent of my fall from grace. Feeling the bare concrete on my legs, I shamefully thought back to those times when I'd had to be picked up from the platform by the porters at Waterloo station and carried on to the train.

I began to see that I'd spent the previous two decades in a spiritual desert, blinded by sandstorms. As I looked at the shining faces of the devotees all around me, I was reminded of my favourite parable from St Luke's gospel, of how, when the Prodigal Son returned to his father's mansion, he saw that even the servants were better off than him.

> How many of my father's hired men have food to spare, and here I am starving to death! I will set out and go back to my father and say to him: Father, I have sinned against heaven and against you. I am no longer worthy to be called your son; make me like one of your hired.

Just then I noticed that Sai Baba had flattened his hand palm downwards and he was swirling it in a circular movement. He then closed it into a fist, only to open it again. Then what looked like white powder flowed out from his palm like a fountain, and sprayed over everyone in the vicinity. My jaw dropped.

My neighbour, the grey-haired Australian woman, nudged me.

"I can see you're new," she said, brushing my arm kindly.

I told her it was my first day.

"I've been coming here every year for the past nine," she told me.

"How old are you?" I asked.

"Seventy-three," she said proudly.

"And you don't mind sitting on the ground?" I asked.

"No way," she grinned. "It's well worth it."

"So what was all that with the white powder then?" I asked.

She threw her head back and laughed.

"That's called *vibhuuthi* ('vi-booti')," she said. "It's like ash. Sai Baba regularly materialises it out of the air and it has great healing qualities. You can eat it or put it on your third eye," and she pointed to a place on my forehead between my eyebrows.

She went on to tell me that Sai Baba was an incarnation of Vishnu, one of the Hindu gods. She said that he was the most recent in a long line of them. But it was when she got to the part about him being Kalki, a warrior version of Vishnu, that what felt like an explosion went off in my head, and the images from a dream I'd had years before, passed before me.

It was as if a very great battle was about to take place. There were legions of troops drawn up. At the head of them were three mounted horsemen in a line, with one riderless horse next to them. All seemed to be waiting for that horse's rider to arrive before the battle could begin. I was wondering who it could be. Then I suddenly realised that it was me. I was the missing platoon leader. So I quickly ran up and mounted the horse.

Then I looked up to see our general, who was just starting to address us. But he wasn't just an ordinary general. He was a splendid being whose fierce beauty glistened brilliantly against the breaking dawn sun. His radiance was so bright, we could barely look at him. He was smiling so lovingly at us, as if he was so proud of us and loved us so much, that our hearts were like dogs straining at the leash.

Then he began to speak. But it wasn't the usual rousing 'England and St George!' kind of speech. On the contrary, he was telling us that were going to lose this battle. He was making it clear that it was impossible for us to emerge as the victors. It was written somewhere—in the stars, probably—and we couldn't do anything about it.

To each of us soldiers, though, it wasn't the point. We just looked at this divine being and knew we'd follow him into any battle, no matter what the consequences. It wasn't about winning and it wasn't about outcomes. It was about doing the right thing and being who we truly were. We were destined to fight and give our all, and whether it was something about being close to death, or close to him, I don't know. But my senses were so heightened that I could hear every single bird's song in that divine dawn chorus, and the dewdrops that were falling from the leaves sounded like the tinkling of bells in the crisp frosty air.

For the first time, too, I'd felt what it was to be clean, to be pure. I was whole, or holy. It was as if, at last, my life had meaning. It was the first day of the world for me, even though I knew it was my last. And my heart was warm with joy and gratitude that I'd been included in such a noble assignment.

My last memory was being given the signal to charge…and then I woke up.

I woke up next to my boyfriend, with the bruises on my stomach turning black and blue from where he'd beaten me in a drunken rage the night before. I woke to the usual road crash of my life. The life of a tabloid journalist where nothing was ever noble, or true, or worth fighting for. There were half-empty wine glasses and ashtrays over-spilling on the bedside table. Even the bed was a mess.

So I was back to reality.

Over the days that followed that dream, I soon saw that I'd had an experience of truth, of holiness, that had turned my life upside down. Ever afterwards, no matter what I did, it felt shabby, tawdry, empty, meaningless and an utter unholy waste. As the weeks, months and years wore on, I eventually managed to rid myself of such a destructive relationship with a violent partner. But I still felt increasingly bereft to have been given a glimpse of such a noble and worthwhile existence, only to have had it snatched away from me.

It was strange to have suddenly remembered it all again here. But I also had a feeling that for the first time, I recognised the general. As I came out of my reveries, I could see Sai Baba was coming in our direction. He looked so beautiful, so tiny. His soft orange robes were blowing in the breeze and caressing his bare brown feet. His long, black, lion-like mane of hair framed an almost aboriginal Dravidian face that was wreathed in age lines of gentle kindness.

Watching him walk, I was reminded of something I'd read about Krishna. It was said that Krishna walked 'like a wild elephant in must.' I'm not sure that I've ever seen a wild elephant in must but, in a poetic sense, I could see what they meant. Sai Baba's eyes, too, radiated the power of someone who knew the truth, and always lived by it—and it wasn't a power you saw every day. In fact, I'd never seen it in anyone before, except in that dream.

Just then, he started walking towards us. So I mentally wrapped up the image of the general from my dream and projected this thought form towards him, with the question:

"I think that was you, wasn't it?"

He stopped abruptly and then checked himself just a little, as if he'd heard something. Then he cocked his head slightly quizzically to one side, like a bird. Then he grinned in recognition, looked up again and over at me and nodded and smiled, and then waved his hands at me in the gesture of showering blessings.

I was stunned. But he just glided off on his way as if it was nothing—as if it was just a normal, everyday occurrence for him to turn up in someone's dream and completely destroy their life; no sweat for him to give a person feelings that they've never had before and what's more, realise that they liked them! No, I could almost hear him thinking, it wasn't going to be any trouble at all to take this raddled old tart and turn her into an absolute paragon of virtue.

As soon as he'd gone, I got up, tore out of the gates and ran down Lake View Road. I couldn't wait to get back to the hotel to tell Miranda.

Young stallholder boys were out selling Sai Baba posters, Sai Baba tea-towels, Sai Baba badges, all kinds of Sai Baba paraphernalia and as I ran, they'd suddenly loom up in front of me with their big posters of his face and practically trip me up. I had to keep stopping and swerving. But the net effect of all this was that Sai Baba's face and eyes were smiling at me, laughing at me, teasing me and, surprisingly, loving me, all the way back to the hotel.

I finally made it back to the hotel and ran into our room, panting. Miranda was still in bed. Her sleepy head emerged from under the sheets.

"What is it?" she yawned. "What time is it?"

"This is it!" I cried. "This is it!"

I just stood there. I couldn't find any other words. Luckily, I didn't have to explain any further. We'd both been looking for the same thing for so long, and she could tell by my face that I thought that I'd found it.

"Well, okay," she said. "But I'm going to have to see for myself, to make up my own mind."

I could tell that she was trying not to get too excited or anything, in case it turned out to be a big disappointment. On top of that, she was almost as jaded and world-weary as I had been—which, at the age of twenty-one, was going it some.

So we went out for *dosa* breakfast (stuffed rice pancakes). Afterwards, we rummaged around various bookshops for some literature on Sai Baba that could tell us more about him in a language that we could understand. In the end, we found a biography and also a book on Vishnu, which, after my conversation with the Australian devotee, I was keen to start reading immediately.

So we soon returned to our hotel and settled down on our comfortable double bed to our books. Very quickly, something struck me. According to the Vishnu book, one of the things for which Vishnu was famous was that he never failed at anything he turned his hand to. And, I was relieved to find, he'd had a lot bigger challenges than me.

For instance, there was a fascinating story about the demon and the enchantress. It went something like this:

Once upon a time, Shiva, who was one of the Indian gods, had very unfortunately granted a power to an extremely evil demon. This power enabled the demon to instantly incinerate, on the spot, anyone he felt like. All he had to do was put his hand on their heads. And the first person the power-crazed demon tried to destroy with his power was Lord Shiva.

He had tried to place his hand on Shiva's head. But Shiva had quickly ducked and then he flew off to the beautiful and sacred planet of Vaikuntha ('Vye- kunta'). On Vaikuntha lived the only being in the universe that could save Lord Shiva from this terrible demon. It was, of course, Lord Vishnu.

Vishnu listened carefully to Shiva's tale of woe and then immediately hit upon a plan. He disguised himself as the most beautiful, seductive woman ever, and everyone soon fell under her enchantment. Even Lord Shiva made a bit of a fool of himself over her—and *he* knew it was Vishnu!

Naturally, the evil demon was equally enamoured with this divine diva. As Mohini started to perform her seductive dance, his eyes nearly popped out of his head at the mere sight of her tiny, delicate feet, her lithe, wriggling hips and her pert, jiggling breasts. In fact, he became so mesmerised by her beauty that he started to imitate everything she did.

So Mohini waved her hand in the air, and the demon waved *his* hand in the air. Then Mohini circled her arm around her head, and the demon circled *his* arm around his head. Then Mohini placed her hand on her head, and the demon placed *his* hand on his head. Oh! His face had barely the time to register his mistake when—pfffff! All that was left of the demon was a pile of smouldering ashes.

This story struck a deep chord with me, although I wasn't quite sure why. But I was starting to think that the demon might be an allegory for the selfish and proud ego, and I was beginning to wonder if Sai Baba was going to dance mine to death, too, when our alarm clock suddenly rang.

At last, it was time for the afternoon *darshan* session. So we grabbed some cushions and set off for Sai Baba's bungalow.

Once again, though, because I still hadn't worked out the queuing system, we were the first ones to arrive at his gates, and the last ones in. So Miranda and I were sitting well back in the crowd when Sai Baba finally appeared on his porch.

I couldn't see him very well, but enough to notice that he turned his head in our direction. Then Miranda's chin suddenly tipped up and her head fell backwards.

Later, she told me:

"His eyes were boring so deep into mine, the force of it actually pushed my head back."

"So what did you think?" I asked.

She was silent for a few seconds, and then replied:

"Well, he's obviously no ordinary man, although like you, I can't put it into words. But I think you might be right, and this could very well be it."

So there we were, both of us not sure what was going on, although knowing that something was up. But at least there was one thing we had worked out as we turned in that night. Dear practical Miranda had figured out their queuing system, meaning that we could have a bit more of a lie-in the next day.

So we felt quite refreshed and rested the following morning, when we arrived at Sai Baba's bungalow. We were among the first in through the gates this time, and found places quite near the front of the crowd.

But no sooner had we got comfortable on our cushions than we noticed that something quite different appeared to be happening. There was a strange buzz in the air. The ushers kept running into the house and then out again. They were looking very secretive.

Then Sai Baba was late. So we all started shuffling around, wondering what was going on. I was even thinking that he'd probably given up on us as a bad job. I wouldn't have been the least surprised to have been told that he'd dematerialised his human body and returned to Vaikuntha.

But then he suddenly appeared on the balcony, grinning fit to bust, his long dark curls blowing in the breeze, with a tea towel flung casually over his shoulder.

The next thing that happened was that long lines of ushers started coming out of the kitchen, and into the courtyard, and they were carrying paper plates of steaming food.

"We're all going to be fed!" said Miranda.

I couldn't believe it. The logistics of the exercise were overwhelming. It wasn't exactly the feeding of the 5,000, but it was close enough.

"How's he going to feed all these people from just an ordinary bungalow kitchen?" I replied.

Well, the plates of steaming food just kept coming and then were passed back and back until they reached the back row. As soon as the back row was satisfied, the plates were passed to the second-to-back row, and so on, until it was finally the turn of the front row. Within less than an hour, we all had a plate of delicious rice and curried vegetables on our laps, and were eating with relish.

Throughout the whole process, Sai Baba walked continually between the kitchen and the balcony, still with his tea towel jauntily tossed over his shoulder, as he looked over into the crowd, in a motherly sort of way, to see how the meal distribution was going. Then his tiny orange form would glide, swan-like, back to the kitchen.

Knowing that he was famous for materialising things out of the air, like his *vibhuuthi* ash, I whispered to Miranda:

"Maybe he's just conjuring up this food…maybe they're not cooking it at all."

It certainly tasted divine.

Just then, Sai Baba came out on to his balcony again. Seeing that the ushers had now more or less collected back all the used paper plates, he waved his hand in the direction of the kitchen—and another long line of helpers started to appear, this time carrying our dessert.

It was wonderfully sweet, sticky, deep-fried and impossibly rich and fattening—it was a *laddhu* ('la-doo'). And then it stuck in my throat as I got the joke, and tears came into my eyes.

Miranda looked at me questioningly.

"He's vegetarian," I said. "He couldn't serve the fatted calf. So instead, it's the fattening *laddhu*!"

Chapter 4
On with the dance!

Miranda and I spent the next few weeks doing nothing but going to see Sai Baba at his bungalow. I was in bliss. It was as if I'd finally managed to banish all the 'white noise' of my life in order to concentrate on what really mattered. I was loving it.

We'd managed to get hold of several books on Sai Baba by now, and as the day would revolve around when we had to be at his bungalow garden, the rest would be spent lying on our enormous double bed, going through these books in the hope of understanding more about this seemingly divine enigma. There was no doubting his charm, his beauty, his all-attractiveness. In my opinion, he was drop dead gorgeous. But who was he?

As we were spending so much time with them, we also got to know some of his devotees. So our first impressions of pure, unalloyed devotion gradually gave way to a deeper understanding about why people go to Sai Baba (or Swami, as they called him).

There turned out to be quite a mixed bag of motives. It was as if, just like Mohini, Sai Baba had a universal magnetic force. Everything and everyone was drawn to his greater density. They all appeared to be just orbiting around him in a grand processional dance. And just like the sun, the rays of his love seemed to fall on the righteous and unrighteous alike. They all seemed to desire it equally.

However, we did get to meet some real dedicated seekers after truth. There were some authentic-looking yogis, bearded sages and saffron-robed monks that seemed to have devoted their whole lives to the pursuit of God. There were even other *gurus* who said that they'd come to the conclusion that their own powers were as nothing compared to his. We discovered that he was known as 'the *guru's guru*'.

But then there were also those who appeared to be there for less esoteric reasons. Some just wanted Sai Baba to heal their illness or disability. Others were hoping that he would materialise a piece of jewellery out of the air for them, which he often did. In fact, you could always recognise the rings given by Sai Baba because they were usually inset with brilliant green stones.

Then there were followers who would beg Sai Baba to use his powers to get them a promotion in their jobs, or find them a wife, or a husband. And there were even some who appeared to have come all that way just for the ego trip of being in the company of such a holy man—"Wait 'till we tell the folks back home!". The idea in this case being that once they got his blessings, they could just blithely continue with whatever they were doing before, right or wrong.

Anyway, the strange thing about it all was that Sai Baba just appeared to be going along with most of it. As we saw it then, he seemed to be giving everyone exactly whatever it was that they wanted. I'd been wracking my brains to think of who he reminded me of, in his behaviour. Then one day it struck me. It was all a bit like *Charlie and the Chocolate Factory*, with Sai Baba playing the part of Willy Wonka.

He would miraculously materialise rings, necklaces or watches out of the air for some. For those who wanted their illnesses cured, he would just wave his hand and *vibhuuthi* would magically spring like a fountain from his open palm into that of the eager recipient. Middle managers would return home to find that they'd been promoted to senior managers. Single women of a certain age—the Shirley Valentines, as we dubbed them—who'd long given up hope of ever finding a husband, were united with their soul mates. Everyone would go away happy.

But besides all of us common-or-garden spiritual seekers, he also seemed to be surrounded by a sort of inner circle. And while this was mainly composed of some really quite beautiful, extraordinarily spiritual people—a shining example to us all—there was also quite a serious bunch of individuals who you really wouldn't want to cross.

In fact, we'd heard that there had been some deaths there, a decade or so before. It was quite difficult to untangle exactly what went on. It appeared to have to do with all the money sloshing around Sai Baba, what with all the rich (by Indian standards, anyway) Western devotees giving donations to his hospitals, colleges and universities. But being a total renunciate, Sai Baba never had anything to do with this money, leaving it all to be handled and managed by his staff. So human nature being what it is, something was bound to occur, sooner or later.

It had all happened years before. But we heard that one faction of them was challenged by another, and it all ended up with four young men getting bullets through their chests. Now whether these were four young men who sacrificed themselves in the line of duty, or four young men trying to make off with the loot, depends on who's telling the tale. Suffice to say, it all seemed very murky at the time. It doesn't look as if the police came out of it very well either. Apparently, they initially filed one report, and then changed their story and filed another.

So, as I'm sure is becoming apparent, this wasn't your classically calm and meditative Indian spiritual set-up. It was often quite busy and noisy and we would all be bunched up together so tightly in Sai Baba's bungalow garden, and for such long periods of time, that sometimes arguments would break out. It was so bad at times, that I began to wonder whether there would be other ashrams in India that would be more suitable, quieter and more focussed. But then I would think about Sai Baba, and think:

"No ... let's stay a while longer and see what happens."

I was becoming so fascinated by him that leaving wasn't really an option. But the chaotic pot-pourri of variegated agendas around Sai Baba reminded me of an old Indian story, and it went something like this:

> Once upon a time, there was a very rich king called Janaka. King Janaka, as you would expect, had several grand, magnificent palaces throughout his enormous kingdom. But the one in the city of Mysore was a veritable treasure trove.
>
> Its extensive pleasure gardens of scrupulously manicured lawns boasted priceless marble statues dotted among the fountains. Peacocks paraded around gushing waterfalls that flowed into lotus-covered lakes, which were bordered by vast beds of exotically coloured roses and lilies.

The outer facade of the palace was a luxurious riot of pink marble and golden domes, delicately curved arches, bow-like canopies, magnificent bay windows and columns in the Byzantine style. It was all lit up at night by ten thousand light bulbs.

Inside, the pietra dura mosaic floors were inlaid with semi-precious stones and the hallways lined with the most sought-after antiques, like rare Queen Anne walnut veneered bookcases and cabinets of Flemish scarlet tortoiseshell. These all led to an enormous beautifully carved rosewood door that was the entrance into the magnificent throne room. Inside it, the light streamed through a high arched stained glass ceiling, and bounced off precious diamond-encrusted golden chandeliers that set off exquisite Chinese silk tapestries hanging from the walls.

But despite being so immensely rich, King Janaka was actually a very spiritual and holy man. So he eventually grew tired of all his treasures. In fact, one day, he woke up and realised that what he needed was a really good clear out. So he called his secretaries and bade them to send out a proclamation to all his subjects that they should come and take whatever they wanted.

It read:

"Please come to my palace and take whatever you desire. Whatever is mine is yours. Signed, King Janak."

So his subjects came in their droves and, as they poured through the golden gates, it was just like the first day of the Harrods' sale. They ran through all the beautiful opulent rooms in his palace. They rampaged along his mosaic-floored hallways and fought over all the gold-and-diamond encrusted chandeliers. All the hand-woven silk Persian rugs were quickly despatched, as were the Lalique vases, the French Louis XVI ormolu clocks and the golden dinner plates, and even the crystal drinking goblets were spirited away without a single breakage.

In fact, as the day drew to a close, there was little that had not been snapped up. They'd even taken King Janak's Rolex Oyster watch. But just as everything was almost gone, and the townspeople were staggering through the golden gates with their spoils, they noticed a small woman walking towards them.

"You've left it very late," they cried. "There's hardly anything left."

But she calmly walked past them, through the gates, past the fountains and the denuded flowerbeds and on through the palace doors. Her footsteps rang along the now empty corridors. Barely sparing a glance for the ugly patches on the walls from where the old masters had been removed, she carried on until she reached the throne room.

There she found King Janaka sitting cross-legged on the floor in meditation—his enormous peacock throne having been snapped up by one particularly insistent shopper.

"King Janaka," she said, approaching him. "I have come to take you up on your offer."

"That's fine," he replied, hardly bothering to open his eyes. "Please take whatever you want."

"Thank you, King Janaka," she said, and she stood right in front of him with both feet planted firmly on the ground. "I know very clearly what I want. I want you. I want nothing else but you."

King Janaka was quite wide-awake now and frantically looking round for a likely substitute.

"Look, what about that nice Ming vase over there? Surely you'd like that? It would fetch an excellent price at auction."

"No, King Janaka," she replied, firmly. "Please let me refresh your memory. You said, 'Whatever is mine, is yours.' Well, you belong to yourself, and so I would like you."

Well, King Janaka couldn't argue with that. She was right. And what's more, in choosing the king, the source of all the riches, she also became entitled to everything he owned. So they lived happily ever after.

As the days went by, I began to be aware that I had the same mixed bag of motives held by the other petitioners here. Sure, I wanted Sai Baba to help me to find the eternal divine love of God. However, I wouldn't have minded if he'd also found me, while he was about it, a halfway decent husband—or at least one who didn't get drunk, run around with other women and beat me up. I also wanted his blessing on the work I was doing as a Reiki Master. But, above all, I wanted him to help me become more 'true' spiritually, so that my words and actions were more aligned with my beliefs.

I'd become painfully aware that my inner core was rotten. I'd think one thing, say another and do something else entirely. I was completely out-of-synch, dysfunctional if you like, and it made my life meaningless. For instance, I was probably the only Reiki Master who was still smoking 20 Marlboros a day. I knew that, if I was to become more 'spiritual', at the very least I'd have to give up cigarettes—and I was dreading it.

My plan, therefore, was to soak up as much of the spiritual atmosphere as possible so that, after a few months or so, I could start to think about trying to give up smoking. In other words, it was all a long way off and I didn't need to worry too much about it. Or so I thought.

We'd only been at Kodaikanal for a few days when Sai Baba gave a talk. It was quite difficult to make it all out. Sai Baba spoke in his native south Indian Telegu tongue and the translator was continually being drowned out by a) Sai Baba butting in just as he was getting to the most crucial part of each sentence, b) the screeching feedback from the sound system and c) the rumbling of the generator used to power said sound system. On top of that, I was sitting cross-legged in the pouring rain.

Despite all these distractions, though, there was one stream of words that managed to penetrate and put down roots in my mind, no matter how much afterwards I tried to dislodge it. Sai Baba said:

"You will never make any progress on the spiritual path until you give up all stimulants, like cigarettes, alcohol, coffee and tea."

Ow! That was really unfair! I'd barely unpacked and there he was, demanding I give up smoking....now!

The alcohol wasn't so much of a problem. I'd been going off that anyway and now that we were in a 'dry state', I rarely even thought about it. Coffee and tea, too, were only drunk as an accessory to the cigarette. But smoking! How on earth could I possibly do what he asked? It was totally unreasonable of him! I'd only just got there!

That night in bed, hot streams of tears flowed down my cheeks.

I was right all along, I sobbed inwardly. *I'm nowhere near spiritually advanced enough for this great teacher. There's no point in being here if I can't do what he says. I might as well pack up and go home now.*

My thoughts turned to the great send-off that family and friends had given us. It had also been my parents' golden wedding celebration and, because none of our relatives had ever been to India, friends and relations that we hadn't seen in years were, in turn, impressed, intrigued and fervently wishing us well on our journey. So the thought of having to return after just a few weeks was galling. In the end, I prayed:

"Dear Lord Sai Baba. They say you are all-powerful, so please hear my prayer. If it's true what they say about you, then you know, even better than I, the reason why I smoke and what it will take for me to give up. Only you will know the pain I'm trying to numb by these means. Only you will know how that pain got there, in the first place. Please help me, because I cannot do it myself. I really don't know what to do! Please help!"

I went on in this vein for quite some time until, eventually, I realised that a still small voice had been trying to make itself heard for some time, through all the turmoil:

"You can do it. You can. You just have to say you'll do it…that you'll *do* it, not just '*try to*'. That's important. Just say that you will do it. I'll do the rest."

But my ego wasn't going down without a fight. It was flying around like a lawyer desperately searching for a loophole. So it was well into the early hours before it realised that there wasn't one, and I was finally forced to say:

"Okay, then. Yes, I will do it."

The next morning, I woke up…and I had no desire to smoke. Now, this wasn't so extraordinary because I'd never really been one of those people who immediately lit a cigarette upon waking. However, breakfast came and went, and still there was no sign of the nicotine monster. The eleven o'clock period, too, when I would normally have to have a cigarette with a cup of coffee, passed without incident. All was going brilliantly well. Then Miranda and I went out to lunch.

We found a small local restaurant and sat outside on a tiny patio that overlooked a pretty little garden lined with *pipalla* (fig) trees. At the next table, there was a merry trio of very beautiful-looking people; the sort of folks who, in those days, would appeal to my idea of what 'spiritual' looked like.

And after we'd finished our meal, the woman of the group turned and beckoned us over to join them.

"Hi, I'm Eva," she said, standing up and pushing her chair along to make room for us.

We could see then that she was a tall, slim and model-like young Englishwoman with huge honey-flecked brown eyes and glossy dark brown hair swept back into a chignon at the nape of her elegant neck.

The taller and darker-haired man of the party was leaning over the table and extending his hand.

"William, Eva's brother," he said, "pleased to meet you," and he chuckled as he gestured to a sandy haired older man with a lived-a-lot glint in his eye. "And this is American Joe, as we call him."

American Joe gave us a cheery grin. Both the men were wearing the traditional white Indian *dhoti* and *kurta*—long pieces of cloth tied at the waist, and hip-length shirts.

Miranda and I introduced ourselves, and then sat down while the group carried on chatting.

"Anyway, as I was saying," said Joe. "We really should see the Chidambaram temple."

"Is it like that one at Madurai?" asked Eva. "That was really cool! But I really do want to go to Srivilliputur too."

"What's at Srivilliputur?" asked Miranda, her face brightening with the realisation that we'd stumbled upon such a knowledgeable and experienced group of fellow travellers on India's spiritual circuit.

"Srivilliputur is where Andal lived. Do you not know the story of Andal?"

"No, do tell," she said, her face alight.

Eva smoothed the skirts of her green silk *sari* and cleared her throat as we all made ourselves comfortable for the story.

"Andal is one of the most famous young women of Tamil Nadu. She was a foundling who was discovered under a basil plant by a priest. He took her in and became her father and, when she became older, Andal would help him in the temple with the worship of the idol of Lord Vishnu.

"Every morning, Andal would go to the temple to do *puja* to Lord Vishnu. She always brought him fresh flowers and basil leaves, and used them to decorate his statue. Sometimes she'd sit for hours just looking at him, and talking to him. She even began visiting him after school when she was supposed to be doing her homework.

"Eventually, Andal grew into a beautiful young woman. So her father, the priest, began to make enquiries with other families about their sons. He soon got a couple of highly suitable and compatible marital candidates lined up. But it was no good. For it was then that Andal realised that she'd become so in love with Lord Vishnu that she really couldn't marry anyone else."

Eva paused for dramatic effect—and the silence around the table was almost audible as four people waited for her next word.

"On hearing this, her father became extremely worried. He told her that if she didn't marry, she'd end up alone with no one to look after her. This was and still is, to a large extent, a very serious matter in India. However, Andal was adamant.

"Then, one night," she continued, "Lord Vishnu came to Andal's father in a dream. He told him to see that his daughter was dressed in all her bridal finery and that he should then send her to the great temple at Srirangam.

"The father was shocked. But because of his devotion to Vishnu, he knew it was no ordinary dream. So the next day Andal was robed in her red and gold wedding *sari* and bedecked with her golden ornaments and jewellery. Then her father put her in a horse-drawn palanquin and she was taken to Srirangam."

Eva paused again, and took a sip of water before going on.

"Andal sat as nervously as any bride in her palanquin. She didn't know whether to shout with joy or run with terror. But as the palanquin approached the temple gates at Srirangam, Andal could wait no longer. She jumped off it and ran straight into the temple towards the idol of Vishnu—and within seconds, both had disappeared in a blaze of light."

There was a silence as we all absorbed the surprising pay-off line. Then Miranda said:

"Wow! That's a great story! But do you think it's true?"

"Well, who knows," laughed Eva. "But if we go to Srivilliputur, we can see the basil garden where Andal was first found. The house where she was brought up has been turned into a temple dedicated to her."

"Okay," said William. "And then maybe we could then go on to Tiruchendur for the Skanda Shashti festival? It's fantastic! It's on the beach and it goes on for twelve days."

"So when are you going?" asked Miranda, her eyes wide with interest now.

Joe gestured to the waiter for coffee.

"Well, I think we've just about done Sai Baba now," he said.

"Yes, he was cute, wasn't he?" said Eva.

"So maybe we'll leave tomorrow ..." Joe continued. "Now Ishtar and Miranda, black coffee or white?"

It was then that I noticed that Eva was offering an open silver cigarette case in my direction.

I must admit, I hesitated. Then I said:

"Well, er ... actually I'm trying to do what Sai Baba said yesterday."

"Oh yes," said Eva, smiling knowingly across the table at William, who burst out laughing. "Well, we would all like to do what Sai Baba says, wouldn't we..." and she left the unspoken "but no-one really expects us to, do they?" hanging in the air between us. There was even a slight hint of ...

"... of course, those of us who are spiritually sophisticated in these matters understand these things."

You can see how I was tempted. I would have loved to believe her. But I knew, by then, that Sai Baba—and my own conscience—was not going to let me get away with it. It was then that I started to realise that a change was taking place. I was beginning to get the feeling that it didn't matter what others chose to do. If I didn't obey Sai Baba's directions, then I could trail around every temple in India and offer homage at every shrine. But I would still be at the bottom of the dunces' class as far as spiritual progress went.

So I declined. Shortly after that, we wished them luck on their travels and made our goodbyes.

Miranda, I could see, was a bit torn. I think she'd been considering going with them. She was slightly disgruntled that she wouldn't be going to any wild Indian beach festivals. But she was also pleased that I resisted the cigarette.

After that, I more or less breezed through the afternoon tea period. By the time dinner and the post-prandial period had passed, I knew I was free—and I was.

So, he had kept his promise. He'd made it so easy for me—almost embarrassingly so. I'd escaped the nicotine monster and made a clean getaway.

However, I was left with the feeling that my spiritual journey was not always going to be so straightforward and easy. Everyday, the *dhobi*, or washerwomen, would come to collect our *saris* for soaping and pounding on the banks of the river. I was beginning to suspect that there would be times when Sai Baba was going to need to purify me, to clean me up, to give me a good scrubbing too—and that there would also be times when he wouldn't spare the soap.

CHAPTER 5
NATARAJA, THE DIVINE DANCER

One of things that Miranda and I couldn't get over about Kodaikanal was that, along with the Sai Baba contingent, there were also hoards of regular Indian tourists who'd come there to escape their own hot climate and to bask in the cold and the rain. Some days, we would be shivering in our newly-bought *saris* and feeling slightly let-down as it was a bit too much like what we'd just left behind—especially Miranda, who'd joked in Goa that her main reason for coming to India was to get "thin, brown and spiritual." We were doing quite well on the "thin" bit, though, as one or the other of us seemed to be forever going down with bouts of sickness and could barely keep a meal down.

It turned out that Sai Baba was also there on holiday from his main ashram, Prasanthi Nilayam, which was currently sweltering at over 90 degrees down in the agricultural plains of the Andhra Pradesh region. His definition of 'holiday', though, seemed to be quite unique in that he never took a single day off from seeing to the needs of his devotees.

He was due to stay at Kodaikanal for only another couple of weeks and then the whole cosmic caravan was due to leave for his second ashram called Whitefields, which was near Bangalore.

Until then, though, Miranda and I were more than happy to continue with our daily schedule of reading and going to visit Sai Baba. I had just got started on his biography.

I learned that he was born as Sathyanarayana ('satya-narai-arna') Raju on 23 November 1926, in the village of Puttaparthi ('put-a-party') in the sheep-grazing region of Andhra Pradesh. Apparently, the Rajus had been a well-known pious family of chieftains in that area for generations. They'd built and dedicated many temples and would often take part in local religious plays, which were the main form of entertainment in those days.

It is said that Sai Baba's grandfather, Sri Kondama Raju, spent the whole of his 110-year life in constant contemplation of God. As a master of music, he knew, off-by-heart, the whole of the *Ramayana* epic (the story of a previous incarnation of Vishnu, Lord Rama). Whenever the villagers put on the play, Kondama Raju would always be called upon to play the part of Rama's brother. When he died, in 1950, they say he passed away peacefully singing verses from the play.

In those days, there was also a professional group of players who would travel from place to place, putting on religious entertainments. And while Sathya was still very young, one of these groups came to visit Puttaparthi, and their plays began to pull in such enormous crowds that they soon became the talk of the whole district.

One of the highlights of their show involved a young girl who was part dancer, part gymnast. Her *piece de resistance* was a routine in which, keeping track of the timing and the tune, she danced with a bottle balanced on her head and performed various contortions. She would bend low, then sit down and lay herself face down on the floor, open her mouth and bite on a handkerchief placed on a matchbox on the floor and, with the handkerchief between her teeth sit back again, then rise and stand, with the bottle still balancing perfectly on her head. It would win her a standing ovation every night.

Now one day, apparently, the little Sathya was taken by his family to see these plays and he also saw the girl dancer. And when he got home, so the story goes, he tried to perform her routine himself. To everyone's immense surprise, he could do it without much trouble at all. However, when his parents asked to see this new item in Sathya's repertory, the little boy withdrew within himself and hesitated.

But the news got out into the village. So some of Sathya's more persuasive friends managed to talk him into dancing the famous feat at the Cattle Fair, and to pretend to be the young girl dancer.

When the big night finally arrived, Sathya's sisters dressed and made him up to look like a pretty little girl. Then they took him to the Cattle Fair. And when the curtain rose and the 'girl dancer' tripped her way on to the stage, the audience was too wild with excitement to notice any difference.

So the famous dance piece began...but Sathya had improved upon it. Instead of the handkerchief on the matchbox, he had put a needle—and he lifted that needle by his eyelids.

And, the story continues:

> '... the audiences applauded His acting, singing and, above all, His dance. For there was rhythm in his feet, a sense of time and tune, they had seldom seen; a litheness and a loveliness which made them feel, "He never touched the earth, He belonged to some ethereal region."'

It occurred to me that none of that was any big deal for the original Mohini. In fact, since reading about Vishnu's manifestation in the form of the seductress who'd fooled the demon, I'd recently learned that he had taken on any number of guises including those of at least ten incarnations of God.

Apparently, Vishnu had first appeared on earth as Matsya, a fish; his second incarnation was as Kurma, the Divine Turtle, an amphibious creature; and thirdly, he came as a land animal, the Divine Boar. Then came Narasimha ('nara-seema'), the man-lion incarnation of God, which bridged man and animal. After that, man-cum-dwarf was represented by the diminutive Vamana, ('var-marna') the fifth Vishnu incarnation.

Prithu, ('pree-two') the sixth incarnation of God, was the first consecrated king of mankind and he taught man agriculture. Parusarama, ('pa-roosha-rarmer') the seventh incarnation, was said to have been a bit of a hothead who carried an axe and used it to conquer Persia. Rama, the eighth Vishnu incarnation, established the dharma, or Divine Law, and Krishna, the ninth incarnation, brought the message of Divine Love.

And this brings us up to date, with the tenth incarnation, Kalki, whose purpose, I was learning, was to bring the Golden Age upon the earth by destroying the opposing demonic forces. Some say that he is yet to arrive, others that it is Sai Baba. But we were still making up our minds about that.

It was difficult. Sometimes I'd wake in the night thinking that Sai Baba seemed a bit too good to be true. I would have wonderful experiences in his bungalow garden every day. But as soon as I left, my head would fill with doubts, not least because it seemed incredible that as soon as Miranda and I had decided to head off on our search for God, we'd almost immediately bumped into his representative on earth. I'd think, surely we should have to spend lifetime upon lifetime, sitting in very painful lotus positions in the Himalayas or something, to warrant such an outcome?

Anyway, as the days rolled by, there was a slowly growing body of speculation in the bungalow queue about when Sai Baba would be moving on to the Whitefields ashram, a day's drive away. One woman was already packed, so as not to miss the off. Some were convinced that it would be "next Tuesday"; others were equally adamant that it couldn't be because "he never travels on a Tuesday. It's an inauspicious day for travelling."

The timing was important to these devotees. They needed to have their act together so that they weren't caught by surprise when Sai Baba left. They liked to follow his shiny red BMW, as he would often stop off on the way and talk to them.

Finally, though, the day dawned and at last Sai Baba was off to Whitefields. There was a chaos of cars, taxis, jeeps and brightly-painted trucks, a riot of honking horns and cacophonic klaxons, as we waved off the whole cosmic cavalcade and watched as it begin to wend its way down the steep mountain road.

Miranda and I had decided to follow on later. We wanted to take a small detour first, to see a bit more of India. Being so close, we couldn't resist the idea of going to see one of its greatest temples at Madurai. So the following morning, after the dust had settled, we boarded a bus going south.

It was the usual bone-shaking, death-defying ride. We didn't dare look out of the windows. We spent most of the journey with our eyes shut, praying. Against all odds, though, the bus did finally reach Madurai, late in the afternoon, and we were pleasantly surprised to find that, finally, we'd hit 'old India'.

The buildings lining this city's narrow, cobbled, labyrinthine and bustling streets went back to the great Padya kings from the Tamil era over a thousand years ago. We found, at its centre, the huge Meenakshi temple, which turned out to be actually more like a small village with its shops and stalls. Dedicated to the fish-eyed goddess Meenakshi, the temple was enclosed by twelve enormous towers rising from granite bases. They were covered with stucco figures of gods and goddesses, and strange mythical creatures and monsters in vivid and gaudy colours.

So leaving our sandals in an enormous pile (from which I doubted we'd ever recover them) we entered through the high eastern gate into a great hall. It was like walking into a dark cloud of incense, camphor and spices. The sacred and arcane atmosphere was intensified by the chanting of shaven-headed monks. Until our eyes adjusted, all we could see was their saffron robes glowing like candle flames in the gloom.

There turned out to be four great halls. Each one was supported by thousands of pillars, all beautifully decorated with typical Dravidian sculptures of figures from Hindu mythology. We also saw and heard the extraordinary Musical Pillars. Each one, when struck, sounded a different note.

In fact, just like India's main religion, Hinduism, this temple seemed to contain something for everyone. In the course of our explorations, we came across a swing, a parrot cage, a gigantic idol of Ganesh (the elephant-headed god) and even, when we arrived in the centre of the complex, a real elderly, wrinkled elephant that regarded us with a somewhat rheumy eye.

In another of the halls, we came across an enormous tank of water. According to our guidebook, this was where the ancient academy of poets used to meet. Apparently, they would test the merit of any new piece of work by throwing it into the tank. Only those that did not sink to the bottom were deemed worthy of further attention.

Not being members of the Hindu religion, we were only allowed as far as the corridor outside the inner holy-of-holies. This inner sanctum contained the idols of the goddess Parvarti and her husband, Lord Shiva, which, this being the spring festival, were being readied for the annual marriage ritual. We were allowed into the outer corridor, though. And it was along this, in the Silver Room, that we found a beautiful silver statue of Nataraja, ('nat-a-rarja') the four-armed Lord of the Dance, his long locks of hair flying madly as he dances in ecstasy within a circle of flames.

One of the monks must have noticed us examining the Nataraja. He came over. He looked very young.

"Would you allow me to explain the symbolism of this statue," he asked sweetly.

We said that we would.

"This is the aspect of Lord Shiva that is the source of all movement in the cosmos," he explained. "The cosmos is represented as the circle of flames, and Shiva is responsible for its creation, sustenance and eventual destruction."

"Why has he got four arms?" asked Miranda.

"Each one is symbolic," the priest replied. "The upper right hand holds the drum from which creation springs forth. The lower right hand is raised in blessing. This represents his sustenance aspect. The upper left hand holds a flame, symbolising destruction. The lower left arm gestures towards his own raised foot, which is the source of grace for everyone."

Then he leant closer to the statue and pointed to the Nataraja's waist. It was then that I noticed that there was a snake winding around it.

"This cobra represents the power within all of us," the priest continued. "It's not just empty symbolism. The Nataraja is dancing within each and every one of us, at an atomic level, at all times. Our scriptures say that the birth of the world, its maintenance, its destruction and the soul's journey towards liberation are all contained within the Nataraja's dance."

Immediately, my thoughts turned back to my own spiritual journey, and to the teacher in which I had such high hopes.

I suddenly felt as though I was in a dream. Then I realised that I'd been feeling a bit like that for days now. The visit to the Madurai temple had just intensified the feeling. Miranda would often have to say the same thing twice to me. I couldn't seem to concentrate on anything, except Sai Baba. Part of me felt that because I was in India, I should visit these temples and experience something of the rest of the country and the culture. The other part, though, just wanted to be with him, and I found myself thinking about him all the time.

Luckily, Miranda felt the same way.

"I really miss Sai Baba," she sighed.

"Hmmm. So do I."

We thanked the priest and left the temple.

That night, we slept on hard wooden seats. We were on the last train out, heading towards Sai Baba's ashram at Whitefields.

At Bangalore railway station, we had to hold our noses because of the festering filth on the tracks. As we came out of its modern white edifice, we were amused to find dozens of taxi drivers rushing up to us with "Sai Baba? Sai Baba?".

Was it really that obvious? I thought, as we were driven off in a motorised rickshaw. But then I was pleased to find that it was only because the Whitefields ashram was just a half hour's drive away.

When we arrived at the ashram, its beauty surprised me. Pale pink and blue buildings that looked like large iced cakes were arranged around a huge courtyard.

I felt as though we'd come home and my heart rose—only to be immediately dashed again by a small Indian man at the gate that stopped us.

"No room," he said. "There's no room."

We reluctantly turned to leave. But just then, a middle-aged European-looking woman, dressed from head-to-toe in white, came rushing up.

"No, no, come with me," she said. "There is still some room."

She led us into one of the pink and blue buildings, which, she said, was the women's hostel. We followed her along a long blue corridor until she showed us into what she said was a sort of overflow room.

There were about a dozen women already in there. They had already laid out their sleeping bags and belongings. So Miranda and I did the same.

"They're a party from Sri Lanka," the woman in white told us. "They've just arrived too."

Then she took us to the canteen. The evening meal was in full swing. Lots of women were standing behind trestle tables dishing out food. One of them was a surprisingly sweet-faced Western woman who kept smiling lovingly at us. We held out our plates as she spooned on to them ample helpings of curried vegetables, lentils and rice. At the next table, we were given yoghurt and chapattis.

After such a good meal, we were feeling very satisfied and sleepy as we returned to the overflow room. We'd hardly slept on the overnight train to Bangalore. So we were looking forward to making up for it.

But it turned out to be impossible to sleep that night. We were stiflingly hot. The mosquitoes were feasting on us. So it was about four-thirty in the morning before we managed to fall asleep. Unfortunately, though, this was just when the Sri Lankans were waking up and switching on the harsh overhead light. They then proceeded to chat away among themselves as they prepared themselves for the day. From what we could glean, it seemed that they were hoping for an interview with Sai Baba. So they were going to no end of trouble with hairdryers and sickly smelling clouds of spray lacquer.

The lacquer was the final incentive to force us up and out, into the courtyard. We sat on a low wall and watched the *darshan* queues start to form.

Then the canteen opened for breakfast. We were amazed to find that we could have toast and marmite. A Canadian woman had brought a large jar of it from a specialist shop in Bangalore, and she was passing it around. As it had been over a month since we'd been able to have our favourite breakfast, Miranda and I were soon feeling much better.

We'd been advised by some of the Sri Lankans to go to see Mr Rao, the accommodation administrator, to ask if he could allocate us a room. We found his office easily enough. But there were quite a few ahead of us in the queue.

Finally though, it was our turn, and Mr Rao turned out to be a kindly and bespectacled Indian man who seemed to take his role very seriously. He pulled up two wooden chairs, bade us to sit down and then proceeded to ask a stream of questions about ourselves, all done in the most friendly manner as if he was genuinely interested in us.

He made us feel so welcome that by the time we left his office, I felt as if we'd made a friend and was convinced that if any room should become available, he would personally see to it that we were told immediately.

After that, we explored the grounds. We found a bookshop, a gift shop and also a large green playing field. On the other side of the playing field we could see some large, modern, white buildings. They turned out to be part of Sai Baba's college for boys.

Then we returned to the compound to have lunch.

We were just leaving the canteen afterwards when we saw Mr Rao. He was standing on the steps of the main building and waving something at us. Miranda ran to see what he wanted. When she returned, she was holding a large key.

"He said that two spaces have just come free in room A1," she said. "But he thinks we might not like it as it's right next to the communal bathroom. So shall I just go and check it out?"

"Sure," I said. "At least we won't have far to go when we get the runs in the night."

She dashed off.

Five minutes later, she was back.

"It's fine. It's really nice, and there's that woman you like there, too."

I asked who she meant. But her description didn't ring any bells. Anyway, we went to the Sri Lankans' room to collect our rucksacks and then found corridor A. It was a white washed corridor with half-walls looking out on to a central courtyard garden. We followed it along until we reached room A1, right at the end and, as Mr Rao had said, next to the bathroom.

The door was already open. We walked in, and there was the lovely young woman from the canteen, sitting on her bedroll in the corner. I said:

"Oh, it's you!"

She just grinned.

"Hi," she said, in a broad Bradford accent. "I'm Becky. Are you new? Only when I saw you yesterday, I thought you looked a bit lost."

"Yes, it was our first day," replied Miranda.

"Well, I've been coming here for years," said Becky. "So I'd be happy to act as your guide."

Her offer turned out to be invaluable. She took us out to the shops, and showed us where to get good-priced futon-like mattresses, sheets and mosquito nets. She also showed us how things were done in the ashram. There seemed to be a lot to learn, like which canteen to eat in (Western or Indian) and where to buy meal tickets or get pure drinking water. She was also extremely adept at straightening and retying my *sari*, which never looked as smart, with all the pleats lying perfectly, when I did it myself.

But more than just a guide to the facilities and activities, she also turned out to be such a good example of someone walking the spiritual path.

The floors of the huge Prayer Hall—where the *darshan* sessions with Sai Baba were held—were of a hard grey and white stone. You really needed a cushion. It would become completely jam packed, with the men seated on one side and the women on the other. So once you'd been seated by the ushers, it was difficult to get out again—well, without causing a great fuss anyway.

However, on one such occasion, I was already in the hall before I'd realised that I'd left my cushion in my room.

"Oh no!" I said. "Well, I'll just to have sit on the floor."

"No, no! Take mine," said Becky, and even though I tried to argue with her, she insisted.

Our accommodation was quite basic—just bed rolls and bedding on a stone floor. There were no wardrobes or cupboards to hang up our clothes. Becky showed me how to string up lines of string from which to hang our mosquito nets. Then she tucked the ends in, under our mattresses, so that they looked like little tents. These lines were also quite useful for hanging up our damp towels and our *saris,* even if the room did end up looking a bit like a laundry.

The routine at Whitefields was very similar to that of Kodaikanal, with *darshan* sessions twice a day.

Sai Baba still didn't seem to have noticed us, but we didn't mind. We were newcomers, after all, and so didn't feel as if we merited any special attention. We just loved to watch him as he floated around the hall, taking a letter there, materialising *vibhuuthi* here, reassuring a devotee with a pat on the head or the arm, or stopping to speak to another.

However, there were a few special 'healing events' that happened to me there. One in particular, I shall never forget.

It all started because I was finding it difficult to sleep in the ashram. I'd not minded our room being next to the communal bathroom, at first. I even thought it might be convenient. But that was before I realised how noisy it would be, what with all the comings and goings during the night. Some of the Western women were obviously having the same digestive problems as

Miranda and I, judging by the highly visceral sounds emanating through the walls.

Miranda, though, having only recently been at university, wasn't too fazed by it all. She barely noticed the disruption and was quite happy to stay in the ashram. But I decided to look for a room for myself in the village.

After looking around for a day or so, I eventually found an Indian couple that had a spare room that they wanted to let out. After a little light haggling, we agreed to 100 rupees a night and that I would move in on Thursday, the following day.

But the following morning in the ashram, just before waking, I had dreamt that Sai Baba was talking to me, and he said:

"I'm coming to clean your house on Thursday."

Now in this dream, my home resembled nothing better than a rubbish tip.

There were mouldering apple cores on top of old, yellowed newspapers, stinking ashtrays and half empty wine bottles. The milk in the fridge was off. There was grease all over the cooker, stained sheets on the bed, grime and dust on the windows, mould in the bath ... I'm too ashamed to continue.

But it wasn't yet Thursday in my dream. So I thought that I had plenty of time to clean it all up before Sai Baba's arrival. I casually picked up a duster and started flicking it around. Then I suddenly had an awful thought. It *was* Thursday. I quickly rushed to push some apple cores under a cushion. Then I heard Sai Baba's voice outside the window. I looked up, and there he was. It was too late.

"I'm here," he said. "I've come to clean your house."

The shame of it was terrible, too terrible to describe here.

Luckily, though, just when the full force of my humiliation was about to hit home, I awoke. The true meaning of the dream didn't become clear until later on that day.

That morning, when Miranda and I made our way into the Prayer Hall, we found ourselves placed among three generations of a wedding party. A young Indian woman was about to get married and so she, along with her grandmother and mother, were lined up next to us, in the hope of getting Sai Baba's blessings. Spread out in front of them, on the floor, was all the paraphernalia of a typical Indian wedding: the special red-and-gold *sari*, the necklace of black beads and the sacred grains and spices on silver trays, all waiting to be blessed.

I noticed that people were always bringing things for Sai Baba to bless. I'd also seen that there was absolutely no guarantee that he would—in fact, often the reverse. But the strains of the *darshan* music soon started up and as Sai Baba entered the hall, he appeared to be making a beeline in our direction. It all happened very quickly. The next thing, he was right in front of us. It was as if he flew there. I swear he was floating. Suddenly, there was *vibhuuthi* going everywhere. It was showering out of his hands and spraying, like a fountain, on to all the wedding accessories as well as into the upraised, cupped hands of the daughter, the mother and the grandmother.

It stopped as quickly as it began. Sai Baba turned and glided off. Then the grandmother quietly nudged me and offered me some of her *vibhuuthi*. She shook it into my hand. It was just a tiny smidgen, but it was enough for me to taste its special flavour. It was an interesting experience. It tasted slightly salty.

Later that day, I packed my belongings and left the ashram to move into my new lodgings in the village.

My new landlords were very welcoming and showed me around their house. They'd obviously gone to lot of trouble with the decor. I was pleased to notice that the family bathroom, which I would be sharing with them, had recently been refurbished to such a high standard that there was even a proper Western sit-down toilet, which was state-of-the-art in those parts.

That evening, I went to bed early and settled down to what I hoped would be a really good night's sleep. But after dozing for a couple of hours, I was woken up by the family's television. There was some sleep-defying all-singing-and-dancing Bollywood movie blaring out. So I just lay there dozing and let my thoughts drift.

However, after a while, my thoughts started to run out of control. No matter how much I tried to redirect them, they kept insisting on re-running old videos of my relationship with Pierre, a boyfriend of several years before.

Pierre and I had had a wonderful relationship, except when he was drinking, which was most of the time actually. I kept my flat in Sevenoaks. But as we both worked as journalists on the same newspaper, we usually went back to Pierre's large Victorian house in Hampstead. So I ended up mainly living there.

But sometimes Pierre didn't make it home until very late, or the early hours of the morning. There were also times when he didn't make it home at all.

But it wasn't his irregular hours that ruined our love affair—although I'd never dared to enquire too deeply as to what he was up to during his drunken binges. No, our love affair was wrecked, in the end, because although he had been an incredibly loving partner for most of the time, he could also be very violent when he was drunk.

There had been one time, in particular, when he'd hit me so hard that I'd flown across the room and my head had barely missed the corner of a table. I was always covered in bruises, especially on my legs from where he'd kicked me. I'd hide the marks on my legs under thick black tights. But once Pierre gave me such an ugly black eye, I had to stay away from work.

I should have left him sooner. But on the morning after the night before, he would always be beside himself with remorse, pleading with me to stay and swearing to change, go for counselling, undergo acupuncture, take the pledge, join AA, start a temperance society ... you name it. So because of these regular abject remorse sessions, the relationship had managed to stagger on for a number of years. But he never followed through with any of his promises. And in the end, his attacks became so brutal that I became afraid that one day he would kill me. So I finally ended the relationship and yet another candle—this time a thick, long church one, had had to be snuffed out.

In the days and years to come, I never doubted that it had been the right decision. But it had been an immensely painful one, and one that I mainly dealt with by trying to repress any feelings about it. I was too afraid to feel such emotional pain.

Anyway, that night, my thoughts kept insisting on straying into that area of my memory banks which was usually surrounded by barbed wire fences, guard dogs and signs saying Keep Out! And each time one of these violent episodes came back to me, I started to feel a bit queasy.

I kept trying to think about something else, but I couldn't. In the end, I realised that I was feeling nauseous at just the thought of Pierre. His face would swim up into my mind's eye, and it would make me feel sick to my stomach. It got so bad that I started to think that maybe I was actually going to *be* sick. Of course, it seemed incredible that anyone could actually be sick at just the thought of another person. But just in case, I thought to myself, I'd better be prepared.

So I got out of bed, and opened the bedroom door. Then I walked down the hallway into the bathroom. Then I positioned myself over the loo. It was then that I started to hear a voice in my head that sounded suspiciously like the one that had got me to give up smoking.

"Go on," it was saying. "Think about it. How did you *feel?*"

"Feel what?" I shuddered, trying to avoid the memory.

"How did you feel when he hit you? No, don't try and slide away from it. Think about it. How did you *feel? Feel,* not think."

And all of a sudden, my stomach did a somersault and I just about managed to react in time to aim in the right direction as the contents of my stomach erupted into the loo.

"And how did you feel that time he threw you across the room and your head narrowly missed …."

And I vomited again. I was sick like I'd never been sick before. Then the diarrhoea started. I didn't know which way to turn first. It just went on and on. Every time I'd think that the worst was over, Sai Baba—for it was him—would be there again with:

"And what about that time he………" and I'd be off again.

"And do you remember the time that……".

Sai Baba, as *dhobi* washerwoman, was merciless. I can honestly say I vomited up my insides until there was nothing left. Never mind: 'clean my house'. It was more like Dynorod.

By the end of it, I felt completely empty, and not just in my stomach. On every level, physically, mentally, emotionally, I seemed to be reduced right down to the most basic bare bones of a human being. It was as if nothing remained of the old 'me'. There was just a big hole where 'I' used to be. And, as if that wasn't enough, I felt terribly guilty.

That poor family, I thought. *They barely know me. They've taken me into their home. Now here I am, wrecking their brand new bathroom.*

In the morning, I cleaned it up as best as I could. Then I packed up my rucksack and headed for the door, muttering something about my illness requiring me to go back to the ashram. I'll never forget the faces of that sweet couple, though, as they stood at their door. It was a look of bewilderment and loss.

They'd thought I was a godsend. They could have done with the rent money. Now they'd have to redecorate the bathroom again.

I got back to find the ashram gates closed and locked against me. It seemed symbolic somehow. Then I realised that it wasn't yet six o'clock. Gradually, more people arrived and we were let in. I ran to our building and room A1 where Miranda and Becky welcomed me warmly.

After an hour or so, I felt much better. So Miranda and I decided to go to the Western canteen for a fruit and yoghurt breakfast. However, we were halfway across the compound when, suddenly, there was a great commotion. People were rushing everywhere and shouting. We turned to see four men running towards us. They were carrying someone in their arms. It was Mr Rao. He didn't look well at all. As they came closer, we could see that he was very pale and slumped, like a rag doll, in their arms.

An old grey Ford car quickly pulled up next to us. All four men, still carrying Mr Rao, slid themselves on to its back seat and the last thing we saw were the pink soles of Mr Rao's bare brown feet flying into the air as they settled him across their laps as the car sped off.

I was instantly reminded of something I once heard about why Indian people go bare-footed. It was because that way, when they died and went to God, they'd feel better prepared to enter such a sacred atmosphere. It was then that I realised that Mr Rao was dead.

"Oh dear, poor Mr Rao. He looks very ill," said Miranda, her voice quivering with sadness as we watched the car speed out of the ashram gates.

Neither of us had seen anyone die before. So we just stood there, too stunned to move.

My previous *guru*, Vedananda, had always banged on about the transience of mortal life. But I'd only ever listened with half an ear. I was just like pretty well everyone else as far as leaving this mortal coil is concerned. Although I knew that death was inevitable, it was 'not for me', or at least, 'not today'. So witnessing a real-life instance of a person being there one day and, with no warning, gone the next, was quite shocking, especially after the inner journey that I'd taken the night before.

We went to see Swami that afternoon in a quieter, and more reflective mood.

Afterwards, as we were leaving, we noticed that Sai Baba's red BMW was coming out of his part of the compound. As Miranda and I reached the corner of the road that led to the main gate, it was getting closer and so we stopped to wait for it.

It soon came alongside us. I couldn't see Sai Baba in the back because of the reflection of the glass. But I felt his gaze fall on us. It came over like a cloud and surrounded us both in a warm, loving glow. Then it suddenly penetrated, like a sword.

My heart exploded. I felt it come alive for the first time ever. It was like the first day of spring, and it started to dance with joy. I had been in a desert. But there had been seeds lying dormant under the parched sands and now they were suddenly sprouting, ready to bloom under the rain shower of his love.

We both folded our palms in greeting and bowed our heads as his car purred slowly by. Then he was gone.

Miranda and I just stood there, dumbstruck, for quite a few seconds. Then I turned to her and said:

"He was looking at us, wasn't he?"

Miranda's face looked quite beatific and she spoke quite softly.

"Yes, he was Mum," she said.

CHAPTER 6
LILA, DIVINE SPORT

I used to go to Sunday school as a child. But they never would tell you much about the power of divine love. It's true that we learned that we should practise loving one another. It had looked to me, though, like a sort of wishy-washy, gentle Jesus meek and mild, turning-the-other cheek sort of affair. So I thought that this was all God consciousness was. Being nice to people. I didn't know then there was a lot more to it than that.

But as my reading progressed, I began to see that there were quite a few similarities between Hinduism and Christianity. It soon became clear that both religions are based on orally passed on stories about divine beings that taught about a God who was, essentially, Love. So when the Christian missionaries first reached India in the 18th century, they were quite struck by the Krishna story. They couldn't help noticing how alike the names were, Christ and Krishna. Neither did it escape their attention that there was also a wicked king like Herod. In the Hindu version, he was called Kamsa and he killed all the newborn males after Krishna's birth because, like Herod did with Jesus, he felt threatened by him.

But perhaps the most striking parallel of all was in the tripartite Godhead. Where the Christians have the Father, the Son and the Holy Spirit, the Hindus have Brahma ('brar-ma'), Vishnu and Shiva. As in Christianity, all three were originally considered to be equally important components of the one Divinity with different, but complementary, functions. Brahma was designated as the creator, Vishnu as the preserver and Shiva, the destroyer. So I learned that God to the Hindus is G-O-D—generator, operator and destroyer.

However, over time, Vishnu's fame eclipsed the others and through the practice of devotional worship, or *bhakti* ('bak-ti') yoga, his worship spread all over India. Here's how Devdutt Pattanaik explains it in his book: *Vishnu – An Introduction*:

> Adoration of Vishnu was an inspiration for the flowering of vernacular literature. The 12 Alvar saints of South India wrote four thousand Tamil hymns in the 7th century AD in praise of the lord.
>
> Around the 13th century, Ramananda took the cult of ecstatic devotion to the north. Soon the fertile plains of the Ganga and Yamuna were reverberating with songs of Krishna's love for Radha, composed by Surdas and Meerabai. In Ayodhya and beyond, Tulsidas enthralled the people with legends of Rama's valour and nobility, rewritten [from the original Sanskrit] into the language of the people, Hindi.
>
> Jnaneshwar's Maratha translation of the *Gita* and Tukaram's devotional poems, the *abhangas*, brought the word of the lord to the western corner of India. This was the period that saw Haridasa minstrels in the forests of Karnataka and Narsi Mehta in the villages of Gujarat. Everyone was singing songs about the blue god, Krishna.
>
> Around the same time, Shankardev took the lores of the *Bhagavatha Purana* to Assam while Chaitanya, enchanted by Krishna's charm, danced in the streets of Bengal and Orissa. Eastern India echoed with the desire to unite with the divine.
>
> *Bhakti* carved out routes across India, linking North and South East and West, taking pilgrims to distant lands where Vishnu danced and sang. It united *Jambudvipa*, the rose-apple continent of India.

I should add that Sai Baba himself did not appear to favour any one school of religious belief. He seemed to honour them all. He had a logo that was carved into some of the ashram buildings. It was of a lotus flower encircled by the symbols of all the major world religions. He would say that he wasn't here to change people's religions, and that when they returned to their home countries, they should resume practising their own faith. However, I came to understand that, because he was in India and, therefore, mainly speaking to Indians, his discourses were tailored to their needs and referred to their own scriptures, the Vedas, ('Vay-das') of which he is regarded one of India's foremost authorities.

So perhaps if Sai Baba had been born in the West, the stories that circulated about him would have been about how like Jesus this saintly little boy was when he was young. But, because *bhakti yoga* is still the predominant route to God realisation in southern India, I heard that the villagers of Puttaparthi in those pre-partition days often compared the child Sathyanaryana Raju to the young Krishna. And, in the same way that there were parallels between the Krishna-story and the Jesus-story, so, according to Sai Baba's biographer, there were similarities in the childhoods of both Krishna and Sai Baba.

Like Krishna, he said, the young Sathya was a total charmer. The villagers loved him so much that he would often have to eat his dinner in up to 10 different houses on the same day, just to keep everyone happy. He even managed to leave each family with the impression that he had been their guest, exclusively. This reminded me of the story about Krishna and his wives. Apparently, Krishna had 16,108 wives. This set-up could have been fraught with family discord. But, it is said, he managed the situation so skilfully that each wife thought that he loved her alone.

There is also a story about Krishna raising a hill and sheltering the cowherds and milkmaids under it, to protect them from the torrential rain. Well, a not dissimilar story appears in Sai Baba's biography. One day in Puttaparthi, some people set fire to a thatched hut where the young Sathya was staying. But he just summoned the rains from the sky to put it out. The rain just fell on that hut, and nowhere else.

Actually, I was continually hearing tales of him commanding the elements like that, even while we were there. Power cuts would happen on a regular basis, as they do throughout India. One day, Sai Baba was talking to some people in his interview room, and the lights went out. He just clapped his hands, and they came on again.

But going back to his childhood, I found a really enchanting story in his biography.

It involved an Englishman who had been hunting in the forests around Puttaparthi. He had managed to bag a tiger and was just on his way back to his hotel, with his trophy in the boot of his car. But suddenly, his car broke down, right in the middle of the dried-out bed of the river Chitravathi, ('chit-ra-vati'), which ran through Sai Baba's village.

The man got out and looked under the bonnet. Nothing doing there. He topped up the water in the radiator. Then he tried cranking the engine. All to no avail. No matter what he tried, he couldn't get the car to start. He didn't know what do. But just then he remembered a rumour that he'd heard about a young 'God-boy' in the area. So he decided to set out to find him.

It didn't take him long to track him down. The young Sathya was already heading towards the Englishman and his car. So as the boy drew nearer, the Englishman asked:

"Can you start my car for me? It's just stopped and I can't get it to go."

"I know," replied little Sathya. "Yes, I can help. But on one condition."

"Name it," said the Englishman, anxious to be on his way.

Sai Baba continued:

"That dead tiger you have in your boot was the mother of two small cubs. Now they are completely bereft without her. They are wailing in agony at her loss. They are at the mercy of any predator. So if I start this car, you must promise me that you will go back and find those cubs. Then you must take them back with you to a zoo in your own country."

The Englishman agreed. So Sathya waved his hand over the engine, the car started and the Englishman drove off. But he kept his word. He went back into the jungle, found the cubs and took them back with him to a zoo in England.

Anyway, the days at Whitefields were going quickly, and I was really enjoying getting to spend this time with Miranda. However, on some days, it was apparent that there was a struggle going on between her head and her heart. She was as impressed with Sai Baba as I was. But sometimes I'd float out of the Prayer Hall on a pink cloud of bliss to find her sitting in a corner, her forehead screwed up and her eyes looking troubled. At these times, we would go to a café over the road for a nice chilled Fanta and a good chat.

Miranda had never really been well since we'd arrived in India. The food didn't agree with her and neither did the climate.

LILA, DIVINE SPORT

We really tried to follow all the rules in our *Rough Guide*, which included not drinking any of the water. But it seemed that she was always either recovering from one stomach bug, or going down with another. So that didn't help her state of mind either, and it was ages before I worked out the problem. It was all those Fantas—or rather, the chunks of ice we always had in them.

With her high, angular cheekbones and translucent ivory skin, Miranda was beginning to look like a stick-thin supermodel. Then one day, we heard that a number of people had died of heatstroke in Andhra Pradesh, and we were due to move there soon, as it was where Sai Baba's main ashram was situated.

So I said to Miranda:

"If you stay in India much longer, you're going to waste away. Maybe it's time to think about taking up that television job that's being kept open for you in London."

She looked relieved.

"Well, I've been thinking that," she said. "But I've also been worrying that you might not want to be left here on your own."

I didn't. But I also knew that it was right for her to go.

"Of course I'll miss you," I said. "But your health is more important. Your immune system has taken such a battering that, if you go down with anything else, you could end up getting seriously ill. Anyway, I'm also worried that you won't be able to stand the heat once we get into Andhra Pradesh."

So our days together at Whitefields began to draw to a close. Miranda was preparing to go back to England, while Sai Baba and his entourage—me now included—would be moving on to Prashanti Nilayam ('pra-shan-tee nil-ee-am'). This was his main ashram in his home village of Puttaparthi, more than 100 kilometres north of Bangalore.

I was devastated at the thought of Miranda's departure.

"I'm going to miss you so much," I said to her a few days later, tears filling my eyes. "This is like an alien world here. Nothing is normal here, apart from you."

"But Mum," she said, putting her arm around my shoulders, "you won't be alone. You've got Becky. She'll look after you, and it's quite a protected environment here."

"Yes, although it's not just that," I replied. "I'm also a bit nervous about what the next few months are going to bring. I have a slightly ominous feeling that we are about to get down to business."

"How do you mean?" asked Miranda.

"Well, you know ... with Sai Baba," I hesitated, uncertain myself about what I meant. "I don't know. So far, it's been a bit of a play here, a bit of a tease there. Nothing too strenuous or demanding. Just a taster. But I've a sneaking suspicion that once we get to Prasanthi Nilayam, he's going to start work on me for real, and it scares me."

"Look Mum," said Miranda quickly. "If you really feel that bad about it, you should come back to England with me."

"No, no," I quickly replied. "I can't do that. This is the only proper meaningful thing I've ever done in my life. If I blow this out, there'll be nowhere for me to go and I'll always wonder about it. I have to stay and face the music."

So a few days later, the time finally came for Miranda's departure.

I was in floods of tears as we went out of the hall to her waiting taxi. Sai Baba was on the stage, leading the *bhajans*, but I could barely speak for grief. I kept using the shawl of my *sari* to wipe my eyes. I must have looked a pathetic sight.

It was so bad that we'd decided that Becky should accompany her in the taxi to Bangalore airport. I couldn't face it myself.

So Becky got into the taxi, and the driver kept its motor running while Miranda and I just stood holding one another.

"It'll be alright, Mum," she said, stroking my hair off my forehead.

"I know. I know. Don't take any notice of me. I'm just a silly woman."

Then she got into the back seat with Becky and they drove off.

I slowly walked back into the Prayer Hall. The *bhajans* were still being sung and Sai Baba was seated on the stage, staring straight ahead. Then his head turned slowly in my direction. He seemed to be looking at me in a very powerful and Vishnu-like way, with a strange, knowing expression. Looking back on it, it seemed to say something like this:

"What will I do with this mad Englishwoman? She comes to me for God realisation only to dissolve into floods of tears over her attachment to her daughter?"

Now when I think about it, it seems that I was very lucky that he didn't just pack me off home, there and then, with just a new husband or a necklace, or something. And who would have blamed him? I mean, he was surrounded by all these great yogis and sages that had renounced everything in their pursuit of God realisation. They owned nothing besides their loincloths and their small water jugs, or *khumbas*. They'd walked barefoot for hundreds, if not thousands, of miles in the scorching heat to get to this guru of gurus, to beg for the ultimate blessing.... and then there was me.

How he let me remain there, I'll never know. But he did. And the next day, another of these great sages arrived.

It was a sight to see as Jaroslaw Penderecki swept through the ashram gates with his shoulder-length blond hair and grey greatcoat flying out behind him like a Magyar. All the devotees seemed to scatter out of his path as he strode masterfully through the compound, looking very intense and handsome, a true heroic spiritual warrior.

I'd just happened to be sitting on the wall, outside my accommodation block, drying my hair in the late evening sun. So when Jaroslaw came and sat down on the wall next to me and asked, in a guttural Slavonic accent with an American inflexion,

"So what goes on around here?"

... I nearly fell off the wall with surprise that someone like him would even bother talking to me.

Anyway, I started to fill him in on the routine and finished up by telling him that he could see Sai Baba in the Prayer Hall the following morning.

"Yes, I need to see this guy," he said. "I gave up my lecturing job in California a few years ago. I've been up in the Himalayas, studying the *Vedas*. Anyway, I've discovered a whole new section of it that has been lost, until now. I'm in the process of translating it. But I need to discuss it with someone knowledgeable, and I understand your Sai Baba is something of an expert on the *Vedas?*"

Wow! Was I impressed? The Himalayas, the *Vedas* ... I immediately felt quite inadequate, in fact, a real fraud. I'd been too distracted about whether my *sari* was tied right to even concentrate long enough to get on to this spiritual path, while here in front of me was the real thing.

I explained that it would be best to write his request in a letter to Sai Baba and give it to him at *darshan* in the Prayer Hall the next day. So he thanked me, and we said goodnight.

I didn't expect to see him again. But the next morning, as I came out of my hostel on my way to the Prayer Hall, he was there on the steps.

"Oh good, there you are," he said. "I have the letter," and he showed it to me.

I was flattered that he felt that he needed my help. So I showed him where to queue for the men's side of the hall and then carried on to my own lines.

The *darshan* session went off as normal. Sai Baba was his usual lovely self, wafting around the hall and taking letters. I couldn't see Jaroslaw for the enormous crowd on the men's side. But he soon found me afterwards.

"He didn't take my letter," he said, looking upset.

I tried to reassure him.

"Don't worry, I'm sure he will soon," I said. "As you can see, there are thousands of people all wanting his attention. But he will get to you when he can—maybe this afternoon."

The crowd was so big at Whitefields, much bigger than at Kodaikanal. So I privately thought that he would be extremely lucky if Sai Baba took his letter so soon. But I didn't want to discourage him and, anyway, there was always a chance.

"Okay," he said, somewhat mollified. Then, "Where can I get breakfast?"

I took him to the Western canteen and showed him the men's queue. He looked surprised.

"But can't I eat with you?" he asked.

"No," I explained. "That's not the way it works here. Men and women eat separately, just like they sit separately in the Prayer Hall."

"God, this country!" he almost shouted. "Why are they so afraid of sex?"

"Well, that's not quite my understanding of it," I replied. "I don't think that they're afraid of it. It's probably just that it's easier to concentrate on spiritual matters when you're not being constantly distracted by the opposite sex."

Anyway, we went off to our separate breakfasts, and then the day went on as usual. I took my clothes to the *dhobi*. Then I went to the hospital to pick up some antibiotics for Becky, who'd gone down with an infection.

Later on, I went to one of the wooden huts to hear a talk from a devotee about the practice of *bhakti* yoga. As I walked in, I noticed Jaroslaw was also there, sitting uncomfortably on the men's side. As the talk proceeded, I could feel that he was constantly glancing in my direction.

I went up to him afterwards. I felt sorry for him. He looked so lost and confused.

"Maybe Sai Baba will take your letter at this afternoon's *darshan* session," I said.

"Well, I certainly hope so," he replied, puffing himself up a little. "I'm a busy man. I can't just put my life on hold to hang around here like all you lot. I've got more important things to do. When my book is published, it will revolutionise the way the world views India and its religion."

But Sai Baba didn't take his letter that afternoon. Neither did he the following morning.

Jaroslaw met me as I came out of the hall.

"Do you want to go over the road for a drink?" he said.

"Sure."

So we went out and over the road to the Fanta café, and as soon as we sat down at one of the pavement tables, he lit a cigarette. He then proceeded to tell me more about this new, undiscovered part of the *Vedas* and, although I sat there trying to nod knowledgeably, I didn't really understand much of what he was saying.

"I must say," he said after a while, he eyes glancing longingly over my best ivory silk *sari* top, "I find you very beautiful."

Really? Wow! I gazed at him in astonishment.

However, things seemed to be moving a little fast, even for my tastes. So I got up, telling him that I'd just remembered that I had to give Becky her antibiotics. However, I also made sure that I gave out the necessary signals to indicate that I wasn't completely closing the door to future possibilities.

That afternoon, at *darshan*, Sai Baba didn't take his letter again. In fact, according to Jaroslaw, Sai Baba had come over to where he was sitting and had taken everyone else's letter apart from his. Jaroslaw was distraught.

"Come out to dinner with me," he begged. "Please! We can't eat together here and I need to talk to you."

We went out of the ashram gates. Then Jaroslaw hailed one of the waiting taxis and told the driver to take us to Bangalore.

As we drove into the city, the monsoon suddenly erupted with all the fury of a Wagner opera. Enormous peals of thunder shook the roof of the taxi. Forks of lightening flashed and reflected like the trident of Shiva on the now virtually flooded roads. Sheets of water were pounding down, reminding me about the story of Krishna holding up the mountain to shelter the gopis from the rain. Then I began to get an uncomfortable feeling that we were not going to be afforded any protection here, divine or otherwise.

The taxi finally stopped outside a modern-looking building with a restaurant on the first floor. We jumped out and rushed up the stairway into its warm and welcoming spicy and pink-lit interior. The waiters gave us thick towels to dry ourselves off. Then they brought us platefuls of delicious south Indian vegetables in coconut curry sauce, and bowls of white fluffy rice.

"I want you to understand something," said Jaroslaw after we'd eaten and were wiping our plates clean with the big, soft *naan* breads. "I want you. I want you really bad. I can't stop thinking about you."

"But you hardly know me ..." I tried to say. I don't think he heard.

"Look, you can't be that comfortable, having to share a room in the ashram," he continued, dabbing around his mouth with his napkin. "Now, I'm staying in a nice, quiet place outside the village and, guess what?"

He looked knowingly at me with twinkling eyes, and then continued.

"They have another room there. Now I think that would be much better for someone like you, who needs their privacy. And I would be right next door, so I could take care of you."

My eyes widened. Take care of me? Crikey! Did he have any idea how gorgeous he was?

"Look, I do understand," he went on, "you're here for your spiritual growth. But you shouldn't have too many hung-up ideas about how it should be. You and I could be really good together. I could teach you a lot about the *Vedas*. Then, when you've had enough of this Sai Baba guy here, we could go down to Sri Lanka. You'd love it there. There are some beautiful deserted white sand beaches...."

"Well, I don't know ..." I hesitated, playing for time as I examined my own feelings. It was turning out that they were not quite as straightforward as they would normally be in such a situation.

"Okay, but let's stay in a hotel here tonight," he went on, ignoring my doubtful tone. "That will give us some more time to discuss it. The roads are going to be flooded back to Whitefields anyway."

I stared down at my white linen napkin. I was struggling to find words to describe feelings that I'd never known before. But I eventually found them. I looked him straight in the eye.

"How many times have you said that to a woman?" I asked. "How often have you said 'I want you'?"

Jaroslaw looked shocked. Then he started twisting uncomfortably in his seat, and his napkin fell on the floor. So I couldn't see his face as he bent to pick it up and then reply:

"Well, you know ... maybe a couple of times."

"Only a couple of times?" I teased him. "Hmmm. Let me see. You're a few years older than me, with probably a marriage, if not two, under your belt."

He quickly looked up then, surprised. I continued:

"So I reckon you've said that more than a couple of times. Because I have to tell you, I've lost count of how many times those three words, or something very similar, has been said to me."

Jaroslaw's cheeks reddened slightly, but he wasn't about to give up.

"So what are you saying? That you're looking for a virgin?"

I burst out laughing. It eased the tension slightly.

"No, no!" I protested. "You misunderstand me. What I'm saying is, if you and I go off together, how long do you think it would last? Because I have to tell you, I tend to get through these little romantic interludes pretty quickly these days."

He still looked confused. I felt sorry for him. So I leant over the table and took his hand.

"Look, you were right yesterday when you said before that I'd put my life on hold," I said, trying to go more gently. "But I've done it for a reason. I've been forced to take this course because of the way my life has panned out. I don't want to feel hurt, anymore, and I don't want to hurt anyone else. I don't want any more pain of lost love. I'm looking for a divine love that's eternal, like Krishna talks about. Not a worldly love that always runs out on you in the end, or just keeps you around to wash its socks."

"Divine love? Are you kidding?" Jaroslaw looked utterly astonished. "Surely you know that all those stories about Krishna are just fairytales? I've been studying the *Vedas* for years and years, and I can tell you that categorically!"

"Yes, they may be fairy tales," I replied. "But I don't believe that they were fairy tales that were told just for the sake of entertainment. They were stories that were told to teach a deeper truth. They're spiritual allegories—in other words, there is a sub text, an under-story if you like. By learning about these hidden meanings, I'm hoping that I will understand more about how to reach God's love."

"Okay," Jaroslaw's tone told me he was going to try another tack. "But how do you expect to find God's love among people who can't even manage the normal worldly kind? Look at how they treat their women. They only marry them for money. Sometimes, the dowries demanded by Indian men are so extortionate, the bride's family is reduced to poverty. Then when the wife's dowry is all gone, the husband tries to get rid of her by setting fire to her…and what about the children?" He was building up a real head of steam now. "They maim them deliberately and then send them out on the filthy streets to beg."

I couldn't deny this. But I couldn't go to the hotel with him either.

"You may be right," I replied. "Believe me, I'm no apologist for India. But, although I don't understand what's going on with Sai Baba, I have to follow this through to the end. I have a feeling about him. If I don't act on it, I'll never find out, and it will bug me for the rest of my life. I'm here for just six months. After that, my visa runs out. During that time, I need to concentrate on what he's trying to teach me. I can't have the distraction of a relationship going on. I'm sorry. But that's how it is."

"And what about when the six months are up?" enquired an incredulous Jaroslaw with the air of a man who'd never had to wait for a woman in his life.

"After that, who knows?" I replied, because I certainly didn't.

We did eventually manage to make it back through the floods to Whitefields that night, and so it was a very disgruntled and frustrated Pole that I left on my hostel steps when I went to bed. I also wasn't feeling too well by then, as I still hadn't made the ice-in-the-Fanta connection.

So I spent most of that night gingerly stepping over the unconscious bodies of my roommates and dashing in and out of the bathroom. The night seemed to go on forever. Then, as the minutes and hours crawled slowly by, I began to doubt my decision, and to wonder whether Jaroslaw hadn't been right after all.

Perhaps Krishna was just a character from an anachronistic fairy tale. And maybe I did need my privacy—although the way he'd been looking at me, I probably wasn't going to get an awful lot of that. He probably also didn't realise, I thought, that the only reason I looked so attractively slim was because I had almost constant diarrhoea.

But maybe I could do with someone to look after me, I thought, and who could be better? What's more, with all my journalistic experience, I could even help him with the editing of his groundbreaking work. Gosh, who knows? We could even become famous as the couple that brought a whole new section of the Vedas to the world....

That morning, once again, I found Jaroslaw waiting impatiently on my steps, still clutching the now crumpled-looking letter. And so off we went to the Prayer Hall. But, oh dear! Sai Baba didn't take it again!

Jaroslaw by now was beside himself. We went over the road again.

"You have to try and understand," I tried to console him over the Fanta. "Sai Baba has so many people wanting his attention and there's only one of him. Some people wait months to get even so much as a look from him. So it's really not that he's snubbing you...."

"I do understand that," Jaroslaw thundered, his grey eyes darkening, "and I can see all those other stupid people queuing up. But *you* don't understand! This is *me!* It's *me* he's keeping waiting!"

"But can't you see who he is ...?"

Jaroslaw interrupted me.

"He's an ordinary man, just like me!" he shouted, banging the tin table top with his hand so hard that the Fanta bottles chinked against one another. "I don't know why you daft morons can't see that. He must be laughing his head off at you all! My God! He's got a nice little racket going on here!"

And that was when the scales fell from my eyes. I just stared at him. Then I stood up and said:

"Well, I really do have to go now."

I got up, left the cafe and walked across the road to the ashram and straight to the Prayer Hall where the *bhajans* were in full swing.

I thought that I'd be safe on the women's side of the hall. I assumed that surely, even the Great Pendericki wouldn't have the nerve to follow me there. So as the *bhajans* rang out around me, I started to pray very hard:

Sai Baba, I'm truly sorry. I've got it wrong again! I've attracted this man to me. Now I realise that I should have been more careful, more modest in my behaviour. I need your help to rid me of him. I don't think he'll go until you take his letter. Of that much, I'm almost 100 per cent sure. So please Lord, I know it's a lot to ask. He's only been here for three days. But please, would you be so kind as to take his letter?

Jaroslaw, by now, had arrived in the hall and was leaning, sullenly, up against the wall on the men's side. I didn't need to turn to look at him. I could feel his eyes boring into my back. This went on for some time—me praying, Jaroslaw boring—until, eventually, Sai Baba entered the hall. Then he very sweetly went straight up to Jaroslaw and politely put his hand out for Jaroslaw's letter.

Afterwards, I returned to my hostel building. There was Jaroslaw again, waiting on the steps.

"He took my letter!" he said.

"I know," I replied.

"So I'm going now. I've given him my address, and so I hope to hear from him very soon. I'm sure he will want to discuss these matters with me. Meanwhile, I must continue with my work. It's very important and I've left it long enough. But, please," he said, thrusting a piece of paper at me, "take my address and if you're ever in the area, it would be good to see you."

I took it and thanked him. We shook hands goodbye. He walked out through the ashram gates, and turned to wave to me. After he'd gone, I turned gratefully into the hallway of women's hostel and bowed humbly to the picture of Sai Baba on the wall. Then I walked down the corridor to my room, opened the door and chucked the address into the bin.

* * *

A few days later, we were off to Prasanthi Nilayam. The departure scene was a story in itself and this extract from my first letter home to Miranda gives a good account of it:

> … Anyway, one of the things I wanted to tell you about was that last day at Whitefields. It was so sad! Sai Baba came out that morning to give us his *darshan* as usual and all those who were staying on—the permanent staff at the hospital, the police—were crying! One policewoman was on her knees, holding on to Sai Baba's arm. You could just see that she was begging him to stay. Even the dog (you know, your favourite) was howling! It felt like the end of the world.
>
> But Sai Baba was just like a mother to them. The look on his face was so kind and concerned, but firm. I obviously couldn't hear what he was saying, but it looked like:
>
> "I'm really very sorry. I do have to go. But it won't be for too long and I'll be with you, anyway."
>
> His face was a picture of mercy and compassion.
>
> Straight after *darshan*, it was chaos—absolute pandemonium. We'd been warned about the departure the day before, so we were packed and ready to go. But the taxi drivers immediately jacked up their prices to 950 rupees. They wouldn't budge. Some of us tried to hang back and wait them out. But they were past masters at this kind of blackmail. They knew that every devotee wanted to be in the convoy behind Sai Baba. So we all had to cave in, in the end.
>
> Then suddenly, Sai Baba was being driven out of the main gates in his red BMW, and everyone was in the road, stallholders, shopkeepers, taxi drivers, the mayor, everybody. The police, through tear-sodden eyes, made a vague attempt at holding everyone back. But their hearts weren't in it. It was total mayhem. I nearly got trampled in the crush and there were people practically swooning all around me.

Then as his car swept past, the crowd took coconuts and smashed them, dramatically, in the road, just in front of his car. They were shouting something in Hindi. Apparently, it meant: "All glory to the Lord, Sai Baba!".

Sai Baba's car went so close to me it almost ran over my toes. But I couldn't see him for all the smeared coconut milk on the car's windows. I'm told that he was smiling and waving. Then this great, long convoy of taxis swung out after him with all the devotees, including myself, scrambling to get into one. It was wild!"

Thus, the whole cosmic caravan was off again. I went on to tell her that, just before we got to our destination ashram in Puttaparthi, the whole convoy ground to an abrupt halt. Sai Geeta, who has been Sai Baba's pet elephant ever since he was a boy, had escaped from her enclosure and was out on to the road, waiting to greet him. As Becky told me: "She always knows when he's coming."

CHAPTER 7
THE WISH-FULFILMENT TREE

Poor Sai Baba had an awful childhood. Well, anyone else would have thought it was awful. I expect he just regarded it with the same equanimity as he appeared to everything else that summer. He never seemed to care whether the weather was good or bad. He was always the same. There were times when I had to miss seeing him in the Prayer Hall through illness or tiredness. But he never flagged. He didn't miss a single day for the whole three months that I was at Prasanthi Nilayam and always arrived bang on time. You could have set your watch by him.

But according to his biography, like any young boy that was different, he was bullied by those that were jealous of him. He'd often come home from school looking decidedly rumpled and roughed up. Apparently, though, he would then just make up a tale about falling out of a tree, or walking into a door or something, and he would never complain about or name his oppressors.

He also had problems with his parents, in the beginning, anyway.

Initially, the Rajus hadn't known what to make of their son's strange powers. They were constantly worried about him, especially when he would go off into a trance. Sometimes, they wondered if he'd been possessed by an evil spirit. They would call in the local exorcists. But to no avail. There was one exorcist who came to the Rajus' house and took ages laying out all his paraphernalia with great pomp and ceremony. But the young Sathya just laughed at him, and pointed out all the bits of kit that the exorcist was missing.

One time, the family heard about a very powerful sorcerer in another village before whom, apparently, no evil spirit could survive. So the whole family, with Sathya, set off in their bullock cart, in the hope of a cure for the young boy.

The sorcerer turned out to be a huge man, frightening to behold, with blood red, angry eyes and wild manners. He made little Sathya sit in a circle of chicken blood and then went through his whole repertoire, even trying a couple of techniques that you'd think twice about using on a fully-grown adult.

I suppose, in retrospect, one has to feel slightly sorry for this sorcerer. There he was, up against the all-powerful Vishnu, who was just sitting quietly and smiling politely at all his efforts, when all the sorcerer had on his side was a couple of dodgy incantations and a dead hen. So, naturally, nothing he did made any difference and he began to get angry and desperate. After all, his professional reputation was on the line.

So he announced that his next trick was world famous, as it had seen off many an evil demon. It couldn't fail. And he proceeded to shave the poor little boy's scalp, score the surface with a knife into three big Xs and then pour acid into the wounds. Still, nothing happened. Sathya didn't even make a sound. So then the sorcerer began to beat little Sathya on the joints with a heavy stick.

By now, the family were feeling decidedly uncomfortable. But their little son was signalling to them not to say anything. The torturer then poured a 'magic mixture', made of acids, into a bowl. He then applied the mixture to the eyes of the still uncomplaining little boy. Sathya's head and face began to swell almost beyond recognition.

That did it. The Rajus could stand no more. Jumping to their feet, they swept up the little boy and ran. And, as their bullock cart trundled off, all the family could hear was the sound of the mad witchdoctor raving after them:

"I was within an *inch* of victory! An *inch* of victory!"

So it seems that Sai Baba had great fun playing with the poor bemused adults into whose care he had decided to incarnate. He would enjoy amusing his friends by 'taking', or materialising treats out of the air. His schoolmates, ordinarily, would have to last all day on just a packed lunch of cold curd rice and chapattis. So they would be delighted to receive all manner of sweet delights

THE WISH-FULFILMENT TREE

and delicacies from his hand. But perhaps the most well known story from Sai Baba's childhood concerned a certain tree that also ended up playing a pivotal part in my experience that summer. The locals called it the 'Wish-Fulfilment Tree', and here is a description of what happened from Professor Kasturi's biography on Sai Baba.

> During those days, Baba generally went every evening to the sands of the river with the devotees…and [he] vouchsafed to those who attended…various miracles. It was then that the tamarind tree that grows solitarily at the crest of the hill on the left bank of the Chitravathi, near where the road meets it, got the reputation of being a *Kalpathura* [a Wish-Fulfillment Tree].
>
> Baba used to take the devotees to that height and pluck from that tree many varieties of fruits. He would pick apple from one branch, mango from another, orange from a third, pears and figs from a fourth and fifth! Of course, Baba says he can make any tree a *Kalpathura,* for he himself is a *Kalpathura!*

His playmates, just like those children in *Charlie and the Chocolate Factory,* also found out that you sometimes have to be very careful what you wish for. Once, says Professor Kasturi, one of them asked him for a display of all his previous incarnations. They were fascinated to watch Sai Baba 'shape shift' into all the incarnations of Vishnu, one after the other, until he got to Narasimha, the ferocious man-lion. One of them fainted with shock.

I'd recently been reading about how Vishnu had been forced to incarnate in the shape of Narasimha in order to save his faithful devotee, Prahlaad (pronounced 'pra-lard'). The story goes something like this:

> Although he was the son of Hiranyakasipu, ('Hir-anya-kas-ipu') the most powerfully evil demon king that the universe had ever known, Prahlaad was, in fact, born a saint and even at the age of five, the name of the Lord was constantly on his lips. Naturally, this was a source of great pain to his wicked father. So he sent Prahlaad to demon school to learn how to mend his good ways.
>
> However, even at the demon school, Prahlaad would teach his schoolmates about the truth and would lecture them thus:

"As much as the human body is most rarely achieved, it is also hardly ever used for its true purpose. It is the only form of being in which the soul can become one with God. So instead of wasting our time being the victim of our senses, we should renounce those temptations and dedicate our lives to God, in the form of the lotus feet of Lord Vishnu.

"And we should sing the praises of Lord Vishnu because he is the most beloved, the master of the soul and the true friend to all living beings."

Now when Hiranyakasipu got to hear of his son's teachings, he flew into a violent rage. He was so angry, that he instructed his servants to kill Prahlaad. So the servants proceeded to strike the boy with their swords and axes. But Prahlaad called out to Lord Vishnu, and the swords and axes miraculously turned into feathers.

Not to be thwarted, the servants then tried to push Prahlaad into the path of a herd of rampaging elephants. But once again, Prahlaad called upon Lord Vishnu—and the herd of elephants suddenly came to a halt. So then the servants decided to throw Prahlaad from the peak of a mountain. But still Vishnu protected his devotee. He caught him.

By now, his father was becoming enraged at Prahlaad's ability to survive. So he struck out at a pillar supporting the roof of his palace, shouting at Prahlaad that if his precious Vishnu really was omnipresent, why wasn't he in this pillar? It was a good question.

But then the pillar let out a deep, ominous, otherworldly growl. Then it dissolved into a million pieces as the terrifying figure of Vishnu in the form Narasimha, the man-lion, smashed his way out of it.

Prahlaad's father's knees weakened as he surveyed the fearsome leonine form of the Lord. He could see that Narasimha's eyes were like furious golden bullets. His enormous mane was gleaming as brightly as his deadly pointed teeth. His razor-shaped tongue swung hungrily from side to side in his mouth. The lion's ears stood on end and were completely still and as his jaws parted, his whole body touched the sky. His arms, like flanks of soldiers, spread in all directions. It didn't take a David Attenborough to see that Narasimha was poised to kill.

Needless to say, Narasimha then proceeded to tear Hiranyakasipu limb from limb, and there's no need for us to go into graphic detail about it here.

But Prahlaad was eventually enthroned in his father's place, and he went on to become one of the great kings of India.

Sai Baba would also instruct his school friends in the way to God. When he got to his senior school, he was even teaching his schoolmasters. His elder brother was already a teacher at this school, which was in the nearby village of Uravakonda ('you-rava-konda'). He had a plan to push Sathya through High School to make him eligible for Public Service.

But when the young Sathya went to Uravakonda and moved in with his brother and his sister-in-law, he found that his reputation had preceded him, and it wasn't long before he had accumulated a large following. They didn't really know who he was. But they acclaimed him as a mysterious prodigy, a tiny prophet. They would turn up with offerings of fruit and flowers, filling the house until the early hours of the morning. Even Sathya's headmaster would come to the house. He would prostrate himself before his pupil, and along with his assistant masters, sit placidly at Sai Baba's feet, listening to his words of wisdom.

Then one day, when Sathya was only fourteen years old, he threw away his childhood forever. He declared to everyone who he was, and why he was here. But the story of his momentous announcement is better narrated by his biographer, Professor Kasturi:

> On the 20th day of October 1940 ... Sathyanarayana started for school as usual. The Excise Inspector of the place, who was very much attached to little Baba, accompanied Him as far as the school gate and went home, rather reluctantly. He seemed to see a superb halo round the face of Baba that day, and he could not take his eyes away from that enchantment.
> Within a few minutes, Baba too turned back to the house. Then standing on the outer doorstep, he cast aside the books He was carrying and called,
> "I am no longer your Sathya. I am Sai."
> The sister-in-law came out from the kitchen and peeped out. She was almost blinded by the splendour of the halo that she saw around Baba's head! She closed her eyes and shrieked.
> Baba addressed her,

"I am going; I don't belong to you ... My devotees are calling Me; I have My Work; I can't stay any longer."

And so saying, He turned back and left, despite her pleadings. The brother hurried home on hearing all this. But Baba only told him,

"Give up your efforts to 'cure' Me; I am Sai. I do not consider Myself related to you."

A neighbour also heard the noise. He listened and realised that it was something serious. He ran in. He saw the splendour of the halo and fell at Baba's feet. He too heard the Historic declaration,

"*Maya* [illusion] has left; I am going; my work is waiting."

But the Baba's brother was non-plussed; he could scarce collect his wits to meet this new situation. A boy just fourteen, talking of devotees, Work, *Maya* and the Philosophy of belonging! He could think of only one plan. Sathya was entrusted to him by the parents and it was therefore his task to inform them. Sathya could leave the house only after they came to Uravakonda.

But Sathya would not step into that building again. He moved out into the garden of the Excise Inspector's bungalow and sat on a rock in the midst of the trees. People came into the garden from all directions bringing flowers and fruits. The whole area resounded to the voices of hundreds, singing in chorus the lines that Sathya Sai had taught them. The first prayer that He taught them that day was, as many still remember "*Manasa bhajare guru charanam, dhusthara bhava saagara tharanam.*" ("Meditate in thy mind on the Feet of the Spiritual teacher that can take you across the difficult sea of worldly belonging.")

Eventually, Sai Baba's parents arrived. But their son would only return home with them on the condition that he would be free to continue his work. They agreed, somewhat reluctantly, and so the whole family returned to Puttaparthi. However, Sai Baba's announcement must have been some sort of signal for the floodgates to open. From then on, spiritual seekers from all over India started to flock into Puttaparthi.

At first, a small temple was constructed to accommodate these guests. The only road to the village soon began to overflow with traffic. Feeding these crowds became a fulltime job too. Sai Baba's mother and the wife of the head man of the village did most of it and, when it looked as if there wasn't going to be enough to go around, Sai Baba would be quietly informed. He would just go into the kitchen, crack open a coconut and sprinkle its milk on to the rice and vegetable dishes. Apparently, the food never ran out.

But before too long, the crowds were so vast, the available overnight accommodation so overstretched, that it was decided to buy some land on a hill outside the village. This turned out to be the Prasanthi Nilayam ashram. It was built and inaugurated in 1950.

From there, the village of Puttaparthi just grew and grew. Sai Baba used the money from donations to build hospitals, schools, colleges and even a university. The village itself was modernised. So when I arrived there from Whitefields, nearly half a century later, I was delighted to find it a beautiful, peaceful place, more like a small market town than a village. It was spacious and clean with well-tended gardens, tree-lined avenues and temples housing statues of figures from the scriptures.

The Prashanti Nilayam ashram area itself was more like a university campus. Multi-storey modern buildings, providing accommodation for devotees, bordered an expanse of grass. It was here, every morning, that the coconut man would set up his pile of fresh, green coconuts, and break them open with a hammer to provide us all with welcome cooling drinks.

When it came to food, there were three canteens to choose from. The Western canteen served salads, burgers, pizzas and so on. The Indian canteen provided typical South Indian fare with lots of very hot chillies. But for those that preferred their spices milder, there was the North Indian or Punjabi canteen, which also did great deep fried *puris*.

In the centre of the ashram, there was also a small shopping centre with a bank, a bakery, a grocer, a shop that sold *saris* and another selling spiritual books, music and videos. There was also a post office with telephone booths for making overseas calls.

As in Whitefields, Becky and I shared a room again. We would also help out together in the kitchen of the Western canteen. My job was to scrub the stoves. But otherwise, our days were much the same as they were before. We would go to see Sai Baba, first thing in the morning, in the enormous gilded Prayer Hall which was even bigger and much grander than the one at

Whitefields, its huge marble columns and decorative frescoes a match for any maharaja's palace. We'd then go to lunch together in the Western canteen and, after helping to clean up, would return to the cool of our room for a quick nap before afternoon *darshan*.

One morning, on our way to the Prayer Hall, Becky and I stopped off at the coconut stall, and that's where we were standing, sipping our milk through straws, when a middle-aged man with dark hair and intense-looking eyes approached.

"Er, excuse me," he said in an upper class English accent. "Are you Ishtar?"

I nodded.

"Only I heard that you're a Reiki Master?"

"Yes, I am," I replied.

"Good," he went on. "I'm also a Reiki Master, and I've got so many people queuing up for my workshops, I wondered if you could give me some help?"

I should briefly explain. Reiki is a healing technique that purports to use spiritual energy to heal others, and people can learn how to become Reiki practitioners at one-day workshops.

The English Reiki Master went on:

"I really only need some assistance when I get to doing the actual initiations, to turn them into Reiki practitioners. I usually reach that stage by about lunchtime. So I was thinking. We could line them up in rows and then perhaps you and I could work along them ..."

"I don't know if I can," I replied. "I'm busy at lunchtimes. I have to scrub the stoves in the kitchen of the Western canteen."

He drew back with almost a shudder.

"You're as spiritually advanced as a Reiki Master and you're scrubbing stoves," he said in a faintly horrified tone.

Becky burst out laughing. Then she said, in her full Bradford accent:

"It's because she thinks she's a Reiki Master that she has to clean the stoves!"

The Zen humour of Becky's remark was lost on the English Reiki Master. So he turned to me again.

"Look, I get £300 for every person I teach. I could give you a 20 per cent cut. I had over a hundred trainees last weekend. Why don't you at least come along and see what we're doing? We're over in that building there," he said, pointing to a hostel block in a corner of the square, "on the second floor, in Room 6."

My intuition was telling me something wasn't quite right. But I couldn't quite nail it. My brain, however, couldn't resist doing the math.

"Okay, maybe later," I said, still doubtfully.

So he took his leave and went off to join the men's queues.

We went to *darshan*. Then, just before lunch, Becky and I decided to pop into this Reiki session. It was partly just out of curiosity. But it was also because I was considering taking him up on his offer. It seemed crazy to turn down such easy money.

So we crossed the grassed area and climbed the stairs to the second floor of the hostel building. Then we walked along the white walled corridor until we found a blue door with the number six on it. Becky knocked on the door, and we heard the English Reiki Master shout, "Come in!" So we did. And even before I was barely through the door, and into the room itself, I felt the energy around me nose-dive.

There were about ten people in the room, all lined up in a row and waiting to be given the Reiki initiation. But there was no healing energy or spiritual atmosphere in the room. None at all. In fact, there was about as much inspiration and joy as you'd find in a station waiting room on a cold February morning when the 8.24 is forty minutes late. The air felt thin, like at the top of a mountain. The Reiki candidates looked like they'd been waiting forever for a God-ot who was never going to come.

It was so bad, I felt as if I was going to suffocate. So I quickly grabbed Becky and said:

"Let's go."

Becky looked surprised. I vaguely remember that she recovered herself to manage a few polite noises to cover our hasty departure. But I can't be sure, as I was already out the door and racing down the corridor.

She caught me up at the bottom of the stairs.

"Phew," I was panting, and not just with the effort of the run. "That was a lucky escape! Did you feel what it was like in that room?"

"Well, I have to admit that it didn't feel that great, now that you mention it," replied Becky, as we headed off, arm in arm, to our lunch and our cleaning duties.

"I suppose I just didn't realise what a high spiritual atmosphere we've been in," I went on. "It must have just sort of crept up on me gradually."

"You could be right," said Becky. "Maybe going into a room where it didn't exist was like walking into a cold shower."

"But until I came here," I replied, "my Reiki sessions were the highest experience I ever had!"

She just laughed knowingly.

Later that day, we were sitting in the hall when a message came around. It came along the row to us like Chinese Whispers. Sai Baba was requesting that all the various types of spiritual healing workshops taking place around the ashram should henceforth stop.

I looked at Becky, and she smiled. I said:

"If I'd heard that a few days earlier, I would have been quite puzzled. But after our experience today, it makes perfect sense to me. Perhaps Sai Baba has already answered one of my questions, without even granting me an interview."

"What was your question?" she asked.

"I was going to ask him how to be a better Reiki Master," I replied.

"Oh, right then," she chuckled. "So you got your answer then: 'Don't do it!'"

And we both burst out laughing.

I think it was then that I first began to see something of the immense power of this tiny, beautiful man, if man he was. He'd taken me into his home—no questions asked, no payment required—and allowed me to experience the pure, divine atmosphere that seemed to permeate from his every pore. As each day passed, I began to see more and more that I was in the presence of a strangely unique being who seemed to be turning my world into a magical wonderland of blissful love.

Every morning, I would wake with such a sense of excitement, knowing I was only a few hours away from seeing Sai Baba. I would happily spend hours queuing up at the crack of dawn—it wasn't even light when we first arrived—to get into the Prayer Hall. Then I'd spend even longer just sitting cross-legged and gazing at him in the distance, as he glided up and down, selecting devotees for the privilege of joining him in the interview room. His beauty cut me to the quick; it was so pure. It was as if it sprang from an intrinsic integrity and goodness I'd never known before. When I looked into his face, I saw everyone that I'd ever loved.

The whole day would revolve around him.

Morning *darshan* sessions would last for a couple of hours. Then there would be just enough time for a few household chores, a bit of shopping and a bite of lunch before retreating to my room for a nap. Then I would lie on my bed thinking dreamily about Sai Baba's face as I drifted off on a cloud of bliss.

In the afternoons, we would go to see him again. The hours would go so quickly. Before you knew it, it was time for dinner, a shower and finally, to bed and wafting off to sleep on waves of love. However, it soon got to the point where I couldn't bear the separation from Sai Baba even for those few hours of the night. So I would pray to him, asking him to come in my dreams. He very often did. And this is how, very slowly, I began to realise that I was falling deeply in love with Sai Baba.

In all the preceding months, I'd not been aware of this slowly unfolding emotion. I'd not intended it to happen. But looking back, I can see that the feeling had been creeping up on me for months. It had stolen into my heart through the back door when I wasn't looking, like a thief in the night. Then one morning, long after it had taken off its boots and put its feet under the table, I woke up, and I knew that I was in love with him.

Of course, I realised that it was utter madness to fall in love with someone who was so inaccessible, and I was more than a little confused by it all. It wasn't making any sort of sense, on any level. Sometimes I felt stupid to have developed a ridiculous infatuation for a 72-year-old celibate who, from being so physically close to me at Kodaikanal, was now appearing to be retreating further and further into the distance. The crowds at Prasanthi Nilayam were about five times the size of those at Whitefields. At other times, I thought that I'd gone crazy. A mere mortal woman had fallen in love with the great, all-powerful Lord Vishnu—and how suitable a match was that? There is a Jewish saying:

"A bird can fall in love with a fish. But where will they make their nest?"

Anyway, I couldn't make any sense out of it all. But mostly, when I wasn't driving myself mad with it, I would manage to convince myself to relax and not worry about it. After all, I had what I wanted. I was with the man I loved for most of the day—and much of the night. I was living in his home, with him, learning his teachings. What more could I want? So the days would just carry on in the same blissful routine, until I forgot that there was an outside world and my whole existence was just centred on Sai Baba. I could have lived like that forever.

Then one day, after we'd been there about a month, I noticed that people were putting up some brightly-coloured banners and flags all around the ashram grounds. I asked Becky about it. She told me that a very big festival was coming up. It was called *Guru Poornima* ('poor-nee-ma'). Thousands upon thousands were expected to converge from all over India. It was the biggest festival of the year.

Then gaudily painted buses began arriving and disgorging their multi-hued passengers. People were arriving from all over the subcontinent, from the taller and paler Nepalese hill people to the smaller and almost black-skinned Dravidian types from Tamil Nadu. There were also some Indian women with shaven heads.

"They've just come from Tirupati," said Becky. "There's a shrine there to another incarnation of Vishnu, Lord Venkateshwara ('ven-kat-e-shwara'). When people make pilgrimages there, they shave their heads. It's part of the ritual."

It was all quite colourful and fascinating. But I'd never been much good in crowds. So, hoping to avoid the worst of the crush, I decided to move out of the Prasanthi Nilayam ashram and into an apartment in the village.

Becky was a bit doubtful about such a move.

"We're always recommended to stay in the ashram," she told me, "so that we can stay under Swami's care."

"Really?" I replied. "But how can that be? The power of an incarnation of Vishnu should be such that it would be able to reach us wherever we are in the world. Now you're telling me that Sai Baba's power won't even reach down to the end of the road?"

She just gave me one of her "you're too clever for your own good" looks. But it didn't stand in the way of her helping me on the day of the move. She and a few other fellow kitchen helpers followed me in procession out of the ashram gates, each carrying an armful of my possessions, the most valuable being my plastic bucket.

I'd found a spacious apartment in Chitravathi Lane, an unmade up road lined with shops that led off from the ashram down to the river from which it took its name. During the days, there was a market selling everything from freshly squeezed lime juice, tinted glass bangles, brass Buddhas and joss stick holders to deep fried samosas, cheap watches, swathes of multi-hued *sari* material, brightly coloured spices and sandalwood *japamalas* (rosary beads). In other words, the same kaleidoscopic and chaotic pot pourri you would expect from any Indian market— beggars, mangy dogs and all.

My new apartment was huge—much bigger than my flat at home in England—and its beige stone tiled floors made it cool and welcoming. I bought an enormous dark red and gold silk embroidered Kashmir throw in the market and spread it across the floor of the living room. Then I just topped it off with lots of different-sized cushions. I was on the ground floor. So I hung mosquito nets on the windows to give me some privacy. On the far wall, I hung a portrait of Sai Baba that I'd haggled over in one of the shops. Then I put a small table underneath it with a white candle and a brass joss-stick burner, to make an altar.

I would sit in meditation in front of this altar, and was relieved to find that I didn't notice any diminution in the spiritual energy around me. Vishnu's powers did at least stretch as far as 77 Chitravathi Lane. I happily followed the same blissful routine as before, the only difference being that the walk to the Prayer Hall was a little longer. Afterwards, I would buy my breakfast mangoes and some strings of creamy jasmine flowers for my hair from the market, and then plough through the crowds and on down to the quiet of the river and the solitary spot where I now lived, at the foot of the steps leading up to the Wish Fulfilment Tree.

Initially, I'd been too busy furnishing my apartment to think much about this tamarind tree. If I did, it was only to regard it as a bit of a gimmick. I'd enjoyed the story about Sai Baba plucking the different fruits from it for his childhood playmates. I'd assumed that that was all it was—a story. But one day, I felt like taking a walk. So I decided to go and have a look at it.

I'd already noticed what looked like about a dozen concrete steps winding up and round the back of my building; I'd imagined the tree would be at the top of them. I was wrong.

Once these steps ran out, ahead of me rose what turned out to be a long, steep, meandering climb. I wasn't the fittest of people. So I was soon puffing and panting my way upwards. As I climbed higher, I found that some parts of the path were unstable and dangerous, with the steps crumbling away to nothing. I was surprised that such a famous tree didn't have a more 'tourist-friendly' route to it, and there was litter everywhere.

When I finally reached the top, there was yet another obstacle. The tamarind tree was actually up on a high rocky ledge of a steep white rocky crag that overlooked the valley. You were supposed to jump up and grab hold of this ledge. Then haul yourself bodily up.

I couldn't see any railings or other protective equipment. So I hesitated for a good while. I looked up and tried to see over the top, but I still couldn't see the tree. So there was nothing else for it. I had to continue.

Summoning up all my courage, I jumped and grabbed hold of the ledge. Then I gradually managed to pull myself up on to it. I had to wriggle along it on my belly and then swing my legs up. Once safely on the ledge, I just sat there in a daze, too shocked to enjoy the view of the patchwork quilt of fields in the river valley below.

After a while, though, I managed to get my breath back. Then I remembered why I was there. I turned to look at the tamarind tree.

It was similar to an oak. Its trunk was gnarled and withered and its copious green-leaved branches spread themselves low, providing welcome shade from the midday sun. An altar had been carved into the rock face and painted in maroon, blue and white. The lower part of the tree's trunk had also been daubed in these colours.

Then I was surprised to see that there was a large bell hanging from one of its branches. Nobody had mentioned the bell.

A small Indian man was sitting under it. Seeing my questioning look, he stood up and explained to me:

"You have to ring the bell and make a wish."

Then he disappeared over the edge of the ledge.

THE WISH-FULFILMENT TREE

I was now alone with the tree. The wind was ruffling my hair and caressing my cheek. The fragrance of jasmine filled the air and all I could hear was the singing of the tiny bulbul birds nestled in the tree's branches.

I took hold of the bell and started to think hard. It was then that I suddenly realised that I was at a very important crossroads. I'd approached this tree like an ordinary tourist. But now something else was happening; a deeper level was opening up. I felt almost as if I was standing on the top of the world and that every being living within it was waiting with cocked ear to hear my request.

I started to think about what I'd like to ask for. But I couldn't think of anything. There seemed to be just emptiness where my thoughts used to be. It felt faintly ridiculous that here I was, finally getting the chance to get what I wanted, and I'd forgotten what it was. Then, something came into that void and I knew ... I knew exactly what to do. So I took hold of the bell and pulled it right back, so that it would make the most noise possible. Then, as I let it go, my soul shouted:

"Marry me! Marry me! Please, marry me!" and I gave the bell an extra push for good measure.

The bell rang out loudly over the valley. As I stood there, I just knew that Sai Baba heard it. It felt as if the whole universe heard it. Then what followed was a deep, deep silence that seemed so much more than just an absence of noise.

I just stood there for quite a while, feeling the atmosphere. Then I swung myself back over the ledge and made my way back down the sloping path to my apartment.

I remember feeling a little surprised at what had happened. But I tried not to think about it. Instead, I went to bed and fell into a very deep sleep.

Luckily, I'd set my alarm, or I never would have made it to that afternoon's *darshan* session. But as I walked up Chitravathi Lane, the memories of the morning came flooding in and I started to question myself.

Of course, I thought to myself, it was highly unlikely that Sai Baba would marry me. For one thing, I was just a mere befuddled mortal, while he was supposed to be a glorious incarnation of God. But there was also the small matter that he'd never, to my knowledge, ever shown the slightest inclination to marry anyone.

Perhaps avatars of Vishnu don't marry, I thought. Then, *But no, that can't be true. Krishna had 16,108 wives and as soon as I manage to get an interview with Sai Baba, I'm going to remind him of that!*

However, despite my deep conviction that he'd heard the prayer of my heart at the Wish Fulfilment Tree, Sai Baba didn't pick me out for an interview that day.

A few days later, though, I came across a book by someone using the pseudonym of Lotus Petal. I was intrigued to find that she also felt the same way. She would refer to Sai Baba as her Beloved, which I thought was incredibly bold of her. I had no idea, though, when this book had been written as it had quite a timeless quality.

Then one day, I was sitting in the queue for the Prayer Hall reading the book. A woman behind me leant over my shoulder and in a throaty French accent said:

"I see you're reading Lotus Petal's book."

I turned round to see that she was an attractive woman with a short blonde bob. She could have been a few years older than me. It was difficult to tell because she had the typical Frenchwoman's knack of knowing how to look amazing at any age.

"My name's Sophia and I'm a friend of Lotus Petal," she said, putting out her hand.

"Oh, I'm Ishtar," I replied. "But I didn't realise that Lotus Petal was still around."

"She is, but she doesn't live in the ashram anymore. After she wrote that book, some of the ashram elders misunderstood her intentions. Things got a bit uncomfortable for her. So she decided it would be easier to move out and live in the village."

"Oh, I see," I said, warming to this new acquaintance. "Well, I would enjoy discussing this book with you."

"Why not discuss it with the author directly?" she asked.

"I wouldn't want to put her to trouble …" I said, already feeling a stab of butterflies in my stomach about meeting such a great devotee and starting to panic about what I'd say to her.

"It's no trouble," Sophia replied. "I'm seeing her this afternoon. So I'll arrange it for you."

The next morning, tens of thousands of people had arrived in the hall to see Sai Baba. But by a series of the usual so-called

THE WISH-FULFILMENT TREE

'coincidences', the ushers sat me right next to Sophia. She looked as pleased as I was.

"I've been looking all over for you," she said, handing me a small slip of paper. "Here's Lotus's address. She's expecting you at three o'clock."

So that afternoon, I found myself nervously clutching a bunch of yellow roses at the top of a small flight of stairs and ringing Lotus Petal's doorbell. I had no idea what to expect. So I was surprised and relieved when a kind-faced Western woman with grey hair opened the door and said in a warm Canadian accent, "You must be Ishtar."

She invited me in and was so pleased with the roses, she instantly set about arranging them into a vase. At the same time, she gossiped away quite merrily, mainly about Sai Baba who, it appeared, lived in her flat! The way she was talking, you'd think he'd just popped out to the newsagent and would be back at any second. But I wasn't too surprised by this. She'd written in her book about Sai Baba materialising in front of her at odd times. However, as it was still some time before he would appear in my flat back in England, I still wasn't sure what to make of it.

" ... anyway, when I was about five miles from Puttaparthi," she was saying of her car journey from Whitefields, "he suddenly appeared in the passenger seat. As large as life. There he was. Just sitting there. Then he said: 'you'd better slow down or you'll hit a traffic jam. Sai Geeta's escaped from her compound again.'"

She carried on like this for some time, talking like any woman would about her husband. She'd say things like, "Well, he would do that, wouldn't he?" and "Trust him to say that!", smiling and shaking her head with affectionate disbelief as she made us *chai* spiced tea and buttered some ginger cake, and then joined me on her soft cushioned sofa.

We chatted away quite easily and soon found much to laugh at. But I was also beginning to wonder if Sai Baba had used his Vishnu powers to set up this meeting. My overwhelming feeling was one of relief. At last, I realised, as I started to relax under Lotus Petal's chatter and giggles, here was someone with whom I could share my guilty secret.

I eventually found the courage to tell her. I just blurted it out:

"I think I'm falling in love with Sai Baba," I said. "I know it's wrong, but I think of him in 'that' way, you know what I mean. It's definitely a romantic kind of love and not at all spiritual."

She threw back her head with an earthy laugh.

"Oh my dear, don't worry about it," she said. "It's not wrong. Everybody has to start from where they are, not where they'd like to be."

Noticing my quizzical expression, she continued:

"I have a gay man friend, and a few years ago he was telling me the same thing. He said that he'd fallen in love with Sai Baba. He was quite worried about it, I can tell you! But now, that love of his has transformed into something much purer. It's just that, apart from maternal and family love, romantic love is the only love you know. You cannot conceive of anything greater. But Swami will take you from there and then he will raise you up to his level. You will still love him. But it will be a much purer love."

"I don't quite understand..." I replied.

"Well, Swami always gives everyone what they think they want..."

"I've noticed that!"

"...so that afterwards he can give them what he wants them to have," she continued.

Then she stood and reached up to pull a huge book off the shelf.

It was the *Srimad Bhagavatham*, my old book about Krishna that Sri Srinivas, the sitar teacher, had given me.

"I had this book!" I almost yelled.

"Now there's a coincidence," she laughed as if she didn't think it was a coincidence at all. She continued to flick through it until she found the page that she wanted, and then she handed it to me.

"Read this," she said.

I curled up in her armchair and started to read. It turned out to be about a guru who is instructing a king in spiritual enlightenment by telling him some stories from Krishna's life. But the king is confused by the nature of the milkmaids' love for Krishna, and he is saying:

"Oh wise man, I hope you can solve this knotty problem for me. I don't understand why the milkmaids, who were so spiritually advanced, regarded Krishna as their lover, and not as the all-powerful incarnation of God. So how could these trivial-minded dairymaids, with their concentration drowned in their material senses, rise above this worldly attachment to attain spiritual enlightenment?

And the teacher replied: "Sir, it doesn't matter which way people concentrate on the incarnation of God, so long as they do. You remember, I told you about one of Krishna's cousins, who hated Krishna so much that he would spend every day seething about him, and planning his downfall? Well, even he achieved realisation of God. So why not the Lord's dear devotees, too?

"Lord Vishnu is infinite and cannot be measured. He is above worldly attachments, because He is their controller and he has been born as an incarnation of God into this world for the purpose of granting the highest benefit to man. So those whose thoughts are constantly directed towards him—whether in lust, anger, fear, protective affection, feeling of impersonal oneness or friendship—are sure to eventually become absorbed in his true form, which is the sole aim of their existence."

In other words, it was exactly the right treatment for a love junkie. In fact, I was beginning to realise, it was probably the only way he could get my full and undivided attention.

"But what's this about Krishna's cousin?" I asked. "How could someone who hated Krishna achieve spiritual realisation?"

"That was Sisupala," she said. "He hated Krishna because Krishna stole his fiancé, Rukmini ('Rook-meany') just before the wedding ceremony. Rukmini wanted him to," she added quickly, seeing my face. "She loved Krishna, not Sisupala."

"So then what happened?" I asked.

"Well, Sisupala spent the rest of his life in a complete rage about Krishna. He could think of nothing but how much he hated Krishna. He was totally obsessed. Then, one day, a great sacred ceremony called a *rajasuya* took place in a royal palace and all the kings, sages and great men of India attended. And in the middle of that august assembly, Sisupala stood up and proceeded to give a speech in which he roundly insulted Krishna."

"Do go on."

Seeing I was rapt, she continued.

"Well, when everyone heard what Sisupala was saying, they were ready to tear him limb from limb. But Krishna realised that that would ruin the auspiciousness of the ceremony. So there was nothing for it—he would have to kill Sisupala himself. Krishna took his razor-sharp discus, and threw it at Sisupala. And at the moment Sisupala's head separated from his body, his spirit flew from his body and merged into Krishna."

"Merged?" I said, surprised at this new idea. "Why would he want to merge with Krishna?"

"At death, we go to where or what we've most concentrated on in our life, to what we've dedicated our life. Sisupala's mind and emotions had constantly dwelt on Krishna, albeit in anger and hatred, and so he achieved liberation by merging with the Supreme Godhead."

But this brought up another doubt.

"I'm not sure that I'd actually want to merge with Sai Baba," I said.

"Well, there is also the option of devotion rather than merging," she said. "This means that every time Vishnu incarnates into a human body, you come with him and help him in his task."

"That's the one I'd choose," I quickly replied. "I just want to be with him."

"Yeah," she said wryly. "You just want to marry him and have his babies!"

"That's about it," I had to admit, and we both exploded with laughter.

When I left Lotus Petal's apartment that evening, I felt quite relieved and content, for the first time in weeks, that all was under divine control. I didn't yet understand how this love for Sai Baba's human, physical form could possibly be transformed into a purer love for his infinite, transcendental Vishnu form. But I was beginning to realise that greater powers were carrying me along on my journey, and that they knew what they were doing.

But only a few weeks later, Sai Baba said something to me about it that seemed so utterly radical, I was shocked to the core. It was just after the *Guru Poornina* festival and he played such an enormous, but truly wonderful game with me over that time ... but I'm getting ahead of myself.

Chapter 8
The Lotus Feet of the Lord

Once, when we were still in Kodaikanal, Swami had padded barefoot past us, and Miranda had leaned over to me and innocently whispered:

"Doesn't he have lovely feet?"

I'd burst out laughing. She probably didn't realise it at the time, but countless poems and songs have been written about the beautiful feet of the Lord. To lay their head on them is the highest aspiration of any devotee. The milkmaids, for example, so adored the feet of Lord Krishna, that they sung their praises thus:

> "O dear Lord Krishna, even the Goddess of Wealth considers it a divine privilege to touch the soles of Your Lotus Feet. You are very precious to those who live in the forest, and so we would also love to stroke those Lotus Feet. After that, we will have no interest in any other man, for we will have been totally fulfilled by You.
>
> "Even your consort, whose attention is craved by the gods, and who has attained the unique position of always remaining on your chest—even she constantly longs for the dust of your Lotus Feet, despite having to share it with many of your other devotees. In the same way, we humbly ask you to allow us to live under the dust of Your Holy Lotus Feet."

But adoration of the Lord's feet is not just an ancient, Vedic phenomenon. I'd discovered from Sai Baba's biography that there was a modern-day story of equal significance:

One day, when Sai Baba was just 17 years old, he went to visit some devotees in Bangalore. Shortly after he arrived at the house, a visitor turned up, a certain Krishnamurthy (pronounced 'Krishna-murtee') who was a clerk at the Mysore Secretariat. And over a period of several hours, Krishnamurthy gradually became quite fascinated by Sai Baba. So he started to join enthusiastically in the singing of the *bhajan*s.

This went on for a few days. Krishnamurthy would come to the house and join in the *bhajan*s. But the whole time, he would also be closely watching Sai Baba. After a while, he seemed to be getting quite agitated. Then one day, he arrived at five in the morning and excitedly confronted Sai Baba with:

"I know You are God. Show me Your real form!"

Sai Baba tried to avoid him, but he couldn't. So he told Krishnamurthy to go to the inner room and to sit quietly and to meditate, while he left the house to give *darshan* to some devotees in another part of the city.

The clock was just striking midday when Sai Baba returned. He had barely crossed the threshold when he heard a loud noise from the inner room. He found Krishnamurthy who, deep in meditation, had let out this huge cry of joy before fainting with ecstasy and collapsing on to the floor.

When Krishnamurthy came to, he was shivering and shaking and breathing heavily. But, keeping his eyes tightly closed, he insisted on following Sai Baba from room to room, all the while asking, sometimes plaintively, sometimes authoritatively,

"Give me your *Pada* (Feet)! Let me touch your Feet!"

He was locating Sai Baba by his sense of smell. Not being able to see exactly where Sai Baba was, he was sniffing his way towards him. But Sai Baba would either gently push him away, or he would hide himself or keep his feet firmly under him. The others would ask Krishnamurthy to open his eyes, but he refused, saying that he did not want to cast his eyes on anything else. He wanted only to touch and see Sai Baba's feet.

His excitement and joy continued unabated for days. But Sai Baba said that if he touched his feet while in that ecstatic mood, his frail body would be unable to stand the ecstasy of it and he would die. So he refused to let Krishnamurthy anywhere near his feet.

But eventually Krishnamurthy was quietly persuaded to return to his home with the promise that he would receive *darshan* there. Then Sai Baba went to stay with some other devotees who had a house in the Civil Station.

However, Krishnamurthy could not contain himself. He couldn't bear to wait patiently for Sai Baba's visit. So, with his eyes still closed, he somehow managed to sniff his way on to a horse drawn cart and he directed the driver to the Civil Station. On arrival, he slid down from the cart, ran into the compound and by sniffing around, managed to find the building where Sai Baba was staying and began to bang at the very window of his room.

But Sai Baba was still very concerned about the danger to Krishnamurthy's life. He said that his human body would not be able to contain the overpowering joy of his experience. Then, after a while, Krishnamurthy's relatives turned up and they managed to drag him back home. But Krishnamurthy was still keeping his eyes closed and praying for Sai Baba's feet. So intent was Krishnamurthy by now on his heart's desire that he gave up all food and water. He eventually became so weak that he had to be taken to the hospital. Sai Baba, on hearing this news, sent him a little water that had touched his feet, and when Krishnamurthy drank it, he quickly became fit enough to be taken home.

Once home, he asked everyone to sing *bhajans* while he laid himself on the bed in the same room. But when the singing was over, Krishnamurthy did not rise. The body was completely still. He had touched the feet of the Lord; the river had merged into the sea and the thousands of lives that had culminated in that of the clerk Krishnamurthy had reached their fruition. He wouldn't be coming this way again.

So Miranda was right. Sai Baba did have lovely feet. Each day, the women would spread jasmine blossoms on the ground to soften his path into the hall. After he had passed, I would collect up handfuls of them, take them back to my room and infuse them with boiling water to make jasmine tea, which I would then drink with my mango breakfast.

I was also praying that the upcoming *Guru Poornima* festival would bring me into even greater proximity to these feet.

Guru Poornima was said to be the most important festival of the year for spiritual adepts. It was traditionally the time when the spiritual teacher accepted the devotee as his own. So I was hoping against hope that Sai Baba would signal his acceptance of me by granting me *padnamaskar* ('pad-na-mas-car') which meant touching or kissing the feet.

It wasn't looking very likely, though. Sai Baba usually only seemed to grant interviews and *padnamaskar* to official groups who had formed in their own home country and travelled there together. How to get into one of these groups was a complete mystery to me. However, I did try to join one.

This particular group was from Tunbridge Wells in Kent. They'd only just arrived, all looking quite smart and respectable, as if they'd just got off the 8.22 to Cannon Street. My hair, on the other hand, hadn't seen a hair drier in months and because I'd been working in the kitchens, cleaning the stoves, my face and arms were smeared with black grease and Ajax. So it was probably that—as well as the wild woman love glint in my eye—that caused them not to believe me when I told them that I was from Sevenoaks. They politely but firmly declined to let me join them.

In the end, they weren't granted an interview. But one group that was were the Russians. In fact, it seemed as if every day, the Russians would be called into the interview room—sometimes, twice a day. We all used to get quite annoyed and jealous, wondering what they'd done to warrant such exclusive attention. We didn't know it then, though. But at that very moment, their country's economy was collapsing, their banks were foreclosing and they were losing just about every rouble they'd ever owned. Sai Baba appeared to have known it, though, which might have been why he was showering so much of his love and attention on them.

As the days flew by, though, I began to realise that I no longer cared about getting an interview. Even I was starting to see that Sai Baba was so much more than just his physical body. It wasn't necessary to be in a room with him to have contact. Eventually, all I really wanted was to touch Sai Baba's feet and I used to pray to him regularly to that effect:

"Sai Baba, please would you give me *padnamaskar*? I know it's not easy. I know I'm not part of a group. But, Lord, you are all-powerful, so you can do anything. So please, could you find your way clear? If you would just grant me this one thing, I'll never ask for anything else ever again. I promise, Lord. I'll shut up after that, and stay out of your way."

I was as bad as Krishnamurthy, really. I just kept banging on and on at Sai Baba about it. I was like a dog with a bone. Sai Baba, however, was oblivious. He would glide into the hall every day, go straight past me without so much as a glance in my direction, and then beam widely and have a great time with everyone else. I could have been invisible, as far as he was concerned, and I was quite used to this way of things. So I thought, anyway, until one fateful day.

It was just two days to go before *Guru Poornima*. I'd settled into my place in the hall as usual, fully expecting to be totally ignored and not feeling especially bothered about it—no more than on any other day, anyway. But the *darshan* music started up, in wafted the all-perfect Lord, straight past me as usual...and I exploded into tears.

It was so unexpected. It was as if a dam built of denial and 'stiff-upper-lip' had suddenly given way with absolutely no advance warning. I found myself sobbing and sobbing, real hot tears. But, of course, Sai Baba didn't seem to notice and carried on as usual, going round the hall, gathering up those he'd selected for the interview.

This eruption of emotion must have gone on for at least fifteen minutes. I was still crying when Sai Baba returned to the front of the hall, on his way to the interview room. But as he drew opposite me, all the pain inside me, all the bitterness, the resentment, the feelings of not-good-enough seemed to draw themselves together into a tight ball. Then I fired it like a missile from the depths of my being and it emerged as a mental wail of agony.

"I don't think you care about me at all!" I screamed at him. I hasten to add, it wasn't a verbal utterance. It was probably my first attempt at telepathy.

Anyway, Sai Baba stopped immediately. Then he frowned slightly in concentration, as if he was listening to something. Then he shook his head, as if to disagree. Knowing he'd heard, I went on:

"Well...I don't think you *do*!"

Then he shook his head again, this time more vehemently. Then he turned in my direction and raised and lowered his hands in blessings.

I still wasn't satisfied. That evening, as I left, I could feel the rage starting to boil inside me. I marched down Chitravathi Lane, staring straight ahead, completely ignoring the shopkeepers and stallholders who were bidding me "good evening". I charged straight into my apartment, slammed the door behind me and then went absolutely berserk.

It was as if Sai Baba was in the room and I was nagging him, yelling at him and storming at him, like a wronged wife. The picture of him on my wall was soon hanging askew from all the things I was hurling at it. Then I threw myself on the floor, and rolled around in agony. It went on for hours. I didn't even stop to eat. Then after the anger came the tears—hot, bitter ones splashing down my cheeks and on to the floor.

I felt so hurt that I had fallen in love so deeply with someone who was never going to reciprocate my feelings. I felt absolutely desperate about it. I'd never felt so deeply before, about anyone. I couldn't see a way back. I blamed Sai Baba for it. It seemed that he had seduced me into becoming infatuated with him …but why? Just so that he could then ignore me? After all, I thought, he had millions of people, worldwide, to love him. Why should he need me? He was so beautiful, so attractive, that it had made him cruel. That must be it, I decided. And why was I so stupid as to fall for someone like that?

I remembered some counselling sessions that I'd had several years ago when I was trying to extricate myself from the relationship with alcoholic Pierre. The counsellor had come to the conclusion that I always fell in love with unsuitable men, or unattainable men, because I was actually frightened of having a real relationship.

Well, I thought to myself, *I've hit rock bottom now! They don't come much more unattainable than Sai Baba!*

I had such pain inside me. The inside of my throat felt as if a cat had scratched it with its claws, and the pain stretched right down to my chest. I was breathless and hiccupping. Then all the hounds of self-doubt that I'd been holding at bay for years and years suddenly all rushed in howling. I could no longer keep up the pretence of my self-image, that of a free Western woman who chose her own destiny along with her sexual partners. I saw instead what I thought he saw when he looked at me. I had wasted my life by prostituting myself to countless men. I was now just an empty, worn-out husk only fit for the rubbish tip.

It was as if my whole life had come to end. I couldn't see any way back. I just carried on in that way, sobbing and sobbing, until, eventually, I must have cried myself to sleep.

When I awoke in the morning, I immediately tried to slip straight back into unconsciousness, to escape from the pain. But I couldn't. It weighed so heavily on me, I didn't want to get up or do anything. I certainly didn't want to go to see Sai Baba.

I lay there for ages, turning it all over in my mind. Then with a heavy heart, I made the fateful decision. It was time to go home to England. There was nothing else for it. So I got up and went to the kitchen and pulled my rucksack out of the cupboard. Then I took it into the bedroom, and started pulling my *saris* out of the wardrobe and stuffing them into it.

I was about to start on my underwear drawer when, suddenly, there was a knock at the door. I thought it must be the landlord. So I quickly grabbed a shawl and wrapped it around my shoulders and then went to open the door. It was Sophia, and her smile quickly turned to a look of concern as she saw my red-rimmed eyes.

"Hello," she said kindly, and then looked at me closely. "I was just passing and was wondering if you were going for *darshan?* But what's up with you? Are you ill?"

"I'm not going to see him ... ever again, in fact," I said, stepping back to allow her in. "I'm going back to England just as soon as I can book a flight at the travel agents. I'm already packing."

Sophia went straight into the kitchen, while I just flung myself face down on to the cushions in the living room, determined not to co-operate.

"I suppose at times like this, in England, you'd have a nice cup of tea," she called out brightly, rattling some glasses. "Well, we can have some mango *lassi*."

I heard her peeling and mashing up the mangoes and a few minutes later, she came in with the drinks. She passed me one and then made herself comfortable on a cushion.

"Now Ishtar," she said, "tell me what's going on."

I couldn't really look at her. So I just stared at the floor. After a few false starts, I started to explain it all to her. It didn't take long, though, for the whole sorry saga to erupt, like a torrent. My voice gradually built in pitch as I left nothing out—the falling in love, the pain, the not feeling good enough, the utter desperation that I'd totally wasted my life in giving myself to any man who wanted me, and the heartfelt sobbing of the night before. Then finally, there was an agonised shout:

"It's just that I don't want to be me anymore! I want to be somebody else!"

This, to me, was a cast iron case for going home. So when I finally looked up at her face, I was expecting to find an expression of empathy. But she was just smiling knowingly.

"My dear," she said, "you're just going through *metanoia*. This is a very important landmark in your spiritual progress."

"Meta what?" I replied.

"Well, the Greeks called it *metanoia*," she said. "The Christians call it 'repentance'," and then seeing me shuddering at such a concept went on quickly, "but I don't think the Christians really understand its true nature. It's actually a precursor to an initiation. An initiation is like a change of gear, an acceleration upwards. It's an immensely important step forward in the relationship between the disciple and the teacher."

"Relationship?" I practically shouted. "I don't have any relationship with my teacher. He just completely ignores me."

"The relationship is not on this level. It's not one that anyone else here can see. You have to learn to find that place where you can be with him. Remember, Jesus said that the kingdom of heaven is within. He knew what he was talking about!"

Then she touched my arm lovingly.

"Come on, I'll help you to get ready. It's going to be really fine you'll see."

I sighed, not wanting to admit to myself that I was slightly intrigued by Sophia's new spin on things. I didn't want to go to *darshan*. But I did need breakfast. The toast and marmite in the Western canteen were beckoning to my growling stomach.

"Okay, I'll go up to the ashram with you, but I'm not going into the Prayer Hall," I said. "I'll get some breakfast while I'm waiting for the travel agent to open."

She waited while I showered. Then I came back into the living room with a towel wrapped round me. She was pulling out of her bag a number of expensive-looking French cosmetics.

"Sit down," she said, indicating the cushion next to her.

She then proceeded to magically transform my stricken face with creams from pots that had magical-sounding words on them, like *anti rides*. After that, she brushed my hair into a sophisticated French pleat. Then she helped me to tie my *sari* neatly and, before too long, we were walking up Chitravathi Lane together, arm in arm.

It was then that I realised that I was feeling a bit brighter.

"Anyway," I said, with a hint of irony, "what's all this about 'I just happened to be passing.' No-one just happens to be passing down this end of the lane."

"Well, yes," she giggled. "The truth is, I was having tea with Lotus Petal yesterday and then, completely out of the blue, she said: 'You must check up on Ishtar.'

"Then, when I got back to the ashram, I looked for you in the Western canteen, but you weren't there. Becky told me that you'd moved down here and she wrote the address down. It was too late by then and so I planned on visiting you later today. But then when I woke this morning, I had a very strong feeling that I should come right away. So I did."

"Intuition," I said. "If only I'd listened to my mine half as much as I should have, over the years, my life would have turned out completely differently. Instead, I listened to everyone else."

The dawn was barely breaking as we walked through the tall, wrought iron ashram gates. Then she took her leave to go to see Sai Baba, while I carried on up the hill to join the queue already forming outside the Western canteen.

I couldn't think. I couldn't speak. I only wished that I didn't have to feel. But within quite a short time, I heard a voice that seemed to be getting louder as its source came towards me. As I peered through the early morning gloom, I saw that a tall blonde woman was walking down the canteen queue and making an announcement in an American accent. As she came closer, I could hear her more clearly:

"Volunteers with medical experience are needed for *Guru Poornima*. We're setting up a medical camp to deal with any casualties or emergencies. Any volunteers please report to ..."

And I thought,

Yes! That's it! That's what I'll do. Sai Baba is always saying that we should help others and so I will.

I didn't actually think *and then he'll be sorry!* I'm pretty sure that I wasn't exactly visualising myself as Florence Nightingale, dressed in white and carrying a lantern. But I was probably close to it. Like any romantic heroine whose heart had been broken, I planned to spend the rest of my life devoting myself to good works.

In fact, I realised, with a sort of grim satisfaction, *I will probably be so busy sacrificing myself, I'll never have time to go for darshan ever again.*

So that's how I became a volunteer at the medical camp.

That afternoon, I reported, with about 50 other volunteers, to one of the smaller halls. It had been arranged with rows of chairs for our first briefing. There was an opening announcement by one of the American organisers.

"Before we get underway," he said, "and we go to the trouble of inducting and training you all, I just want to stress one thing. There's absolutely no point in volunteering for this if you think that it'll help you get an interview with Swami, or *padnamaskar*. The medical camp has been going for a number of years now and Swami has never granted an interview or *padnamaskar* to anyone involved in it. We don't expect that to change."

A handful of people got up and, looking slightly embarrassed, left the room. I didn't budge. After all, getting closer to Sai Baba hadn't been my motive for volunteering. Quite the contrary, in fact.

Why should I care about that? I thought to myself. *I've given up on him anyway, and what's more, I hope I never have to see him ever again!*

So the medical camp was set up in Sai Baba's General Hospital, which was about ten minutes walk up the hill from the ashram. Almost instantly, we were inundated with patients.

Some of them were devotees who had come from far flung parts of the subcontinent. But mostly, they were just the ordinary local people from Puttaparthi and the neighbouring villages who'd been storing up a complaint for months, waiting for this chance to avail themselves of some free American pharmaceuticals.

I'd originally hoped that I would be able to use my Reiki healing skills. But nobody was the least bit interested in anything so nebulous. After all, they could get witchdoctors in their own villages. No, what they wanted were state-of-the-art Western drugs, and some of them had walked a good long way for them.

However, I didn't have any other medical skills. I wasn't even trained to take anyone's temperature or blood pressure. So I was put on the reception desk and, even then, I turned out to be not much use because I didn't speak Telegu, the local language. As a result, I was paired up with a lovely young American woman whose family were originally from south India. Shanti spoke Telegu fluently. So I would just sit there beaming encouragingly at everyone while Shanti took down all their details.

Each day, I would arrive promptly for duty and stay there until the last customer left, often late at night. In my opinion, my beaming duties were far too vital for the smooth running of this hospital for me to be spared to go to see Sai Baba, and I continued like this for about ten days.

I felt extremely privileged, though, to be working with such an expert and dedicated team of professionals. The doctors and nurses had, in the main, come from American hospitals and they were giving up their free time, even seeing Sai Baba, to do this. Many of them were extremely highly skilled and sometimes we found ourselves dealing with some quite serious illnesses.

So all was fine, and I felt I could have carried on forever like this, until the last day of *Guru Poornima* dawned. It was as I awoke that morning that I immediately sensed that something was different.

I felt a little odd, and it got worse as the day wore on. I arrived for work as usual, and Shanti was already there. A woman had been brought in earlier who was extremely ill with 'flu, Shanti told me, and her room-mates were also quite ill with it. She was worried that there might be 'flu bug going around the whole ashram and so we could be faced with an inundation of patients.

One of the doctors, Tim, then came up with the idea that we should treat the problem proactively. So I started to help him arrange teams of doctors and nurses to set up a temporary 'flu clinic in the ashram grounds, and most of the day flew by in this way.

However, I still couldn't determine just what was wrong with me and began to wonder if I was also going down with this 'flu.

Later that evening, an Indian woman came into the reception area. She chatted with Shanti in Telegu. Afterwards, Shanti told me that she'd said that Sai Baba was with all the devotees in the auditorium and they were having a concert. It was then that I suddenly realised what was wrong.

I knew that I had to see him. I didn't stop to reason with myself or even explain to anyone where I was going. I just got up from the reception desk and fled.

I picked up my blue *sari* skirts as I tore down the steps, across the lawns and then down the hill. The young beggar boys began to home in on me like mosquitoes. When I hit the main road, swarms of black and yellow motorised rickshaws started circling me like bees. I continued running in a sort of zigzag, trying to shake them off until I was safely through the ashram gates. Then past the statue of Ganesh, down the side of the Prayer Hall and puffing by now, all the way up the hill to the auditorium.

I knew that the building was open down the whole of one side and that Sai Baba would be at the front, nearest to the stage. So I headed in that direction, towards the front of the hall. But as I rounded the corner, I could see that ushers were standing guard over that whole area. They all stiffened expectantly when they saw this crazed woman dashing towards them.

Then something strange happened.

It was as if Sai Baba had entered my body. Suddenly I found myself walking in the same way that he did. I was using the same gait, the same mannerisms. My face fell into one of his humble, loving expressions. It was as if he was walking me, being me and making a much better job of it than I generally do, which was why, I supposed, that he was doing it. Then I noticed the ushers visibly relax and smile.

"Please," I said, as I approached them, holding my hands in the prayer position, "I've been working in the medical camp and I haven't seen Sai Baba for days. Please allow me just one small glimpse."

Then one of them recognised me. She's been in for a sprained ankle only the day before.

"Yes, she's the receptionist from the hospital," she said. "She's okay," and they softly fell back and allowed me through.

I looked into the hall and saw Sai Baba, still quite a long way off. But I'd been in such a rush, I'd forgotten to bring my glasses. So all I could see was an orange blur with a sort of black fuzzy bit on top. Just then, though, the orange blur turned towards me. I could just about make out the shape of his face and—I'm sure of it!—he was smiling in my direction. I felt the glow from him anyway, as if he was speaking lovingly and softly to my heart. Then all the pain of the last two weeks just fell away as if it had never existed, and I slowly realised that I was truly at peace again.

I beamed back at him and then bowed my head and silently said:

"Lord, I'm so sorry for my arrogance and my anger. I know that a worldly woman like me could never be deserving of your attention. But this auspicious festival of *Guru Poornima* is not quite over yet. If it's not too late, I'm humbly asking you to please accept me as your devotee."

I stayed for a further few minutes, drinking the experience in. Then I quietly slipped away.

The wonderful feeling with which he'd enveloped me remained as I walked, more slowly now, back across the lawns to the hospital. The full moon was just starting to rise in the night blackening sky. The birds were twittering as they settled their young ones down for the night. The seductive aroma of jasmine blossoms was intoxicating the late evening air, as it caressed my cheeks and stroked my hair. I was walking in the garden with my Beloved and I could almost hear the tinkling of the divine milkmaids' ankle bells. All the pain of the last two weeks had just disappeared, and was replaced by a blissful feeling of contentment and fulfilment.

I walked into the hospital lobby and happily resumed my place again at the reception desk.

But then I noticed that everyone seemed to be in a great state of excitement. The doctors and nurses were all standing around in groups, and jabbering away to one another.

"What's going on?" I said to Shanti, whose eyes seemed unusually bright. She turned to me and said:

"We all have to be here at five prompt tomorrow morning, and form a queue outside. Then someone is going to collect us to take us into a special, reserved place in the Prayer Hall. We can't believe it. It's never happened before. But Sai Baba has just sent a message that tomorrow morning ..."

"What? What?" I tried to hurry her.

She smiled and said,

"He will be giving all the medical camp *padnamaskar!*"

Chapter 9
Padnamaskar

By six-thirty the next morning, as thousands upon thousands of devotees were being led into the hall behind me, I was the closest woman to Sai Baba's empty chair. The women of the medical camp had been lined up in rows, facing one another, for Sai Baba to walk between us so that we could reach his feet, and I'd been placed at the top of the line. At this point, my eyes were full of tears, my heart was in my mouth and my legs were killing me. I'd been in the same cross-legged position for more than an hour. I was dying to stand up, or at least stretch my legs out in front of me. But I dare not move or raise my head in case somebody in charge noticed me, and then realised that it had all been a terrible mistake.

All night, I'd hardly slept. My mind had been working overtime, trying to convince me that something would happen to prevent me from reaching my goal. It couldn't be true, it taunted me, that I was finally going to touch his feet and be accepted by him. What if it was all a cruel joke, and death was going to claim me, with a sadistic laugh, just before I got to the hall?

Even when I'd managed to dismiss these demonic taunts, I still didn't dare fall asleep in case my alarm clock failed. So I stayed awake and used the time to prepare, and it turned out that my days on the reception desk with the Telegu-speaking Shanti had not been wasted. That last evening, towards the end of our shift, she'd taught me some Telegu words. So, in my right hand, I was now holding a letter that said, in perfect Telegu:

"I love you more and more every day. You are my heart's desire. I prostrate at your Holy Lotus Feet. Your humble devotee, Ishtar."

As I sat there, waiting for Sai Baba to come, I looked around and saw, for the first time, all the decorations that had been put up especially for this auspicious festival. You could sense, too, so much love and devotion from the thousands of devotees who'd come from all over the world and who had been celebrating here for days. The whole hall—even the walls—were warm and vibrant with it. It was as if a wonderful party had been going on while I'd been sulking and nursing my wounds up at the hospital. Yet Sai Baba was now going to give me the best present ever, anyway.

But I felt very tired too. Not physically, but on a deeper level. It was like the tiredness felt by someone who knows that they are nearing the end of a very long journey, and absolutely dying to get home. In fact, there is a wonderful speech in my book about Krishna by his cousin, Akrura, which describes this feeling much better than I ever could. He'd been sent to collect Krishna from Gokul. So he was also nearing the end of a long journey and these were his thoughts as he rode along in his chariot:

"What great acts of sacrifice have I suffered? What altruistic acts of charity have I performed? What holy deeds or devotional service has a mere mortal such as myself given, so that today I will see my Lord?

"Since I am an ordinary person involved merely in satisfying my senses, I think it is as difficult for me to have received this opportunity to see the Lord as it would be for one of the Untouchables to be permitted to chant the Vedic *mantras*.

"But let me banish such musings! For perhaps, even a low soul like me can obtain the opportunity to see the all-powerful Lord. Perhaps one of the ordinary mortals, with little or no spiritual training, who is being carried along in the river of time is allowed, sometimes, even by chance, to reach the shore.

"Whatever the cause, today all my sins will be destroyed and my life will be redeemed, since I will be able to worship at the Lord's Lotus Feet, which all the great yogis meditate upon. Merely by the grace of these beautiful feet, many souls in the past have risen above the darkness of material existence and achieved full spiritual enlightenment.

"Now all the moments of my life have been made meaningful…"

The narrator continues:

So thinking deeply in this way about the Lord's Feet, Akrura reached Krishna's village, Gokul. It was sundown and all the cowherds were returning from grazing their cattle in the far pastures. Akrura drove his chariot into the cowherd pastures, and there he saw the footprints of those feet whose pure dust the rulers of all the planets in the universe long to have on their foreheads. Becoming blissful just by seeing the Lord's footprints, Akrura's body hairs stood erect with delight and his eyes filled with tears. Then he leapt down from his chariot and began rolling about among those footprints, shouting, "Ah, this is the dust from my Master's Feet!"

I knew how Akrura felt. These were also my feelings as I stared at Sai Baba's chair longingly, wondering how much longer he was going to be. Then suddenly, the music started up and I knew he was on his way.

At last, he entered the hall. He did his usual circuit, first the women's side, then over to the men's side, all the while taking letters, materialising *vibhuuthi* and selecting devotees for an interview. Then, as usual, after gathering up all the interviewees, he started walking towards the interview room by way of his chair.

Very soon, he was just behind me. He'd slowed down a little, just enough to allow the interviewees to go ahead of him. I didn't want to stare, so I was looking down at my lap. But something then made me turn and look over my shoulder. I was just in time to see that he was standing beside one of the pillars and staring at me very intently. The look was so intimate. It was as if he knew me, as if he'd always known me. As our eyes met, he quickly swivelled his. But it was too late. I'd already seen it. I'd seen the look of longing, of yearning, the look of pure love for his devotee who, I now knew, he just wanted to come home to him. And from that moment on, I was his.

Swami led the devotees into the interview room. Then the seconds, minutes, hours slowly ticked by as he conducted his interviews. But, like a ravenous dog watching his master at table, my eyes were firmly glued to the door of his room.

Finally, at 8.09 AM, he emerged. Then he slowly walked over to the men's side where he started going up and down the rows of the male medical camp volunteers, giving them *padnamaskar*.

Aeons later, or so it seemed, he finished on the men's side. Then he started to walk towards us on the women's side. First of all, he went along the row behind me. It was all I could do to keep my head looking forward.

Then finally, it was our turn. He turned and started to walk up our row, beginning at the furthest end to where I was sitting.

As I watched him coming nearer and nearer, something almost tangible in the atmosphere changed. It was as if he was altering the atomic make-up of the air as he passed through it and the resulting ripples, like when you throw a pebble into a pond, were flowing towards me. My heart started burning and spinning like a catherine wheel. It was a strange sensation, one I'd never experienced before. It was as if the area behind my breastbone was on fire. As he came even closer, I realised that I was losing my personality. By the time he was in front of me, even my gender had gone. I felt just like an empty shell—apart from this ferocious burning sensation in my breast.

But then, horror of horror, he'd passed me. He was gone. And without me touching his feet or him even acknowledging me.

My heart was trying to leap out of my chest. It was jumping up and down like a bird fighting to get out of a cage. The only other sensation I felt was one of sheer utter dread. I was beginning to wonder what on earth would be left for me, where I could possibly turn, if he was going to reject me, and my love.

I knew, of course, that my love wasn't pure. It was tainted because it was a worldly love. It was the ordinary carnal love of a woman in love with a man. But it was the only love I had. I didn't have any other love to offer. So if he didn't want that, then I was finished. Totally. It was a terrible feeling. I felt completely rejected.

But just then, when I thought all was lost, he swivelled on his heel and turned around. Then put his hand out for my letter. I can't describe the relief that I felt. My whole body flooded with it, and joy. Joy that he had accepted me, and my love.

"Thank you, Swami!" I said to him in a voice thick with love. My emotions were audible and I felt my cheekbones give way to an enormous smile.

He took the letter and then turned back as if to go on his way, all the while staring intently at the envelope. I wondered if he was reading the letter through it. Then, without even looking up from it, he spoke, telepathically, to me.

"Stay there," he said. "I'm coming back."

In other words, "Don't touch my feet. Stay where you are."

Because he'd never spoken to me before, much less telepathically, I wasn't sure if I'd imagined that he had spoken to me. I began to doubt my own judgment. What should I do? I didn't want to miss touching his feet. But he'd said to stay where I was. I was in a spin. For the first time ever, I had to decide between doing what I thought was best for me and my spiritual progress, and obeying what I thought was his instruction.

I chose the latter. I carried on sitting and looking up at the back of his head. I was practically rigid with the fear that I might be making the biggest mistake of my life. But somehow, I managed to continue to sit there. It seemed like forever. But it was probably less than a few seconds. Then he turned back. Then he leant right over me until he was peering directly into my eyes, so sweetly, so inquiringly.

It was like someone staring down into a deep well to see what was there, to see if there was any water. He wasn't looking at 'me', or what I'd come to think of as 'me' or 'my personality', which had long since made itself scarce, anyway. He was looking way beyond that. I think he was looking at my soul, or *atma*, as he calls it.

I felt my whole being open up to him. My body felt totally relaxed. My heart was doing a song and dance of its own. My eyes were wide open, hiding nothing but not projecting anything, either. I wanted him to see it all, because I knew only he could fix it.

Then he released me from his gaze and turned to the next person. As he did so, I slowly bent over to gently stroke his feet with my hands. They felt deliciously soft and silky. Then as he moved on very slightly, I bent my torso over until it was almost flat on the ground, and went to kiss the back of his foot. My lips were literally just a hairs-breadth away when he very gently moved on, leaving me kissing the air.

After that, I was completely wiped out. We were supposed to go back to the medical camp. But I couldn't speak to anyone. I needed to be alone, although I knew that I would never be really alone ever again.

So I just went back to my apartment and stayed there, meditating and crying and praying with so much gratitude and joy, until I eventually dozed off.

In the afternoon, I got up and went to see Swami as usual, although nothing felt usual. I was ushered into the front row in the hall. Swami came in and as he walked past, without even looking at me, he spoke to me, non-vocally again, and asked:

"Do you want to merge with me?"

He tossed me this question as casually as if he was asking whether I would like to go for a coffee some time. However, it wasn't just a question. It was a proposition and I couldn't have been more shocked if he'd made one of a less respectable kind.

"*Merge?*"

I just stared at him, stunned. But he carried on walking past me, sauntering almost, really casually, until he was lost from view in the temple.

My intuition, which until then had been in the same rosy glazed-over daze as the rest of me, suddenly woke up and started yelling, trying to alert me to the fact that this was my big opportunity. I began to get an uncanny feeling that I'd waited countless lifetimes to be sitting there as the Lord walked past and asked me, "Do you want to merge with me?"

I assumed by 'merging' that he didn't mean merging with his physical body, but the infinite God that it represented. But my feelings about merging had not changed all that much from when I'd first heard about the concept from Lotus Petal's story of Sisupala. So, not knowing quite what else to do, I quickly gathered myself up, left the hall and headed up the hill to what was known as the Meditation Tree.

I often used to visit this Meditation Tree when I needed to think, which is a bit ironic really, because the whole thing about meditation is that you're meant *not* to think. But anyway, in recent weeks, I'd found this to be a congenial spot, away from all the hurly-burly of the ashram, and there was quite a story connected to it too.

Apparently, one day, when Swami had been just a young man, he had been sitting with his devotees on the sands by the Chitravathi river, talking about Buddha meditating under the *bodhi* tree. He began to stress how important it was for spiritual aspirants to have an auspicious place to practise meditation and, as he spoke, he pulled something out of the sands. It appeared to be a thick, copper plate, about 15 inches by 10 inches. As the devotees looked more closely at it, they could see strange markings and letters of many unknown alphabets.

Swami then said that he was going to plant this special plate under a banyan tree in order to help those meditating to develop concentration of mind and control of their senses. This he duly did and, nowadays, this banyan tree has reached quite a height. During those hot summer days in 1998, it had felt wonderful to relax quietly under its spreading branches. But, unfortunately for me that day—special plate or no special plate—there was not the slightest chance of being able to concentrate my mind in meditation, because it was jumping around with questions like a box of frogs.

There were questions like:

"Well, if I merge with you, then how can I be with you, because they'll be no 'me' anymore?"

Or another was,

"Look actually, I'm not really a spiritual sort of person, really. I've just fallen in love with you, that's all. Won't you just let me move in with you and do your laundry?"

Or,

"Okay, look. If that's what you really want, I'll merge with you," as if I was doing him a great favour. Then,

"But how can I merge with you when I don't know how to? I don't even know anyone who's done it, to ask them!"

I did think of asking for devotion instead, as you are allowed to do, according to Lotus Petal. But I was put off by the worry that the next time we incarnate together, he might make me wait another 40-odd years again before showing up. I didn't think that I could go through that again.

I sat wrestling with my thoughts, fears and desires for a long time. But I didn't get anywhere. I returned to the Meditation Tree the next day, and the next, and the next. But it was useless, because what I didn't realise then was that it was no longer up to me. I had handed over the reins of my spiritual progress to Swami when I'd obeyed his command during *padnamaskar*. The process was already underway. I was being prepared for a long journey, a journey of a lifetime, a journey in Swami's red BMW—and he was going to be my driver.

CHAPTER 10
THE SUMMER OF BLISS

I wasn't the only woman in love with Sai Baba that summer at Prashanti Nilayam. As the days went by, I came to realise that there were at least five others. We never spoke to one another. But I knew that they felt the same way. This was partly because of how they were when around him, but also because he always seemed to have us sitting in the same places in the hall every day, despite the 'lottery' seating system, which appeared to dictate where one sat.

By then, I had given up sitting cross-legged with the crowd on the floor. My legs couldn't take it anymore. So I'd joined the older women on the raised-up bench that ran down the side of the ladies' section. This turned out to be a wonderful vantage point for watching Swami down in the hall.

But there was a slightly odd thing about this bench that particular summer. Most of the women sitting on it turned out to be Reiki masters. Now, where I lived in England, I would rarely bump into another Reiki master. Here, you couldn't move for them. There was a very sweet, rotund one from Venezuela, another tiny one from Japan, a down-to-earth Australian one, a cheesy American one, a pretty French one, a quiet, mousey one from Macedonia, two from Italy—well, Corsica and Sicily—another from Kazakhstan (a country I'd never heard of, and wouldn't again until the Afghan war)…I could go on.

I remember, one day, a very tall, haughty Czech woman arriving. She stood in front of us ladies on the bench and then drew herself up to her full height. Then arching her eyebrows, she proudly vouchsafed to us that she was "in fact, a Reiki master."

I didn't have the heart to tell her that we were all redundant.

"Join the club," I said, indicating to either side of me and introducing her to Miss America and the others.

That bench was fast becoming a veritable Miss World of Reiki masters and I was fully expecting a tuxedoed compere to appear at any moment to ask me about my hobbies.

But I was in bliss in my seat. The seating 'lottery' would also apply to how we were seated on the bench. But the prized place, directly facing the path that Swami would always take on leaving the temple, always seemed to be mine. No matter how many women were queuing for the bench that day, and how many lines they formed, and how the lottery turned out, I always seemed to end up in that spot. So I would spend the whole session in bliss, just looking forward to that wonderful moment at the end when Swami would come walking in a straight line towards me. And while he didn't look up at me every single time, he did quite often, and then such waves of love would come rolling from his eyes into mine that I wouldn't be good for anything much at all for days afterwards.

However, from my special vantage point on the bench, I also began gradually to notice these other love-struck women, and I dubbed them the Famous Five. I could clearly see that they, like me, were completely in their own worlds and had no interest in anyone else until Swami appeared, when their whole beings seemed to come alight. In fact, one of them had quite a plain face, bless her. But whenever Swami looked her way, her facial expression would dissolve into such a beatific expression of love that her beauty would have surpassed that of Helen of Troy.

I think I mentioned earlier about Krishna being so attentive to every one of his 16,108 wives that each would be convinced that she was the only one. Well, unfortunately, that wasn't working here. Now that I'd spotted the Famous Five, I would often be consumed by jealousy, wondering if he also talked to them telepathically. I would watch him like a hawk whenever he drew level with any of them, and if he looked at them, the pain would be unbearable, especially if he hadn't looked at me that day.

THE SUMMER OF BLISS

It was all very well knowing that, in theory, he had enough unconditional love for all of us, I'd think to myself. But, because I'd never had any practical experience of such love, I was stuck in the agony of this worldly type for quite some time. Then one day Swami, in his mercy, decided to lance the boil.

One afternoon, in the Prayer Hall, there appeared a group of younger, attractive women who wore their long, silky hair down on their shoulders (usually a no-no) and whose beautifully coloured *saris* clung to their every curve. I couldn't help noticing them because they happened to be seated on the floor in front of me. I was idly thinking to myself that they didn't stand much of a chance of getting an interview looking like that. Then Swami came in, and, breaking his usual habit of going directly over to the men's side, walked straight towards them and with his best winning, film star smile, invited them for an interview.

As you can imagine, the old, green-eyed demon immediately leapt up and began rubbing sticks together to light a bonfire in my chest. Then it burst into flames as this group of beautiful women gracefully got up and followed Swami into the interview room. But worse was to come.

Usually, you couldn't hear any sound coming from the interview room. But today was different. Very soon, all we could hear in the hall was raucous peals of laughter ringing out from the interview room. It sounded as if Swami was entertaining them royally and they were all having a wonderful time. But with each wave of laughter, my agony increased beyond measure. The fun went on like this for almost an hour. So by the time these women emerged from his room with their eyes shining and cheeks glowing, my ego had almost self-combusted with jealousy and rage.

Afterwards, I did my usual angry stomp down Chitravathi Lane. The stall keepers didn't even bother to wish me a "good evening". I think they were coming to know when I'd had a 'bad *darshan*'.

But that evening, I went for supper as usual in the Western canteen, and I found myself talking about it to another devotee.

"Oh, those girls," she said. "Yes, they come at this time every year. They're so wonderful, so dedicated. They live like nuns and completely follow all of Swami's teachings to the letter. They use all their money to help disadvantaged children and keep nothing for themselves. All they have is this week, every year, when they come to see Swami."

Needless to say, I was mortified with shame. I trudged back to my apartment. The awful truth was beginning to dawn about how impure and base my egotistical 'love' for Swami was. I was beginning to realise that I'd hardly progressed at all. All I'd done was taken the tainted, conditional 'love' that I'd always given to other men and tried to offer this filthy thing to Swami. I felt dreadful and started to wonder how on earth I could change. But I didn't know how or where to start.

When I got into bed that night, I was in tears as I asked Swami to help me, to raise me up from this low state of consciousness that I'd been stuck in all my life, and I prayed to him for a long time before drifting off to sleep.

The next day, I went to *darshan* and took my usual place on the bench. Once again, these young women were shown in and seated right in front of me.

What a coincidence! I thought.

Then Swami came in. And just like the day before, he came up and invited them for an interview.

But this time, something different was happening. As he led them off, I was surprised to find myself smiling and the blissful feeling of contentment remained in place throughout the whole hour as the same waves of raucous laughter emanated from the room. I even found myself grinning and laughing along with it. And when the young ladies eventually emerged, glowing as before, and resumed their seats in front of me, giggling and nudging one another, I was still unperturbed, and even thought,

Wasn't that nice for them! How lovely!

Now, I'm not saying that I've never had a moment of jealousy from that day forth. But certainly, in just that 24-hour span, great inroads were made into raising my consciousness. I was also beginning to learn how quickly Swami could get me over seemingly impossible obstacles when I asked for his help. I was also starting to see that, thankfully, and most importantly, the amount of progress made was not dependent upon my own spiritual prowess, but upon his.

As the days went by after that, I even began to feel more sympathetically towards the Famous Five. I'd watch each one come into the hall from my raised vantage point on the bench. I would see them take up their places in their usual spots in the hall, and it would give me a good feeling of satisfaction that Swami had us all safely in our respective places and was taking care of us.

Then, as the days turned into weeks, and then months, I gradually began to get a tiny glimpse of who Sai Baba really was. The more that realisation unravelled, the more I began to see that he had an absolute abundance of love for everyone. It soon became clear that I didn't have to grab on to him and try to own every bit of the love he was giving me. It seemed that there would always be plenty more where that love came from—an unimaginably infinite, to my small mind, cornucopia of delights.

But I was also coming to realise that never again would I be able to have any other boyfriend, partner or husband. I knew that I belonged to Swami through and through. Sometimes I thought that it had always been that way. It began to seem as if this relationship stretched back over several lifetimes. I would wonder if there had ever been a time when he hadn't been with me.

Of course, I also knew that it was ridiculous to think that I was anywhere near good enough for him. It was obvious that there wasn't even a trillion to-one chance that he would ever ask me to marry him. But on the other hand, I would sit there reasoning to myself, if I'd decided because of this that I should then go and marry someone else—well, then there would be even less chance than that. At least, by remaining single, I would be able to lie easy on my deathbed, knowing that I'd given Swami every chance. In any case, all this was just academic. The fact was, I was too much in love with him to allow any other man to touch me.

During that time, I came across a wonderful speech by Rukmini ('Rook-meany') one of Krishna's wives, after he has just teased her on this very subject. Here is just a flavour of it:

> My Lord, I am indeed unworthy of the Supreme Lord of all the universes. How could I compare myself to you, the master and sustainer of all living beings, and myself, a woman of the world who has been wandering for aeons in worldly illusion?
>
> Your actions, which are puzzling even for those saints who are permanently saturated in the fragrance of Your Lotus Feet,

are certainly even more bewildering for human beings who follow their senses like animals.

You own nothing because there is nothing beyond You, even though Brahma and the other demigods pay tribute to You. Those who are distracted by their riches and only intent on fulfilling the desires of their senses do not recognise You. But to the gods, You are the most precious, as they are to You.

You are the personification of all human endeavours and are Yourself the final goal of life. Desperate to reach You, O all-powerful Lord, discriminating people renounce all other quests. What possible attraction, then, could I have to any other suitors?

The delicious fragrance of Your Lotus Feet, which is praised by all the great saints, grants human beings spiritual liberation and is the home of the Goddess of Wealth. Therefore, what woman in her right mind would dream of accepting the proposal of any other man after relishing that fragrance? Since You are the source of all spiritual benefits, what woman with the discrimination to judge her own best interests would ignore that divine aroma and put her trust, instead, in a man who is always exuding insecurity and fear?

Of course, I am not good enough for you. But because you have cleansed me of desire for any other man, and I must have a husband to take care of me, I am begging you to fulfil that role, O Lord of the Universe who grants our wishes in this life and the next. I pray that your divine Feet, which release tormented souls from worldly illusion, will give a home to such a one as me, who has been roaming, lost, from one material situation to another.

O My Dearest Lord, even though You are totally self-sufficient and thus would never need me, or anyone else, please bless me with steady devotion for Your wonderful Lotus Feet.

As those blissful days passed in the summer of 1998, I couldn't imagine that they would ever end. I missed my family, of course. But I couldn't even bear to think about returning home—or at least, to my old life—because I knew that nothing would ever be the same again, and I couldn't begin to imagine what was in store for me.

I just lived in Swami's world, day after blissful day. I would sit on my special place on the bench in the hall and just bask in his presence, until the whole world seemed to tip-toe softly away and there was only the two of us. Often, as I watched him, I would hear the refrain from the Prince song:

"Nothing compares…nothing compares to you."

It would go through my head, over and over again. They were the only words that I knew that came anywhere near to describing how I felt.

Some days would be big festival days, and you couldn't move for the crowds. The Prayer Hall would be beautifully done-up with the most colourful and highly artistic decorations, and there would be concerts and plays in the evenings. In fact, there seemed to be so many festivals and big crowds, one after another, that I used to joke that I was living in the Greatest Show on Earth, with Swami as Barnum and Bailey all rolled into one.

But at other times, there would hardly be anyone there. I came to realise that my favourite days were rainy Tuesdays. This was because everyone who'd arrived for the weekend would usually have left by late Monday. So Tuesdays would be quiet, and even more so if it rained because that meant a whole load of other people who didn't like getting wet also didn't come. And as we were now into the monsoon season, there were quite a few of these days.

So, although on rainy Tuesdays there would still be a couple of thousand people, it somehow felt a lot more intimate. Swami would just walk around and he didn't even need to speak or do anything. He'd just be, and we'd just be, and we'd all just bathe in this be-ness, this being. We were human beings instead of human doings. It would be so quiet. All we could hear would be the drip, drip, drip of the water as it fell from the roof and echoed around the cavernous hall.

The Prayer Hall was a quite enormous structure with a roof held up by gigantic girders. But like the one in Whitefields, it only had half-walls. So sometimes a bird would fly in and swoop gracefully past Swami as he walked around. Or a tribe of monkeys would come squealing and bounding in over the half-walls and then climb up the tall, golden columns to the girders. Then they'd sit there silently, just like us, watching Swami walking around, or looking at the wall motifs of peacocks and snakes, and the elephants and lions nestling together. There were some beautiful sculptures too. There was one of a pair of swans around a lotus flower. Another depicted a pair of deer inhaling the fragrance of flowers. There were sculptures of flowers strewn all around the ceiling, pillars, arches, doors and windows.

But that this hall ever came to be built at all turned out to be one of Swami's lesser-known miracles. Here is an excerpt about it from his biography:

> The Prasanthi Nilayam was inaugurated on 23rd November 1950, the 25th birthday of Bhagavan Sri Sathya Sai Baba. It took about two years to build. Baba can be said to be the architect and engineer who directed the entire work of construction. His suggestions had to be accepted by the engineers for they found them much better than their own. They found that Baba had a greater sense of perspective, a nicer aesthetic point of view than they had. Baba was a hard taskmaster, but, with immeasurable Karuna, too. And His Grace overcame the most insurmountable obstacles!
>
> For example, heavy girders for the *darshan* hall came from near Trichinopoly by train to Penukonda all right. But, how on earth could they be brought over the District Board Road, sixteen miles long, with a sandy stream on the seventh mile? How can any lorry with those long bars sticking out negotiate the acute angled corners of the village of Locherla, on the ninth mile? And, after Bukkapatnam is reached, there are three miles of a track that can be referred to, only by courtesy, as a road. Then the broad expanse of sand across which the Chitravathi river spreads a distance of three furlongs, between Puttaparthi and Karnatanagapalli! There were dilapidated culverts to be gone over; the slushes to be dragged through; and, if and when the girders arrived at the spot, the task of hoisting them up on top of the high walls!
>
> So the engineers gave up all hope of bringing the girders to the village and asked Baba for some alternative proposals for roofing the hall.
>
> But, one night, in the smaller hours, the engineer was awakened by a loud noise in front of his house at Anantapur. He peered into the darkness and was surprised to find a crane from Tungabhadra Dam works, put out of action and unable to move. He ran up to Puttaparthi and told Baba that if only it could be made all right, the owners could be persuaded to travel up to Penukonda and bring the girders along.
>
> Baba materialised some *vibhuuthi* and gave a little quantity of it to the engineer. The engineer piously scattered it over the

engine of the crane and he asked the driver to make efforts to set it going. And with a grunt or two, the engine started, the wheels turned and the crane moved…towards the girders!

Lifting the girders with its giant arm, it somehow passed over all the culverts, turned round the Locherla corners, lurched over the Vankaperu slush, and puffed up the Karnatanagapalli hill! There, the engineers said its strength was well nigh exhausted. It could not possibly draw all that weight through the sands. So Baba himself sat near the driver and handled the wheel, and the crane unloaded the girders near the work-spot.

I was very grateful, fifty years later, to be sitting in this wonderful building that so many had gone to so much trouble to build, and just watching Swami.

Mostly I'd just sit there, waiting for him to throw me one of his smouldering looks. But sometimes, he'd play with me. There was one time when I was trying to learn the Gayathri Mantra ('gay-atree man-tra'). This is the most powerful Vedic chant and it is a potent aid to God realisation. Phonetically, it goes like this:

Om Bhur Buvaha Suvaha
Thath Savithur Varenyam
Bhargo Devasya Dheemahi
Dhiyo Yonaha Prachodayath

It means:

We contemplate the glory of Light illuminating the three worlds: gross, subtle, and causal. I am that vivifying power, love, radiant illumination and divine grace of universal intelligence. We pray for the divine light to illumine our minds.

I had heard the sound of this *mantra* ringing out from Swami's university students. So I'd managed to get hold of a copy of it and one day, I brought it into the Prayer Hall. When Swami went off into the temple, I got it out to practise it. I learned the words by mouthing them to myself. Then I started to mentally recite them. But as soon as I began, Swami came very fast out of the temple, almost running. Then he stood right at the start of the path he always took when walking towards me. He just stood there, facing me, very still and very straight, like an idol in a temple. I somehow managed to carry on with the *mantra*, although stumbling quite a bit.

Another time, one rainy Tuesday, the monsoon came down with a vengeance. The sky suddenly turned almost completely black. The wind whipped itself up and started howling. Then it started to rain. Vast torrents of water came crashing down from the sky, hitting the concrete pathways and bouncing back up again. Gusts of gale-force winds blew the rain into the hall, and as the bench ladies always sat with their backs to the half-walls, we were soon all drenched.

But all this happened just a few minutes before Swami was due to leave the temple and walk towards us. So not one of us moved. We just continued to sit there, and the weather took no pity on us. The wind was so strong, it was as if it was trying to blow us off the bench. But still we sat there. Then it started to blow the rain directly on to us. Very soon, our hair was blown into tangled, dripping messes, our bodies were completely sodden and we were all sitting in puddles, trying to ring the water out of our *saris*.

Swami was late. It was most unusual. He was normally so punctual. But still we sat there. Not one of us was going to miss Swami walking towards them. It would have taken an earthquake to move us.

Finally, Swami came out of the temple. He started to walk towards us. Then he looked up and saw us. He stopped dead in his tracks. A look of utter astonishment spread across his face at the sight of these drenched and bedraggled wretches on the bench. He then extended his hand palm upwards, as if to test for rain. Then he pulled his face into a mock quizzical expression, as if to say, "Hmmm. That's strange. No rain here." It was so funny. We all just burst out laughing. Then he smiled, waved his blessings at us and continued on his way.

CHAPTER 11
THE TASTE OF LOVE

One of the things that puzzled me when I first got to India was why, whenever I went to buy a train ticket, I would be directed into the ladies' queue.

I couldn't understand why there should be separate queues for men and women. I'd assumed it was just a tradition of which the provenance had been lost in the mists of time, until I began to learn more about the Oriental attitude towards body space. Most of the Indian people that I met seemed to love being physically close to one another. So, when queuing for a train ticket in India, even though there would be plenty of space, everyone would be pressing forward and piled up into one another.

It used to bring out the worst of my Raj-ish traits, and I would think:

Good Lord! These people really need lessons in how to queue!

But I did eventually realise why these queues were segregated by gender. It was so that any respectably brought-up young woman didn't have to suffer strange men pressing up against her backside. And it was no different at Prasanthi Nilayam.

Every day, we would spend hours and hours sitting cross-legged in very cramped conditions, waiting for Swami. The ladies would queue separately and be seated on the ladies' side. The men would do likewise, and be seated on the gents' side.

Normally, I would sit on the bench, and it was quite comfortable. But one morning, I arrived late for *darshan* and the bench ladies had already been seated. So I had to take my chances in the crush of the cross-legged devotees on the floor. At times like this, I would usually try to sit next to the Western devotees, knowing that at least they'd make an effort on the personal space front and were less likely to jam their knees up into your back. But on this particular day, I found myself among a whole crowd of Indian women, and just when you couldn't get a Basmati rice paper between any of us, an extremely large Indian woman came along. She must have weighed at least twenty stone. Anyway, she pointed to a five pence-sized space next to my neighbour and prepared to launch herself. All the Indian ladies smiled sweetly, gathered up their knees and their skirts and squashed up to make space for her. So she picked up one foot and placed it down daintily in our midst. Then she plumped the rest of herself down on top of it. Bodies flew everywhere.

I was incensed.

"There's no room!" I exploded to my neighbour, a young, proud-looking Indian woman in a white *sari*. "Surely you people can see that!"

"And you people are always moaning," she snapped back. "Surely you can see that!"

"What do you mean 'you people'," I replied, hurt and angry. "That's a really racist thing to say!"

"But you said 'you people' first," she replied, and I realised, shamefacedly, that she was right.

Until that moment, I'd had no idea that I thought that way. Swami came in just then, and my cheeks were so burning with shame that I could hardly look at him.

Now, if all this sounds as if it wasn't a particularly spiritual, loving-and-giving atmosphere, believe me, that little set-to was nothing. The gents would always be extremely civil and courteous with one another on their side, with their: "After you." "Oh no, I insist. After you." But for some reason, the same could not be said for the ladies. There would often be some sort of spat breaking out on the women's side, usually over personal space, or who was going to be sitting nearest to the path Swami would take. It could even sometimes get quite nasty, and end in shouts, threats and tears.

I'd heard that Swami knew about this. I'd also been told that that was why, although his entrance was on the women's side, he would often not stop. Instead, he would walk straight through to the men's side. I'd even heard that he once threatened to give up entering through the women's side altogether, if we couldn't learn to behave, or at least use it as an opportunity to put some of his teachings into practice.

However, that morning, Swami gave a discourse, and the sentiments he expressed seemed quite apt to my burning ears. He talked about the concept of 'nearest and dearest'. He said that the devotee should aim to be near and dear to the guru. He added that there were some who may have been 'near', physically, but that they weren't that 'dear'.

Oh no! I thought, as this hot prickle started to work its way up my neck. After my run-in with the Indian ladies, I was convinced that he meant me.

Darshan ended, and then I went about my usual chores. But later on that morning, I began to realise that I was in pain. For weeks now, my habitual lower backache had been making its presence felt, and it was particularly bad that lunchtime when I went to lay down for my nap. I was quite worried that, if it got any worse, I wouldn't be able to sit in any more *darshan* sessions. So I prayed, as I dozed off:

"Swami, please help me with my back. I just couldn't bear it if I had to miss seeing you."

I gradually drifted into a dream. I was in a garden that I didn't recognise. Then I heard Swami's voice. It was coming from behind a curtained off area and he appeared to be talking to some men. I wanted to pull back the curtain to see him. But instinctively, I realised it was out of bounds. So I continued listening. They all seemed to be having a really good time, laughing and joking, on their side. Then suddenly, the curtain was being pulled back and Swami appeared. He was smiling at me. Then I noticed that he was holding out a bottle of liquid.

"Here you are, you dear sweet lady," he said. He paused to put emphasis on the words 'dear' and 'sweet'.

I was mesmerised. I couldn't take the bottle. I could only stare at him. But just then, the dream started to fade. So Swami thrust the bottle at me and said:

"Quick, or you'll miss it."

I just had time to grab the bottle and gulp down the liquid. The next thing I knew, I was back lying on my bed with my backache completely gone. More importantly, though, I was also bathing in the wonderful, sweet sensation of knowing I was, after all, dear to my Lord.

But even in the midst of such bliss, I could no longer avoid the realisation that I wouldn't always be 'near' to him, at least physically. My visa had only been issued for six months and by the time *Guru Poornima* had come and gone, I was already halfway through my allotted time. It wouldn't be that long, I knew, before I would have to get used to being far and dear.

I started to wonder if that was the reason why Swami was talking to me telepathically, or coming to me in dreams, rather than inviting me to a face-to-face interview. Maybe he was trying to get me used to how we would communicate when I was half a world away from his physical form, I would think. But chatting with him in that way was fast becoming quite normal, and not just in the Prayer Hall.

One morning, I'd just woken earlier than usual. So I relaxed back into my pillows and started to pray to him. The medical camp had packed up a few days before, and I was feeling that I needed to do something. I began to ask Swami if there was any of his projects that I could involve myself in.

"You don't have to do anything," he replied, "Just love me."

My Protestant work ethic was not going to be satisfied with that, though. So I kept on.

"But I want to be of help. I haven't come here just to take. You've given me so much and I want to give something back."

"Okay, if you insist. What about the orphanage school?" he suggested.

I'd heard from some friends that there was a local orphanage. Most of the children housed there were off the streets. They had arrived in Puttaparthi with their beggar parents who had either abandoned them there, or had died. Some of them had even come there by themselves.

It seemed like a good idea. Perhaps they needed some help with the cooking or the cleaning.

"Yes," I replied. "I'd love that."

"Well, wait for two days," Swami went on. "Then go and offer your services."

It seemed odd that he should ask me to wait for two days. But after my experience in *padnamaskar*, I was learning to trust his telepathic words. So I obeyed.

THE TASTE OF LOVE

Thus, two days later, I was just leaving the Prayer Hall when I ran into Becky.

"I want to go and offer my services at the orphanage today," I said. "But I don't know where it is. Could you tell me how to get there?"

"That's really strange," replied Becky. "I've also decided the very same thing this morning. I want to help out there too. So let's go together."

As we walked along, I explained to her about the telepathic conversation with Swami, and about the two-day wait.

"Why two days?" she said.

"I haven't a clue," I replied, and we rounded the corner to Samadhi Lane.

The lane led into an alleyway with street traders and beggars sitting on the ground on either side. This eventually opened up into a sandy, unmade-up road that looked fairly residential, if a little run-down. Then a large grey stone house rose up on our left.

"There it is," said Becky, her voice suddenly sounding a little less certain. It was then that I realised that she hadn't been there before—she only knew where it was. So then we were both a bit nervous.

Just then, a reddish-haired man shot out of the main door and started walking towards us. He looked really stressed.

"Who are you?" he asked brusquely in a German accent.

"We've come to see if you need any help," replied Becky.

"Do I need help?" he expostulated skywards. "I certainly do! I've just, this very morning, had to sack two teachers who I caught stealing. I've no one to replace them."

I was shocked to hear that people were stealing from an orphanage, which relied on donations. I wondered if it was possible to go any lower than that.

"I've no-one to replace them," the man continued. "I might just manage to cover for one. But I desperately need an English teacher."

"Ishtar can teach English," Becky said.

I jumped.

"Well, I don't know …" I replied, a bit surprised at this suggestion. "I've never taught before …"

"Yes, but you're a journalist. You're confident and your English is really good," she went on, turning to the man. "She can easily do it."

"That's great!" he said and then, looking skywards again. "Oh thank you so much, Swami! I knew you wouldn't let us down. You never do!" and then,

"That's settled then. My name's Max. I'm the head teacher. Be here at 8.30 AM tomorrow and ask for me. 'Bye now, must dash," and he was gone.

I finally found my voice.

"Becky, what have you let me in for?" I complained. "I've never taught in my life."

"You can do it," she said, without a quiver of doubt. "Don't worry."

The next morning, when I reported to Max for duty, my heart was in my mouth. He told me that I would be taking the very young ones, with ages ranging from about four to seven. Then he led me up on to a wide, flat roof and then into a tiny, whitewashed room at the end.

The children were already there, seated cross-legged on the floor. They smiled welcomingly at me as I entered. I'd never seen any children, or anyone for that matter, so pleased to see me before. So I started to feel a bit better.

However, there were problems, the main one being that not one of them spoke a word of English. I didn't speak any Telegu. But I made a mental note to go and see Shanti directly after school, to see if she could help. Then, for the rest of the morning, I had to make the best of it.

It would have been easier if there had been picture books. But the school relied on donations and these had been low for some time. So there were no text books that they hadn't already read a dozen times, no exercise books and only a few pencils that they would share. There was a blackboard, but if you wanted chalk, you had to go from classroom to classroom trying to find a teacher who had some they were willing to share.

We pressed on regardless, and the children were so delightful, it made it all worthwhile—and we found our way through the obstacles. One was that I found it difficult to remember all their names. Many of them sounded strange and had lots of syllables, like Radhakrishna or Subramanyam. So we managed to find some paper and cut it into squares. Then each child wrote their name on a square and then pinned it to their chest.

That first day was exhausting. But as time went on, things gradually got better. The children came to love me so much, it was wonderful. Shanti was happy to be involved and sometimes Becky would also come to help out. In time, I came to realise that I actually had a bit of a gift for teaching and I began to wonder if this would be my new career when I returned home.

For a while now, I'd been feeling uncomfortable about being a journalist. I had begun to realise that many of the things I often had to do in that profession no longer sat comfortably with my newfound beliefs. For one thing, I'd rarely get to write the truth, just a slanted version of it. It wasn't that I actually had to lie, or make things up. But a journalist—any journalist, whether in print or broadcasting—has to construct a narrative and, as life doesn't usually conform to such neat, convenient symmetry, it often leads to a distorted view of the truth, or at least, a narrow perspective on it.

Just a few weeks before leaving for India, I had been offered the position of features editor on a young women's magazine. But I'd turned it down. I couldn't face it. I could no longer bring myself to be responsible for giving young women the impression that happiness in life just lay in finding the right man, or the right lipstick.

So teaching was now becoming a new possibility. I would sometimes discuss this with a few of the other teachers there. One of these was Ted, an Australian, who also taught English.

Ted was a middle-aged, fair-haired, kindly spoken man with a blissful, Buddha-like smile. But he was also a real character. This was mainly because he had a bit of a short-term memory problem (and long to medium-term for that matter!). It could make him behave quite oddly. At times, he was only capable of living in the present moment. So, for example, we'd make arrangements to meet for lunch in the North Indian canteen to discuss changes to the English syllabus. Then he wouldn't turn up. He'd also completely forget things that had only happened the day before. In fact, how he managed to remember to come to school, most days, I don't know. In fact, sometimes he didn't.

So, on one of the days that Ted failed to turn up, I was asked to take his class of older children, and I found it so much easier.

They could all speak English, for one thing. They were all anxious to learn, for another—apart from Devahuti, ('day-va-hooty') the oldest girl in the school, who seemed so upset that she couldn't speak. She just sat facing the door with her back to me, waiting for the bell and her release. I found it very difficult to get any response from her at all at first. But the others were really attentive and animated, especially Sita and Radha, the other two girls, and the boys: Vijaya, Jaya, Naryana, Sukadeva, Vasudeva, Murugan and Prabhu.

The next day, there was still no sign of Ted. So I got to take his class again. I'd brought some books on the life of Ramakrishna, a 19th century Indian saint, which I'd found at the local market. So we used that as our English reader. The children very much enjoyed it, particularly as the way I pronounced Ramakrishna's hometown, Karmarpukar, meant something very rude in Telegu, (I've yet to discover what). So they would all fall about laughing every time I said it, even Devahuti.

This happy state of affairs continued for several more days. Then one bright morning, the door opened, and who should walk in but Ted, closely followed by a small Indian man who I'd never seen before.

"Where've you been, Ted?" I asked, pleased to see him.

Ted just stood there mutely, looking all pleased with himself. I noticed then that he was holding a giant Fanta bottle containing what looked like some clear, gloopy liquid.

"We've been to the Krishna temple at Mysore," the Indian man replied, "and we've brought back some *amrit.*"

"What's *amrit?*" I said.

"It is divine nectar!" he replied. "The ambrosia of the gods! Surely you've heard about how Swami materialises this, from time to time?"

I hadn't.

"Well," the man continued, now addressing the whole class who, I have to say, were agog. "In the ancient Ramayana story, which I'm sure you all know, it is said that *amrit* gives eternal life to all those who are fortunate enough to taste it. Swami has said that when he gives *amrit to* a devotee, it frees them from the cycle of birth and death!"

We all just sat there and stared at the Fanta bottle.

THE TASTE OF LOVE

"But surely," our Indian visitor went on, "you've heard about how Swami blessed the Krishna temple at Mysore with a continuous flow of *amrit*? He went to that temple and blessed it in 1975. Ever since then, a constant stream of *amrit* has oozed out of the ornaments there, on the altar."

The whole class was wonderstruck. But I was still hanging on, by my fingernails, to the last shred of my sensibilities. On top of that, if it really was divine nectar, I would have expected it to turn up in something a bit more ornate and esoteric than a plastic Fanta bottle. But then, I thought, perhaps I shouldn't be so surprised. I'd noticed that many things around Swami had more than a hint of the sublime mixed with the ridiculous. For instance, I would often be amused to see this beautiful incarnation of Vishnu striding up and down the *padnamaskar* lines like a lion, and being closely followed by little, stooped over, grey-haired old ladies giving out sweets from their plastic shopping baskets.

But naturally, I was intrigued to know what this *amrit* actually tasted like.

Ted went round the room with his Fanta bottle and placed a teaspoonful into each of the children's upturned hands.

Up until now, I'd tried to maintain a sort of staid school-marmish image with the class. So they were quite surprised when it came to my turn, and after licking the contents of my palm, I dissolved into an almost orgasmic groan of ecstasy and shouted,

"Ted! Wow!"

Little Narayana was so stunned, and so keen to experience such a sight again that he immediately transferred his own allotment of *amrit* into my palm and then stared up at my face expectantly, like someone waiting for a fireworks display to go off, as I licked it and went into even more paroxysms of delight.

It was absolutely wonderful. But it's difficult to describe the taste because it wasn't like anything else. It was sweet, but it wasn't a cloying, sickly sort of sweetness. It also had a wonderful, almost otherworldly fragrance that, again, is indescribable. But it wasn't just this exquisite taste and smell that was pleasing me so much. It also made me feel so fresh and rejuvenated.

Later that afternoon, as I sat watching Swami from the bench, I could still smell it, even though I'd washed my hands several times since, and eaten a meal. But the aroma was still on my breath, and in the air around me. It even seemed to be emanating from Swami himself now as he walked among the sea of devotees. Then, at one point, he seemed to be the human manifestation of it. It was as if this nectarful liquid had solidified into his form.

This amrit is what love tastes like, I thought to myself. *It must be the taste of love.*

Later on that evening, I had my supper in the canteen and then went back to my apartment and got ready to turn in for an early night. So it was only about nine o'clock, but I was already in bed and reading, when the doorbell rang. I put a shawl around my shoulders and went to open the door. Ted was standing there, and looking quite surprised. He said:

"I can't remember why I'm here."

Now, if that'd been any other man at that time of night, I'd have just said, "Okay, well let me know when you do," and shut the door.

But I just knew with Ted that it was probably true. In fact, if it had been just a line, Ted would never have remembered it. So confident was I in this assessment that I guided him into my bedroom and plumped myself down on the bed, explaining,

"It's just that it's more comfortable in here. I'm not propositioning you."

"And I wouldn't be interested if you were," replied Ted kindly.

He sat himself across from me and then indicating my foot, held his hands open in a receiving gesture. Realising that I was going to get a foot massage, I placed one of my feet in his hands, and then I lay back against the pillows to relax and enjoy it.

"By the way," he said, after several minutes of kneading. "I've remembered why I'm here now. I should have told you last week. I kept forgetting."

"Go on," I said.

"Well, you know there's a monthly magazine that they publish at the ashram about Swami? It's the official newsletter and it goes out to the devotees all over the world. Anyway, I was chatting to its editor the other day and we got on to the subject of you. I don't remember how. I told him that you'd given up journalism because of your spiritual beliefs, and he was really impressed. So he wants you to write an article about it for inclusion in next month's issue."

"Really?" I replied lazily, not really concentrating.

Ted then went on to explain about where the editor lived, how many words he wanted in the article and the deadline for dropping it off at his house.

It was amazing that he should have remembered such a detailed brief. But as I listened, I felt a growing sense of unease. It took a while before I realised what it was. Then, suddenly snatching my foot out of his hand, I sat up with a jerk.

"But how can I write such an article?" I said. "I've given up journalism, and it's only because of Swami's grace that I'm understanding why I should. It's also him that's giving me the courage to do it. So how's it going to look if I not only go back into journalism, but do it by boasting—*in something he may well read*!—about how spiritual I am to give it up!"

It was a sort of twisting, labyrinthine logic. But even Ted had just enough memory to get to the end of it and see that it made sense.

After he'd gone, I went to sleep.

About halfway through the night, I had a dream that someone was massaging my feet. It was such a lovely feeling that I just lay there, enjoying the blissful feeling. Then I gradually drifted into a sort of half consciousness, and the dream continued on. Then, with a start, I suddenly snapped back into normal awareness and sat up. Someone was still massaging my feet!

In the gloom, I couldn't make out who it was. But I was convinced that my bedroom had been invaded. I immediately leapt up and made a furious lunge at whoever they were. Halfway through the dive, when I was just about to land on top of the culprit, I saw who it was. It was Swami.

It was too late to retreat, though. As I landed on top of him, he giggled and dissolved into the floor, leaving me flat on my stomach, feeling a complete fool and begging him to come back. Needless to say, he didn't. Well, not that night, anyway…

CHAPTER 12
THE YOGA OF ACTION

We were now well into August and my birthday was fast approaching. I would ignore it, normally. But as fate would have it, it also fell on Krishna's birthday this year and big celebrations were planned. On top of that, Becky would also be leaving for England the following day. So we decided to have a big *bhajans* session at my place and we invited everyone we knew.

The day before, we'd taken the children on an outing. I'd been concerned that they hardly ever seemed to get out of the orphanage, and that they were always so cramped up. The classrooms doubled up as dormitories, with the children sleeping on the floor and then clearing away their bedding in the morning to get their schoolbooks out.

But the idea for an outing had originally come to me when I was teaching the top class how to write a letter. I thought it would give us a good excuse for an outing if we took them to the Post Office to show them how to buy a stamp and use the mail. It grew rapidly from there, and by the time the hired people carrier rolled up outside the school that morning, Ted, Sophia and Becky had also decided to come, Ramakrishna, one of the trainee teachers, was going to drive us and we had a full itinerary of Post Office, Sai Geeta (Swami's elephant), Swami's dairy farm, the Wish Fulfilment Tree and finishing up at the Telegu teacher's house for tea and tiffin.

Few of the children had anyone to whom they could write a letter, so most had written to Swami and some of them, very kindly, had told him about their lovely English teacher. Devahuti, the young girl who had sat facing the door on my first day, was now a firm friend. She even put in her letter about my visa running out soon and could Swami, therefore, find a way to keep me in India? So, with these precious letters in hand, we all set off for the Post Office in great excitement and with the feeling that it was going to be a day to remember.

The Post Office turned out to be huge and empty. We were its only customers. So it was with great amusement that I noticed the children all queuing up at the counter in the traditional Indian way of piling up against one another. Anyway, they bought their stamps, posted their letters and then we were off to Sai Geeta.

I wouldn't say that Sai Geeta looked that pleased to see us. In fact, she terrified some of the children at first by trumpeting and running towards them. She had a bandage around her left leg and so she may have been in pain. She seemed in quite a petulant mood and not at all divine. But she soon relaxed, and so did the children when they started to feed her her favourite food of bananas.

As we left Sai Geeta to go to the dairy, Hari, one of the younger boys, seemed quite nervous and he fastened his hand tightly on mine. I asked him what was wrong. It took him a while, but he eventually said, "My father lives near here. I haven't seen him since the day he killed my mother. I saw him do it. He tried to set her on fire. The fire went out, and so he strangled her."

It was heartbreaking to see the mix of emotions on his little face—an absolutely irreconcilable mixture of longing for a father that he hadn't seen in years, and sheer terror that he might run into him. I assured Hari that he would be safe with us and kept him close to me for the rest of the day. After the dairy farm, he sat on my lap as Ramakrishna drove us down Chitravathi Lane and parked at the bottom of the steps to the Wish Fulfilment Tree.

Ramakrishna was a lovely young man in his early twenties with a very soft, spiritual demeanour. Both Becky and I were fond of him and treated him like an adored younger brother. He'd been brought up locally and so he knew all the history of the area. So when we were standing under the Wish Fulfilment Tree looking down on the *dhobi* women in the valley below, spreading out their washing to dry, he pointed out what appeared to be a small settlement across the sandy hillocks of the dried up bed of the river Chitravathi.

THE YOGA OF ACTION

"That's Karnatanagapalli ('kar-na-ta-nag-apalli')," he said, "the village where Swami was born."

"We thought he was born in Puttaparthi," Becky and I said, almost in unison.

"No," Ramakrishna went on. "Karnatanagapalli is my village and I've lived there all my life. Everyone there knows Swami was born there. The family moved to Puttaparthi when he was a few years old. I can show you the house, if you like."

This was very strange because all the literature on Swami had him being born in Puttaparthi. I'd even visited a Shiva temple in the village that the locals said was built on the site of his old family house. So Becky and I were intrigued. However, we were expected at the Telegu teacher's house next and so we thought that there probably wouldn't be time.

We pulled into a compound of tiny huts. The Telegu teacher, Mr Krishnamurty, was standing at the door of his tiny house to welcome us all. I didn't think we'd all fit in, but we did, even though some of the children had to sit on the windowsills.

Mr Krishnamurty gave us all very good tea and tiffin—pieces of juicily sweet mango and papaya, and tiny, coloured milk and coconut sweets. Then the children enchanted us with some wonderful *bhajan* singing. But all too soon, it was time to leave.

There was a feeling of sadness in the people carrier as we headed back down the road towards the orphanage. What had just been a fairly pleasant day for us had been an absolutely thrilling adventure for the children.

Then I looked at my watch and noticed that there was still half-an-hour before we were due back at the school. So as we rounded the corner into Chitravathi Lane, I said:

"Okay, Ramakrishna. Let's go to Karnatanagapalli!"

All the children cheered. Ramakrishna grinned and then floored it down the hill towards the river. Then we all lapsed into a nervous silence as we began to negotiate our way across the sand dunes of the dried up riverbed.

We nearly got bogged down at one point. I'd heard many wonderful stories about how Swami would often go down to the Chitravathi sands with his devotees and pull golden figurines of Krishna, Shiva and Lakshmi straight out of the ground. Sometimes, I'd heard, he would even extract phials of *amrit* from these sands. But I was quietly praying, at this point, that he wasn't going to have to come down and extract *us*.

So we all breathed a sigh of relief when we eventually reached the other side, and then found ourselves going along a narrow, winding lane. Within minutes, we were pulling up outside a fairly ordinary looking white house in which, Ramakrishna assured us, Swami's family had originally lived on the ground floor.

The house was locked up and deserted. Ramakrishna then said that there was a way that we could see in. The land dropped away at the back of the house and the basement had a ledge running along the top of its exposed side. Following Ramakrishna, we all shuffled along this ledge. Then we came to a room that was open along one side, apart from some stout iron bars that had been erected. So we clung on to these bars, like chimps in a cage, and peered through them into one of the rooms.

It looked as if it hadn't been lived in for years and years. There were yellowed papers, newspapers, magazines and piles of rubbish everywhere. You'd have thought that some particularly untidy squatters had just left in a hurry. The only link to Swami seemed to be an old, peeling poster of him, pinned to the wall. It was hard to believe that such an important place, the birthplace of such a powerful incarnation of God, would be allowed to get like this. But then the path leading to the Wish Fulfilment Tree hadn't been much better.

Still, we were all quite doubtful as we shuffled our way back along the ledge to the front of the house. But then something odd happened.

A group of young street urchins, led by a stringy-looking boy with longish, untidy hair, came along. Then as I looked at him, I got a very strong feeling of *déjà vu*. He looked at me in exactly the same way that Swami sometimes did. Then he turned to Ramakrishna and asked him, quite authoritatively, "What's going on? Why are you here?"

Suddenly, the whole scene seemed familiar. The houses, the street, even the smell of the air. This place felt like my home and I knew this boy ... I knew this boy very well, but from where?

Ramakrishna explained what we were doing. The boy nodded sternly, seemingly in acceptance of this. He seemed to have an almost royal demeanour, despite his ragged clothes. Then he said something in Telegu which, by the tone, could have been 'Okay'.

So we then moved off towards our vehicle. But the young boy carried on watching us carefully, in a sort of proprietorial way, until we drove off.

As I watched him disappear into the distance, I still had the feeling that I recognised him and the place. I'd known them all before, somewhere and somehow, and I also knew that I would never forget this experience.

The next day was my birthday. There were celebrations for Krishna going on all up and down the land. For us, though, it was a normal school day. So I got up as usual and walked down the lane to the school.

Assembly was always held at 8.30 sharp, up on the flat roof. So when I arrived, the children were sitting in their usual rows and the singing and prayers began as usual. Then, right at the end, and at the nod of the head teacher, several of them got up and came and presented me with a card. Then they all sang "Happy Birthday!" It was quite touching.

I'd come to really love the children, the school and the role that I felt so lucky to be playing in it.

By then, I was the English teacher for the top two classes. So every day I would spend the first two periods with Class 6, the eldest children. Then the bell would go and it was time to move on to Class 5. However, by the time I'd gathered up all my bits and pieces at the end of the lesson and emerged from the classroom, I'd usually find that my sandals, which I'd neatly parked outside Class 6, had been moved. I'd look up to see that they'd been parked by some 'little fairy' outside the door of Class 5. Then several merry little faces would appear, bobbing out of their classroom door.

"Come on then, Ishtar madam," they'd be calling, in great anticipation. "Hurry up! It's our turn to have you now."

Then we'd usually have to play, "Where's Murugan?"

Murugan was aged about eight, although he was small for his age. He was the younger brother of Vasudeva, one of the star pupils in Class 6. I must confess, Murugan had quickly become my favourite, ever since the first day I'd taken his class. He'd been sitting in the front row, nodding off and practically snoring.

So I'd bent forward and poked him gently in the stomach. As he opened his eyes, I said,

"This isn't the sleeping class."

His face immediately relaxed into a big grin. For some reason, he found my remark extremely amusing and he never forgot it. His English was virtually non-existent. But from then on, whenever he saw me, he would just grin at me and say, "This isn't the sleeping class!"

Vasudeva and Murugan had originally been brought to Puttaparthi by their mother. For a long time the whole family had begged on the streets outside the ashram. But their mother could never get enough money to feed them all and so they gradually got thinner and thinner. Then she heard about the orphanage. So she brought them along and asked if they could be admitted. They were allowed to stay and then it turned out that Vasudeva was quite brilliant and, in fact, a model student.

Vasudeva was so hungry for knowledge and anxious to do well that he would study and study. He would tell me that he wanted to go to university and become an engineer so that he could support his mother, and get her off the streets. We were all hoping that, one day, he would be able to enter Swami's university.

Murugan, on the other hand, was not quite so interested in academic pursuits. He'd decided that he would like to be a lorry driver. So we would have long discussions about the places he was going to visit with his lorry. This was mainly so that I could convince him that he would need to speak good English if he wanted to travel the world. He'd also devised and instigated the game of "Where's Murugan?" which we had to play every day. Murugan would hide himself, somewhere in the classroom. Then I'd walk in and the children would all cry, "Where's Murugan?" and I'd have to find him before the lesson could begin.

As to the lessons, well, really I was winging it. Because I'd never taught before, I didn't know anything about curricula, syllabi and lesson plans. So every morning, I'd pray to Swami to give me some inspiration. He always came up with a good idea, and by the time I arrived in the class each morning, I would know exactly what I was going teach them. The children loved it. In fact, solely because of Swami's inspired input, I ended up with such a reputation for being a good teacher that new teachers would be sent into my class to watch how I did it.

I didn't always get it right, though. There was the time when a new boy came, one poor Ram, who was beside himself with grief. He had just lost his whole family in a terrible car accident, and he had been the only one spared.

Ram had sat in my class and just cried and cried. It wasn't just quiet crying. It was loud, uncontrollable sobs and wails. He sat by himself, in the corner, with tears pouring down his cheeks and refusing to be consoled, right the way through the first half of the double lesson.

I didn't know what to do. But then when the children were taking a toilet break, I had a flash of inspiration. I knew that Murugan also missed his mother terribly. So I thought I'd apply some of my amateur child psychology to the problem.

I found Murugan walking back down the corridor.

"Murugan," I said. "You could really help this little boy."

He drew himself up with dignity, pleased to have been entrusted with such an important role.

"You are really the best person to comfort him," I continued. "He's all alone, and you of all people must know how he's feeling. With your experience, I think you could really help him. Why don't you go in there now, and just try and have a chat with him?"

Murugan smiled and willingly agreed. Then he went back into the classroom where Ram was still wailing away.

Moments later, an even louder cry went up from the classroom. I ran to the door to find Murugan, lying on the floor and screaming and sobbing his heart out. Little Ram, finally silenced, was staring at him in horror.

So that didn't work. But I pressed on, usually learning by my mistakes, and sometimes trying out some quite unconventional techniques, especially for the conservative Indian education system.

One day, I came in blowing soap bubbles. The children, not having seen bubbles before, went mad for them. Or whenever they looked like dozing off, which was usually towards the end of the morning, I'd get them up to do the hokey-cokey. Or sometimes we'd do the train. They'd line up in height order and then form themselves into a conga line and then chuff round the room, slowly at first and then getting faster and faster ... until they all fell on top of one another. That was a great favourite.

But I did all this so that they would pay attention when I needed them to. They knew that if they behaved and did their lessons well, there would be some fun at the end. For without wanting to overestimate my own importance in these children's lives, I couldn't help but be aware of the wonderful opportunity they had at this orphanage school to be able to raise themselves up to a better standard of life.

It also occurred to me that, while for a long time English had been the international language of business, it would be even more so with the advent of the new technology and the internet. It was true that the official language of their country was Hindi, and they had lessons in Hindi everyday. But there seemed to be at least as many people in India who spoke English as spoke Hindi. Added to that, with Bangalore fast becoming the software capital of the world, I could see that opportunities would be plentiful in the future for those with the right skills.

So all these thoughts would go through my head and the lessons were designed accordingly. However, while this line of thinking would make perfect sense under normal circumstances, I wasn't under normal circumstances. And a conversation I had with Ted one day completely changed my perspective.

The subject came up when we were clearing up after my birthday *bhajans*.

It had been a wonderful party.

The children had never been to my apartment before. They had been so excited about it, they'd talked of nothing else all through lessons that day. Then, I can still remember the sound of their voices, that evening, as they came tripping and running down Chitravathi Lane, shouting,

"Ishtar madam! Ishtar madam! We're here! At last we're here!"

Shepherded by their teachers, they looked lovely as they walked in, dressed in their best dresses and yoga whites. Then they all rushed straight into my bathroom. Apparently, they'd heard that I'd got a Western-style toilet and wanted to check it out. Vasudeva in particular, with his engineering aspirations, was fascinated by the chain action and the way the water kept reappearing in the bowl. So all you could hear for the first ten minutes or so was the sound of the loo flushing.

Lots of friends then soon arrived, including Becky who brought plates of treats to have afterwards. Ted managed to remember to turn up with his guitar, and Sophia had found some bongo drums from somewhere. So for a good hour or so, the apartment rang out with *bhajans* so loudly that people came in off the street to join us.

I felt so happy that evening. As I looked at the scene around me, I realised that I could never have imagined this when Miranda and I first left Goa. It seemed as if I'd been given such a wonderful new life with such caring friends.

The children sang merrily and clapped their hands along with all the songs. They seemed to have boundless energy. However, it had soon all became a bit too much for Murugan. Exhausted by all the excitement, he had climbed into my lap, curled up and was finally allowed to be in 'the sleeping class'.

It was heartbreaking to have to wake him at the end. He had cried like a baby at being ejected from such a cosy haven. But he wouldn't have wanted to miss the cakes and sweets. The children were like models of good behaviour as they took around the plates of goodies, making sure all the guests had been served before taking any themselves. I was very proud of them.

So all too soon the party was over, and it was when everyone had gone and Ted and I were clearing up that he started telling me about Narada, one of the boys in Class 5.

Apparently, Narada had been a child beggar on the streets of Bombay before he came to the orphanage. He did once have parents. But one day, they had sent him to get some water and by the time he'd returned, they'd disappeared. He'd never found them again. So for many years, Narada had been left alone to beg on the streets of Bombay.

"Anyway, Narada had never heard of Swami before," said Ted, "or even so much as seen a picture of him. But one night, he had a dream about him. In this dream, Swami appeared before Narada and told him to come to Puttaparthi, saying that he would look after him.

"So Narada hid himself on a train and somehow got here. As soon as he arrived, he walked into the ashram and went into the

Prayer Hall. Then Swami came in and walked straight over to him and gave him *padnamaskar* and *vibhuuthi*."

"How amazing," I said, "that Swami should pull him out like that, from such a terrible life."

"Yes, but not that amazing, really," replied Ted. "It was his karma."

Karma, I'd learned, meant the results of our past actions that are accrued over many lifetimes. Apparently, it was our bad karma that kept us trapped and separated from our natural state of God realisation. However, Swami would tell us that you could work off your bad karma by selflessly helping others. This was known, he would say, as karma yoga, or the yoga of action.

"All these children are here because of their karma," Ted went on. "They were all great *yogis* and *rishis* in their past lives. They had asked for this opportunity to be born into a situation where they could be close to the Lord's physical body, but have nothing else, no material possessions, to distract them from him."

How Ted knew this I don't know. But he seemed to say it with great authority. I also knew that he'd had interviews with Swami where the subject of the orphanage had been discussed. Once, through Ted, Swami had sent his blessings to us. So it seemed to ring true.

But it also put quite a different slant on all my thinking. I mean, if this was the case, then their aim to renounce everything in dedication to God didn't really sit that well with my plans for them to end up running Microsoft! Sadly, I hadn't yet realised that I'd gone to help at this orphanage with all the sensitivity of a Bible-bashing missionary in the Congo and, as events would later prove, there would be a price to pay for my mistakes, and not just by myself.

But anyway, if all this sounds as if we were getting a bit too saccharine and misty-eyed about these children, I should perhaps mention that Narada was the worst behaved child in the school. He was ever on the verge of being expelled. So not the actions of a great rishi or yogi, one would think. How he did it, in a place where nobody owned anything, even the clothes they stood up in, I never could figure out. But he was running what was virtually a protection racket. All the children treated him like the Godfather, and, like the Mario Puzo character, he ran his empire by the giving out of treats and favours to those who pleased him—a half-chewed Biro here, a torn out page from a magazine there—and a very hard time to anyone who crossed him.

I couldn't help having certain sympathy towards him, though. Coming from his background, I guessed that perhaps the only way he knew how to survive was by gaining power over others. So it seemed to me that it would be a good long time before he was going to be able to let go, and put his trust in all that unconditional love he was receiving—and I knew just what that felt like.

CHAPTER 13
WHERE TWO WORLDS TOUCH

The next day there were tears in my eyes as I hugged Becky goodbye. Sophia would also be leaving within a few days and Ted shortly after that. So this exodus of my friends was also a signal that my own days of living in the presence of the Lord were also coming to an end. The credits were about to roll on this wonderful movie that he'd allowed me to take part in, with its colourful cast of characters and amazing plot lines, and the thought filled me with dread and uncertainty. I just couldn't imagine how I would live if I wasn't able see Swami every day.

However, I didn't know that he still had one more piece of entertainment lined up for me. And it arrived on the Reiki Masters' bench one September morning in the shape of Agawela.

Agawela was a Cherokee medicine woman and she made everyone else on the bench seem like absolute wimps. I've since learned that Agawela means 'crone' and boy, she was. She'd sit there, staring intently at Swami, her lizard-skinned face screwed up in a furious scowl and her dark eyes blazing like coal embers, shaking out her rosary beads like a rattlesnake and muttering strange-sounding incantations under her breath. There was definitely 'something of the night' about Agawela.

I gave her a bit of a wide berth at first. But every day, she seemed to edge a bit closer. Then during one *darshan* session, I realised that she was sitting next to me, and actually had been for some days. I'd been so wrapped up in Swami, I hadn't noticed. I think she was after my seat, and could probably have easily turned me into a frog or something to get it. But as it was Swami who decreed that I sit there, she didn't really stand a chance against him, and she knew it. Anyway, I wasn't budging, and so I tried to ignore her.

But as the weeks went by, I gradually grew more used to her. Then, one day, I arrived at the ashram to find a gaily-coloured banner strung across the gates announcing: WELCOME TO ONAM. Grumbling to myself that this was probably just another spurious excuse of old Mr Barnum-and-Bailey to get loads of people through his doors, I asked someone what the word 'Onam' meant.

Onam, it turned out, was a festival held every year to celebrate the great king Bali surrendering to Vishnu. Then I was told the story:

> Bali was the grandson of the great saint Prahlaad whose father had been killed by Vishnu in his Narasimha form, the man-lion. But although he took after his grandfather in many respects, Bali was considered a great king. He did, however, have one great weakness. He suffered from having a big ego.
>
> So Vishnu—not one to give up on this family, obviously!—disguised himself as a dwarf named Vamana. Then he went into the court of King Bali and, approaching his throne, begged from him some land. King Bali asked him how much land he would like, jokingly of course. Vamana replied that he would only want as much as it would take him to cover in three strides. So King Bali and his courtiers roared with laughter at the idea of having to give away such a small amount of the kingdom.
>
> But then Bali's spiritual teacher, Sukracarya, ('sook-ra-charia') stepped in. He could see that Vamana was really Vishnu in disguise. So he warned the king that Vishnu would be able to cover the whole earth and all of space, including the heavenly planets, in just two strides. This would then put Bali in the most difficult position of not being able to honour his promise to God, because there would be no land left for the last step.
>
> Bali, however, had other ideas. Perhaps he was mindful of his great-grandfather's savaging by the man-lion. He replied to Sukracarya that, in that case, if Vamana really was Vishnu, then he really couldn't refuse the request. So King Bali agreed to grant Vamana three dwarf-strides-worth of land.
>
> So Vamana took his first step and, as Sukracarya predicted, it covered the whole of the earth. Then he took his second

step, and it took him right up to the edge of the universe. So, with no more land left to give away, how would the hapless King Bali fulfil his promise of the third step? He thought to himself for just a second. Then he realised that there was nothing else for it. He got up from this throne, knelt down, placed his head under Vamana's foot, and surrendered his ego to the Lord.

Each year, the Indians mark this day as a symbol of the ego surrendering to God and the beginning of a new life. To celebrate it, they all wear new clothes. I didn't have a new *sari*, but the festival and Swami's discourses during it did feel quite apt to me. This was because, whether I wanted to or not, I would soon have to leave Swami and Puttaparthi to start my new life—and I didn't know if I would ever see him again.

But it was also during Onam that I started to get to know Agawela. Up until then, she would mostly just sit in a trance. As I was usually in a pretty similar state myself, there hadn't been much need for conversation. However, she gradually started talking to me—just little bits of comments here, and the odd word there at first, nothing too deep. So I began to relax with her.

She was very well off, it turned out. Wives of rich businessmen would pay thousands of dollars for her amazing transformational healing sessions. She would sometimes travel with them and, having recently returned from her last assignment in Dubai with, it turned out, more money that she knew what to do with, she'd had rented a huge apartment and a sporty, cream-coloured Mercedes.

The more I talked to Aggie, as I came to call her, the more I realised that she was one of the most interesting women that I had ever met. As the days went by, I grew quite fond of her. I would look forward to seeing her in *darshan*. We would chat to one another whenever Swami wasn't in the hall and she would explain to me about shamanism and the Native American way. She said that she could see things that others couldn't—whole worlds, or dimensions, that impacted upon us in this one, and that if we only knew how to work with them, our lives would be better, more enriched.

One day, she was telling me about the ritual dancer. The shamanic dancer had the power to bring down rain. She said that it was the same dancer that the Hindus talked about as Nataraja and that this dance had the power to turn so-called 'reality' on its head. It was the key and the entry point or interface, to this more arcane, more mysterious, reality.

I'd been watching Swami walking around the hall as Aggie talked quietly into my ear, but just as she said the word 'Nataraja', Swami's head slowly swivelled round in our direction. Even though he was over a hundred yards away, I knew he was looking at us.

Then that night, I had a very powerful dream. I was sitting in my usual place on the bench in the Prayer Hall and Swami came walking towards me, waving his finger, and saying, sternly,

"No talking in *darshan*!"

I told Aggie about it, and we agreed not to chat in *darshan* anymore. But I was fascinated to know more about these healing treatments for which women would pay so much money. So one day, over an okra and potato curry in the North Indian canteen, I asked Aggie,

"What is it you actually do?"

"My main speciality is clearing karma," she said, "or what we would call dysfunctional genetic patterns that build up over time."

"How do you mean?" I asked.

"The trouble is, in today's world, most people who come to Swami cannot even ask for what he is offering, because they don't know what it is they're lacking. They've never experienced what real love actually is."

I couldn't disagree.

"There is often some sort of genetic disorder that goes back generations. That's why you get problems that seem to run down the DNA in families, like alcoholism. Everyone has their own way of numbing the pain of separation from this love, and families tend to pass on these coping mechanisms. So if, for example, you're the child of an alcoholic, you're quite likely to become one yourself. The genetic codes are stacked against you."

"So you sort all that out?" I asked, doubtful because of my own experience of Swami's views on spiritual healing sessions.

"Yes," she said. "But I have Swami's permission to do it. I discussed it with him once in an interview. He calls me Doctor Love."

I didn't usually pay much attention to people who claimed to be acting on Swami's behalf. You'd get loads of charlatans like that there. But I couldn't help but notice, after that, that Swami did sometimes seem to be communicating with her when he walked past us. She would often say that Swami had just told her this, or told her that. Anyway, because he also talked to me in a telepathic way, I knew that it was a possibility.

But one day, Swami spoke to her about me. It was the last day of Onam, and it had been a terrible day for me at the orphanage school.

I'd got into the habit of setting the children the homework of learning spellings. I'd put up a list of ten words on the blackboard, and they would take them down in their notebooks and learn them. The next morning, I'd give a test and the one who got the most right would get a gold star.

Now, little Hari had been finding it difficult to concentrate for some time and his test results had shown it. The last few weeks, he'd been barely getting four or five out of ten. That day, however, as we did the test, I'd read out the list of words in reverse order, so that number one, 'chocolate', came last. But when Hari gave his work in, I noticed that 'chocolate' was at the top and that the list descended in exactly the same order as I'd given it out the previous day. Hari had just given me the list that he'd copied the day before from the blackboard. Something in me snapped.

"Hari! How could you?" I scolded. "How could you try to trick me like this!"

I raged on and on as if he'd personally done me some terrible injustice. He was hanging his head in shame as I banged on and on at him about the sin of dishonesty. Then I dragged him off to the head teacher. Max put him in seclusion for the rest of the day.

But still I wasn't satisfied. I actually felt betrayed and hurt inside. I was in a terrible mood that I can see, in retrospect, was in no way proportionate to the importance of poor Hari's 'crime'. I went to a meeting of the teachers at lunchtime, and told them what happened. I said that Hari couldn't keep up and that he should be moved down a class. They all agreed to follow my recommendation and Hari was duly demoted to Class 4.

The pain, however, remained. By the time I was due to go and see Swami that afternoon, I was almost in agony. I was feeling physically sick over the whole matter and not really understanding why. I felt as if there were flames of anger shooting out of my eyes and even Aggie looked a bit wary as she tentatively took her place next to me in the Prayer Hall.

Then Swami arrived and *darshan* continued as usual. It was looking as if our time with him that afternoon was going to pass without incident. But it was at the end that the strange thing happened.

Swami came out of the temple and started walking towards us, as usual. But then as he drew close, he looked at me with such a deep and wonderful look of love that I was stunned. Then he slid his eyes over, as if to include her, to Aggie. It was just like we were both wrapped up together in this look, like a warm and soft blanket. I couldn't help noticing, though, that his eyes seemed to be saying something to her.

After he'd gone, Aggie turned to me and said:

"Swami says I've got to give you the treatment."

"Really? Well, I knew he was saying something ... but I haven't got thousands of dollars..."

"No, it's free of charge," she replied. "This is Swami's work. He's told me to do it before you go."

So we arranged a time for the following Sunday. This would be the day before I was due to leave and just before my last *darshan* with Swami. She would come to my apartment in the morning and do the purification treatment. I had no idea about what it would entail, or what it meant. But I was excited about receiving what I considered to be Swami's parting gift to me.

Meanwhile, I could no longer avoid the fact that my last days with Swami were arriving. I couldn't really bear to think about it too much. I couldn't imagine how I would possibly cope in the outside world after living in this protected, holy atmosphere for so long. However, in order to help dilute the worst of the culture shock, I'd decided to break my journey at a sort of halfway house.

On consulting my *Rough Guide to India*, Mahabalipuram ('maha-balee-pouram') looked a likely place. It was on the eastern coast, and well out of the way of the monsoon, so I could spend a couple of weeks getting some rays on my sun-starved body. There were also plenty of ancient temples and spiritual sites there to visit. On top of that, I'd also heard that Swami had once gone there. His biographer, Mr Kasturi, said that when Swami walked along the beach, the sea had expressed its devotion by sweeping up to him and depositing on his feet a beautiful pearl necklace.

During the next week, I tried to take my mind off the inevitable upcoming wrench by concentrating on simple, menial tasks. I packed up all the books that I'd managed to accrue and posted them to my parents' home in England. I then sorted out my apartment and found new homes for my Kashmir throw, ornaments, pictures, kitchen utensils, bedding, and even my bed. Then I went shopping for leaving gifts for the children.

For the past two weeks, I'd been teaching the top two classes to tell the time. So it seemed like an inspired idea when I thought of getting them watches. I went to a local merchant and ordered twenty-four watches with matching straps. They were only about thirty rupees each. Then, for the other younger children, I bought sweets and some cards with pictures of Swami on them.

The last thing I did was to thoroughly clean my apartment. So by the time Aggie arrived to give me my purification treatment on Sunday morning, the day before I was due to leave, it was immaculate.

I'd had no idea what to expect from Aggie's healing session. I was quite intrigued, though, to see that she was unpacking some strange-looking, bluish-white eggs from her basket. They were quite large, much larger than any birds' eggs that I'd ever seen. She put the eggs in a large bowl and then placed them in the centre of the room. Then she told me to wait in the bedroom while she made the correct preparations.

So I went to sit on my bed and all I could hear, for some time, was the sound of chanting in a language that I didn't recognise.

Then, after about half-an-hour, she called me back into the room. I was amazed to find a large circle of burning candles. A beautiful musky aroma, too, was starting to fill the air. Aggie said it was frankincense. Then she told me to stand in the middle of the candles, while she proceeded to walk around me, still chanting, but this time they were more familiar Vedic chants, such as:

"Om Namah Shivayah. Om Namah Shivayah. Om Namah Shivayah," and

"Om Namo Narayana. Om Namo Narayana. Om Namo Narayana."

After a while, she started stroking my body with a huge feather. Then it was as if she was stripping pieces of some sort of material off me, just like you'd tear down old wallpaper. She would pull it down to the ground, and then throw it away, all the while chanting. Then she produced a bottle of a liquid that smelled like ether, and proceeded to rub all the exposed parts of my body with it, chanting the Gayathri Mantra as she worked.

There were other things too, involving her asking me questions, and me answering. But as to the detail, I'm sworn to secrecy. Suffice to say, all this went on for several hours and for much of it, I was oblivious, as I could see Swami standing under my wall clock, and that's all I was interested in. Eventually, though, the vision of him faded. I looked up to see that the hands of the clock had reached one o'clock and that's when I started to get quite edgy.

"We'll have to be leaving for the Prayer Hall soon," I said. "It's my last time to see Swami. I can't be late."

"Yes, yes," she replied, gently. "Don't worry. We'll get there."

But still the treatment continued. Then even when she had finally finished, we still couldn't leave. I had to stay in the bedroom again for a further half-an-hour while she performed the closing ceremony and ritually cleared the room.

Then finally, she was finished. But as she came into the bedroom, I could see that her face had changed. She now had the look of a very sensible, wise old grandmother. She then proceeded to give me a very long lecture. What she told me, in a nutshell, was that I shouldn't have relationships with men anymore. She said that she'd purified me now, that she'd had to get a lot of filth out of me and that from now on, no-one was to touch me. She said it with great authority, as if it wasn't necessarily her idea but that she'd been told to say it.

"Oh, don't worry," I reassured her. "I've finished with all that, anyway. I belong to Swami now."

So all this took ages and by the time we finally left for the Prayer Hall, we were late. I wanted to run. But Aggie just sauntered up the lane, swaying her ample hips and grinning and twinkling at all the young stall keeper boys who, I suddenly noticed, seemed to be reciprocating in kind. When I looked more closely at her, I could see why. She was still Aggie, but she seemed to have shape shifted again. She was no longer the older sensible grandmother. Now she was a much younger, more flirtatious woman and there was, mysteriously, something quite seductive about her. So it seemed that the new rule of celibacy that I'd been placed under did not apply to her. She was just the deliverer of the message and strangely, I didn't find it at all paradoxical.

All too slowly, though, we were progressing towards the ashram and Swami, who by now must have been in the Prayer Hall for at least an hour. Then, when we were finally about to enter through its gates, wouldn't you know it but one of Aggie's clients came along. So we had to stop and talk to her. I was hopping from one foot to the other, wanting to just run ahead but knowing, in all politeness, that I couldn't. Anyway, Aggie told me that there was still one more thing we had to do to complete the treatment.

Finally, Aggie and her client ran out of gossip, and we were on our way again. We walked through the gates and up the hill to the statue of the elephant god, Ganesh. Aggie gave me a coconut. She told me to throw it on the ground at its base, as hard as I could. I did this, and it broke into three pieces. This, apparently, was of some great significance. But I was unable to wait for the explanation. By now, I really had had enough and was so desperate to get to Swami that I just thanked her quickly, and then I just picked up my skirts and ran at full pelt towards the Prayer Hall.

I was still sensible enough to realise, though, that I shouldn't just run in through the main entrance in case Swami was out in the hall. If he saw me, I might be in trouble again. I could just imagine the dream, with him coming towards me, waving his finger sternly and this time saying,

"No being late for *darshan*!"

So I figured that I'd sneak in through the back entrance behind the temple. But I was just tiptoeing round the corner when suddenly, he was right in front of me.

Swami was less than two yards away and facing me and looking intently at a point just above my head. All that was separating us were two rows of his teachers from his girls' college, who were sitting cross-legged on the floor and singing him a song. They were just getting to the final line when Swami interrupted them and, in a sort of hurried, off-hand way, finished off the song himself. Then he turned on his heel, as if he had much more pressing business, and strode back into the temple.

Aggie had caught up to me by now, and we went over to the bench. All the ladies kindly squashed up to make room for us. But then one of the older usher ladies came over to me.

"I've been told that it's your last day, dear," she said. "So come with me. Today, you'll have special *darshan*."

She took me to sit in what must have been one of the most prized spots on the floor, right next to Swami's path as he left the temple. I would be only inches away from him.

My eyes filled with tears and my body shook with the emotion of it all. I could hardly wait for the final *bhajans* to be sung, for the session to be over and for Swami to come out of the temple and make his way towards me.

It seemed to take ages, but eventually the time arrived. Matters were finally coming to a close. The last *bhajan* was being sung, and Swami, at last, was making his way towards me. He was walking very quickly, though. He looked distracted and thoughtful, as if he had to rush off to sort out some very important problem that had just cropped up. As he rushed past me, his feet seemed miles away. Then he swayed his body even further from me, as if to avoid me. He didn't look at me, or at anyone, and within seconds, he was gone.

So this was how I last saw Swami.

My heart suddenly felt as heavy as lead, and an empty feeling of dread was already starting to build up in my stomach. And I hadn't even yet left Puttaparthi.

* * *

I felt no better the next morning when I awoke in floods of tears.

I cried all through breakfast in the North Indian canteen where various friends had gathered for my 'farewell meal'. They did their best to comfort me, but their well-meaning words just seemed to fall to the ground.

However, I finally managed to get my tears under some control when I realised that I still had to go to the orphanage to give out the presents. So I tried to pull myself together, kissed everyone goodbye and then set off down Samadhi Lane for my last visit to the children.

On arrival, I went first into the top class and gave out the watches. Jaya, Vijaya, Sukadeva, Naryana, Vasudeva, Prabhu and the two girls were absolutely stunned by the watches, and not in a good way. They received them in absolute silence, remaining seated cross-legged on the floor. They couldn't even look up at me. Sita and Radha had tears in their eyes. I could see that they didn't want my watches. They wanted me. I didn't know what to say or do. So I hurriedly rushed off to see the younger ones.

The smaller children were delighted with the sweets and the cards, and danced around me with big goodbye smiles on their faces. So that was a relief. Then all the teachers, as well as the children from top class, came out to give me a good send-off.

However, it very quickly became clear to me that I was in deep trouble with a certain person. I'd become aware that two deep holes were being burnt into my back. I turned round to find Narada standing in the doorway and glowering at me intently. I turned back to get into my waiting taxi. But then he stepped forward and threw himself on the ground at my feet, sobbing uncontrollably, and the only word I could make out was "watch".

I bent down to try to lift him. But I couldn't budge him.

"Narada," I tried to gently explain to him, "it wasn't that I didn't think you deserved a watch. I love you just as much as the others." I ruffled his hair. "I only bought watches for the top class, you see, because they've been learning with me how to tell the time, and you're not in that class."

But he wouldn't move. He just continued to lie there, howling. Just then, Max came over and put his hand on my arm.

"It isn't that he wants *a* watch," he said quietly, with a grimace. "He wants all of them."

And then I saw it. I'd unwittingly flooded Narada's economy and ruined his empire.

I could still hear him wailing as my taxi pulled out of Samadhi Lane and headed towards the long and winding road that led to Mahabalipuram.

CHAPTER 14
WHERE TWO WORLDS COLLIDE

I was almost envious of Narada. At least he could express his desolation. Mine was tightly buttoned up in a place somewhere around my heart, and I thought it would burst with the strain.

I was in agony, sitting bolt upright on the back seat and not daring to look to either side out of the windows. So we drove past the ashram and then up the hill, while I steadfastly refused to look at Swami's white university buildings and campus as it swept past, his new state-of-the art, speciality hospital and his planetarium, not to mention Sai Geeta's quarters and the Gokulum dairy at the end of the village.

Then, as the village main street gradually gave way to narrow, meandering country lanes lined with fields and forests, I just lay down and pulled my *sari* shawl over my head, and wept.

I remained in this distressed state for a good few hours. So it wasn't until we pulled over to a roadside restaurant at about midday that I got the joke. A few weeks before, I'd bought a guidebook about my destination, Mahabalipuram. But until then, I'd not had the chance to look at it. Now, thinking that it might make a good distraction from the pain, I pulled it out of my shoulder bag and started to read it—and it was there in the first paragraph. *Maha,* it turned out, meant great. Bali was the king whose surrender to Vishnu we had just been celebrating as symbolic of the beginning of a new life. And *puram* meant city. To start my new life, I was going to the city of the great Bali.

Initially, I'd been a bit worried about the journey. I'd heard terrible tales about female devotees being robbed, and worse, by taxi drivers. But this taxi company had been recommended as safe and reliable and, as soon as my driver arrived that morning, I immediately felt relaxed in his soft presence.

Solomon was from Goa and he seemed a big, kindly gentle giant of a man as he packed all my luggage into the boot. When he'd finished, there was no room for my altar picture of Swami, now standing forlornly on the pavement and looking quite battered from having had so many household items thrown at it.

"I know," he said. "Let's have Swami upfront," and I swear Swami's face visibly brightened as Solomon proceeded to stand his picture up on the passenger seat.

So Swami sat in the front and I sat in the back. As we went along on our journey, just about every time we stopped—whether for petrol, lunch or the loo—the car would be very quickly surrounded by curious villagers who would reach through the passenger seat window to touch Swami's feet. We had a number of these stops and we needed them, as it was a day's long drive to the Bay of Bengal. And as we travelled along narrow roads winding through rice paddy fields and villages set in great forests of coconut palms, there was plenty of time to read more about Mahabalipuram and all the history, myths and legends associated with it.

Apparently, Bali had been succeeded as king by his son, Banasura. There is a story about him going to war against Krishna. Needless to say, he loses. After that, there's a bit of a gap until a king called Malecheren comes to the throne in Mahabalipuram, or so the story goes. Malecheren was responsible for the near destruction of Mahabalipuram by the gods, and this is how it came about.

> King Malecheren became friendly with a *deva*, or a being from the heavenly realms. One day, this *deva* offered to carry Malacheren, in disguise, to the divine court of Indra, the god of heaven. Malacheren was delighted to accept, and so off they both went.
>
> On seeing heaven, boy was Malecheren impressed. He couldn't get over the splendour and opulence of such a magnificent place. So when he returned to Mahabalipuram, he decided to create the same effect there, and eventually the beauty and magnificence of Mahabalipuram became renown and celebrated all over the world.

However, the fame of the city's opulence spread so far that the demigods in heaven got to hear about it, and they were not happy. They felt offended that the beauty of a mere earthly place could rival their own celestial mansions. So they went to complain to Indra, the king of heaven, to tell him that such impudence should be destroyed.

Indra, feeling equally miffed, sent orders to Varuna, the god of the sea. Indra told Varuna to loose his deep blue billows and overflow the city with a tsunami, which Varuna duly did.

And so that is how the old city of Mahabalipuram disappeared under the sea forever ... although not quite. At certain low tides, when the moon is in an unusual orbit, the golden tips of the temple pagodas can still be seen, rearing their heads up above the surf.

It was dusk when we finally arrived at the modern version of this town on the Bay of Bengal, and I was almost swept off my feet by the enchanting evening aroma of frangipani and jasmine. It seemed as if I'd been brought to a veritable paradise.

We pulled into the courtyard of the beachfront hotel and, as I got out of the car, there was a faint rustling and whispering of the leaves of the bushes as if the nature *devas* were chatting among themselves about my arrival. On the beach, tall coconut palms were looming pitch black against the deep orange sunset and silently waving their branches in greeting in the warm, tropical breeze that was caressing my cheek.

All I could hear that night, as I fell asleep, was the sound of the sea god crashing his great waves up on to the sandy shore. So it wasn't until the next day, when I was awoken by the sort of dawn chorus you get in a rainforest, that I was able to go out and see what he'd left of Mahabalipuram.

As I walked around the town, it was clear that this was no ordinary place. There were enormous statues of mythological characters, like Krishna and Arjuna, and ancient temples that had been carved out of the rock face by the Pallava kings more than a thousand years ago.

The town's set piece was a series of temples called the Five Chariots. Each one is cut from one large piece of stone, the largest being about 40 ft high. Some of the tops of these temples were in the Dravidian style of four-sided cupolas. Others were rectangular with pointed arches. One of them, in particular, was very well preserved, having been buried under sand until the British unearthed it in the 19th century.

But the two most famous temples were equidistant from my hotel by about a half-an-hour's walk along the silvery-white, sandy beach. They were the 7th century Tiger Temple, dedicated to the goddess Durga, and the Shore Temple, one of the oldest temples in India. And I was destined to spend the next two weeks trudging through the surf between these two temples with my heart aching, tears rolling down my cheeks and the refrain from "Nothing Compares To You" running in a loop through my head.

By now, withdrawal symptoms had well and truly set in. So it was of no interest to me that I was in one of the most beautiful places on earth and surrounded by priceless pieces of historic art. As the waves crashed around my feet, I would often be passed by beautiful iridescent sunbirds whose colours flashed like rainbows. Squawking parakeets and glistening turquoise-blue kingfishers with long red beaks would appear on the water's edge. Brahmin brown speckled kites would often drift lazily overhead, looking for carrion. Black and white storks would soar above me and an extraordinary great pied hornbill would sometimes sweep past at such a slow, stately pace, I'd fear it was going to stall.

But none of this did anything to heal the gaping gash that seemed to be opening up in my heart. I'd once heard the term 'terrible beauty'. Now I understood what it meant. It was like a wild and gaudy carnival and it was mocking me. It knew that wherever I looked, the true pure beauty that I needed to salve the pain in my heart would elude me. No matter the seeming magnificence of this place, it was flat, stale and meaningless compared to the deep, rich, vibrant, multi-faceted inner world from which I'd just been so abruptly catapulted.

At the Shore Temple, I would fling myself across the black, polished granite feet of an enormous reclining statue of Vishnu and sob,

"Please reveal yourself to me, Lord. Where are you? Please help me. I can't find you. But I can't live without you. Will I ever see you again?"

But his heart seemed to be as hard as the stone from which his statue was made, and I would eventually leave with a heavy step.

One day, as I was lying in this way, and praying, some Indian tourists came in. They were quite a noisy crowd and, probably oblivious to me, they picked up their little boy and placed him on Vishnu's belly. Then the youngster started horsing around while they snapped away at him with their cameras.

I immediately stood up and, I'm ashamed to say, I yelled at them:

"No wonder this country is in such a mess! How can you expect to find inner fulfilment when you don't even respect your own gods?"

They just stared at me in bewildered horror. But, to me, this was the great tragic irony. I'd approach these temples, covering my head with the shawl of my *sari*, in the hope of finding spiritual refuge, only to find Indians dressed in polyester slacks and shirts regarding the statues of characters from their scriptures like any London tourist at Madame Tussaud's waxworks. They would stand there chatting away about the material nature of these statues and buildings. They'd loudly discuss their relative architectural merits, which admittedly, were impressive. Then noting their scale and proportion, they would speculate among themselves about how they had been carved out of the rocks.

Yet, to me, the scriptures that these characters sprang from were not just academic, anachronistic tomes to be got out and dusted off on a Sunday. For the past six months, I'd been intimately connected with them, living and breathing their stories, and learning from them, every single day. They were as close to me as my own breath. Consequently, my heart, which had only so recently been as granite-like and seemingly inert as some of these statues, had sprung into life. So it added to my existing pain to see Krishna and the others being treated as mere architectural curiosities.

However, there were some little delights among this surreal wasteland. While I was away during the day, pounding the beach, the cleaners would come into my room and decorate my altar and picture of Swami. So when I came back, he would be sitting there grinning jauntily at me under an absolute profusion of gaily-coloured, and beautifully aromatic, flowers.

One day, I stayed back to talk to these cleaners. One of them, a very gentle woman, turned out be Swami's devotee, even though she'd never seen him in the flesh. She told me that she couldn't afford the bus fare to Puttaparthi or, when I offered it, the time off work to go. So she was fascinated to hear all about how it was there, and what Swami was like, and I came to admire her greatly. I used to think that it was nice for Swami, too. For while I'd often be swearing, and quite sarcastic to him, throughout the long, hot, dark nights of my soul, she would always come the next morning and redecorate him with fresh flowers and, no doubt, be absolutely lovely to him.

Down the road from the hotel, there was a statue of the mythical Vedic boar, Varaha, another incarnation of Vishnu. Varaha was tossing the planet Earth from one of its tusks to the other. I felt that I'd also been tossed from one world to another. I'd been ejected from the multidimensional world of ancient India, with its holistic understanding of life springing from the Vedas, to a more modern, Westernised, one-dimensional India that was hanging its head in shame over its so-called primitive, archaic mythological roots.

It wasn't that I resented the Indians' desire for progress into the modern world. Far from it—it would have been an extremely patronising attitude from someone whose only experience of hunger was when she was forced to go on a slimming diet. But that this progress had to be at the cost of their inner, deeper identity was in my opinion, tragic. To have your guts ripped out for the sake of a new washing machine just didn't seem a very good deal to me.

The fact that I was, by nationality, complicit in the spiritual downfall of this once great civilisation was also, at that point, sticking in my heart like a knife. Okay, I realised that the British tea traders' mistranslation of the Vedas was not solely responsible for India losing her cultural heritage. But it seemed to me that they pretty well put the icing on a layer cake that had been building for more than a millennia. So my pain was also compounded by guilt and it still hadn't eased when, two weeks later, I arrived back in the hub of Western civilisation.

At Frankfurt airport, where I had to change planes, phalanxes of smartly suited young men with briefcases and mobile phones almost knocked me over as they rushed towards their early morning flights. I stood there stunned, wondering what on earth could be so important to create such urgency. One or two of them did glance back quizzically, or do a double take, when they saw me. I think the stillness around me must have been palpable. I probably looked completely out of the place and time.

Thankfully, when I got to London Heathrow, Miranda was there to rescue me and she fell on me, in tears. She'd been missing me, and Swami, so much that she wanted to hear everything that had happened in the last few months. We went for a coffee, and I poured out everything. Then we took the train to my parents on the Kent coast.

Mum and Dad gave us a great welcome and it felt good to be home. But still the pain wouldn't go away. And it was the next day, when I came into the living room to hear Sinead O'Connor singing on the radio "Nothing Compares To You" that I heard the rest of the words for the first time. I realised then that it wasn't a song of love, but a song of grief, and I was suddenly pole-axed with it.

As the days wore on after that, I was just like anyone with a broken heart, constantly surprised that life could continue as normal around such black and final devastation. But continue inexorably on it did.

I tried to do something about finding a job. But it was difficult. Having dismissed journalism, I had no idea about what sort of career I should take up. So I decided just to do a bit of secretarial work for the time being. A well-meaning agency, trying to find a way to help me benefit from my journalistic skills, placed me in the busy press office of a large multinational company in a modern, glass-fronted office building at Canary Wharf in London.

As it turned out, though, the people in this press office were variously scared stiff of, or couldn't stand the sight of, journalists. So they lost no time in finding me plenty of menial tasks to do and seemed to enjoy using the most perfunctory tone to order me around like a dogsbody. It was pretty awful. But on a deeper level, it didn't matter much to me. Whether I was walking along the beach in the warm paradise of Mahabalipuram or being abused in the cold, mechanical business world of the West, it was all the same, compared to where I really wanted to be.

I was eventually rescued from the press office, and I ended up in a quieter secretarial role where I performed the same small menial tasks every day. But still I wasn't concerned that I was wasting my skills and my talent. At least, I reasoned to myself, if it was boring and easy, I could concentrate on my prayers—or my inner screams would perhaps be a more accurate way of putting it.

One day, an old boyfriend turned up on my doorstep. We'd been out together a few times in a casual way just before I'd gone to India. Now he wanted to reignite the relationship, such as it was. I was extremely doubtful. But he managed to talk me into at least going on a date. So we went out for dinner a couple of times. In the end, though, it was hopeless. I couldn't even let him so much as kiss me. Whenever he went to put an arm around me, or draw me closer to him, I would stiffen and draw back.

We both soon realised that it wasn't going to work.

"But I don't understand," he said. "Did you meet someone else in India?"

"Well, in a way," I said, trying to hedge. But not finding a way out, I was finally forced to admit, "It's true. I *am* in love with someone else. I'm in love with Sai Baba."

"What? Him?" he scoffed, scornfully pointing to the picture on my mantelpiece of Swami who, I suddenly noticed, was looking vastly amused at the whole scene.

"Look, I know it sounds mad," I tried to explain, "but I do love him. And it's in such a way that I don't seem to have any love left over for anyone else. Well, not in the romantic sort of way, anyway."

He was struck speechless. He just looked at me. I could tell what he was thinking:

"But that's never going to work, is it? He's never going to want her! She's going to be a celibate, dried-up nun for the rest of her life!"

"I know," I said. "I know."

So that was the end of that.

However, as the weeks turned into months, I started to get an inkling that perhaps Swami did want me after all. Sometimes, the terrified clamour in my head would quieten down just long enough for a smaller, stiller voice to make itself heard. It was the same voice that I used to hear when he would speak to me in the Prayer Hall. He would often come in my dreams too, and gently soothe me. And there was even one time, when I was meditating, that he materialised himself into my room.

It was first thing in the morning and, as usual, I went to the bathroom to wash my face and brush my teeth. Then I sat cross-legged on the sofa to do my normal daily meditation. Everything about the preamble to the event was unremarkable. I had the same struggle to control my mind that I had every morning and was experiencing the usual wildly varying degrees of success with it. I tried to concentrate on reciting my mantra, to little avail. Then suddenly, something else took over. Now my mantra was being repeated back to me—it was concentrating on me rather than me on it. It went faster and faster until I found myself being shot out of my body.

I whirled through what looked like a number of planetary systems at what must have been the speed of light, or even faster, like a human canon ball. Then, just as I seemed to have reached my destination, the scene changed and I was back in my room again—except that it didn't look the same.

Now, stretched alongside the wall that divided the living room from the kitchen, was a single bed. This bed definitely had not been there before. Then I noticed, just poking out of the sheets at the top, a black, tousled head. On top of that, the room was a lot dimmer than it had been before, as if we'd gone back a couple of hours to just before dawn. So, at first, I couldn't make out the facial features of this sleeping person until he began to wake, yawn and stretch his arms over his head. Then he slowly began to get himself out of the bed. It was then that I saw that he was wearing a flowing saffron robe.

"Swami?" I said tentatively. "Swami? Is that you?"

As he approached closer, I could see that it was him, although he looked much younger than usual. He was totally beautiful and almost iridescent. As he walked towards me, the air gently vibrated and rang like bells with the harmony of the spheres as they danced in bliss along with him.

"Yes, it is me," he said in a voice that dripped burnished honey. Then, as if to apologise for his sleeping state, "I wasn't expecting a communication."

That's when the fire of anger ignited in my chest. What did he mean he hadn't been expecting a communication? I'd done nothing but cry out to him for months! I'd been in agony! Did he not hear me? Where'd he been—off on the golf course?

A whole stream of furious invective immediately started to queue up and was just about to erupt through my mouth like red hot lava when he just put his finger to his lips, and said:

"Not another word, please," in the calm sweet tones of a person whose smallest request had never been refused. I instantly closed my mouth.

Then he knelt down next to me and positioned himself so that he could place his ear against the right side of my chest. He seemed like a doctor listening for something. All my anger had vanished by now, and I just lay back, in bliss, and ran my fingers through the soft black curls of his hair. This wonderful state of affairs continued for several minutes before he disappeared again.

Another time, I woke to find him perched on the end of my bed, grinning.

"Here I am then, my dear," he said, laughing and looking delighted with his surprise.

He wasn't exactly out of breath. But it was as if he'd rushed there and had only just managed to fit me into a hectic schedule.

I immediately sat bolt upright.

"Oh Swami," I cried. "I love you so much. Please stay! Please stay! Don't ever go again!"

But he didn't say anything. He just looked doubtful and apologetic. So then I said,

"Well, at least let me serve you then!"

He looked more interested in this idea and stared down at my bedspread, thoughtfully, for a few seconds, before vanishing again.

That night, I dreamt that I was sitting with other devotees and we'd formed an S shape, like a river, with Swami sitting at its head. Then his loving gaze fell on me and I knew that he wanted to talk to me. So I got up and he came towards me, and then kissed me on the cheek and said:

"Some devotees are wanting to perform a Vedic ritual dedicated to me. They need some help with setting it up correctly, with all the right paraphernalia. Will you do this for me?"

"Of course," I replied. Then I woke up.

Now back in everyday consciousness, I knew that I had no idea about the correct paraphernalia or protocol, which was no doubt laid down somewhere in the voluminous Vedas. But I was fully confident that my astral, or subtle self, would know what to do. So the next night, I dreamt that I performed the task for him. And the last thing I remember is fixing the regulation leaves of the basil to the door, and flying out of it. Then I surfaced into waking consciousness with the satisfying feeling of a job well done.

There were many other dreams, too. Some were pure teaching dreams, where I would sit with other devotees in a classroom while Swami gave us spiritual instruction. There were other really surreal dreams that probably would have confused even Salvador Dali. But Swami would also be there, in the middle of them. In one dream, my head was pressed against the soft orange gown over his chest and vibrating as it was being permeated with the Sanskrit *mantras* that he was chanting. I later learned that that was how gurus used to pass on *mantras* to their disciples.

There were countless other dreams too, so many that they would fill a whole book on their own. In fact, it was getting to the point where my nights were much more fascinating than my days, and I would rather go to bed early than go out.

Tired of being turned down, my friends soon gave up asking me out in the evening, perhaps wondering about the sad life that I now appeared to be living. One of my friends even tried to get me interested in buying a car and learning to drive.

"It'll change your life!" she said, brightly.

"I don't want my life changed," I quickly retorted.

Some would express surprise that I could be content in a job where all I did was type, file and organise meetings for other people. They meant well, of course. But they didn't know about my rich, inner life. And, I used to reason to myself, if I had a so-called exciting or challenging job, I wouldn't be able to sit all day gazing out of the window and thinking about Swami.

So, eventually, I found myself more or less alone and friendless, apart from the orphanage children who would send me wonderful, although heartrending, letters from time to time.

"Please come back, madam," they would plead. "We are praying to Swami daily for your return."

However, I did try to keep up some sort of façade of normality in my waking life and particularly at work.

It was almost a year now since I'd joined the company and I'd yet to take any holiday. There was nowhere I wanted to go, except one place. But the two-day journey to Puttaparthi, and two days back, made it difficult, what with jet lag and so on, when the company had a policy of only two weeks to be taken at any one time. One day, though, I approached my boss.

"I've got loads of holiday to use up," I said, "and I'd like to go to India. But it's difficult because I really need a few weeks, and preferably a month, for the journey to be worthwhile."

"That's okay," he said, to my utter surprise. "Take a month if you like. You deserve it."

Before he had the chance to change his mind, I jumped into the lift, ran out through the swing doors and across the road to the nearest travel agent. By the end of the day, I had a return air ticket to Chennai in my hand for the following Monday.

As you can imagine, that weekend before was spent in a flurry of washing, ironing and packing. So the day of departure soon arrived.

But that morning, my meditation was disrupted by anxiety about the upcoming journey and the risky prospect of being a woman travelling alone to Puttaparthi, a good ten hours by road from Chennai.

So, I started to talk to Swami.

"Lord, please help me," I said. "As you know, I'm coming today. But I'm worried that something may happen to me on the journey. I don't know those taxi drivers at Chennai airport—they're not from Puttaparthi, and I could end up in deep waters."

His reply came instantly.

"Don't worry," he said. "I will organise your car. Just look out for the photograph of me."

Many of the taxi drivers in Puttaparthi carry a photo of Swami on their rear-view mirrors. So I assumed that was what he meant and from then on, approached the journey with confidence. My sister saw me off at London Heathrow, and I was soon comfortably ensconced on the plane next to an older Indian couple that promptly fell fast asleep.

It was a night flight. But I was much too excited to sleep. So I amused myself by watching the film. It was a romantic story about a man who so loved a woman that he drove his truck all night, across Australia, to get to her. The song soundtrack went something like this: "I drove all ni-y-ight, to get to you."

I knew how he felt. I would be arriving in Chennai in the early hours of the morning. So I decided that I would press straight on without stopping to rest and hopefully get to Puttaparthi by that evening.

Now that the prospect was so close, I was desperate to get to Swami. The pain inside, which had temporarily subsided during his manifestation in my flat, had never really gone away, and it was now back with a vengeance. So I intended to throw myself on his mercy and beg him to never let me go again.

By four o'clock that morning, we were finally in the holding stack that was circling Chennai airport and the Indian couple next to me started to stir.

"Are we here?" asked the husband.

"Yes," I replied. Then, as he stretched himself, "You slept well."

"No wonder," he said, yawning and scratching his head. "We were exhausted. We'd just changed planes at Heathrow. We've come from Los Angeles."

"Really?" I said, mildly curious about why such an elderly couple were making such a long journey.

"Yes," he replied. "We live in Los Angeles half the year. The other half we spend at our house in Chennai. Where are you going?"

"Andhra Pradesh state," I replied.

"Oh—whereabouts?" he enquired politely.

"Puttaparthi," I replied, "to see Sai Baba."

The man chuckled. Then I noticed he had a small case on his lap. He opened it up, and inside the lid was a big grinning picture of Swami.

"We're devotees too," he smiled, and offered his hand. "My name is Rajaswamy. Please let us offer you our hospitality in Chennai. We could give you breakfast and then you could get some sleep."

I still hadn't made the connection with my conversation with Swami, and so I replied

"No, no thank you Mr Rajaswamy. It's very kind of you. But I can't stop. I must press on. I want to reach Puttaparthi by tonight."

"How are you getting there?" he asked.

"I'll just get a taxi," I said.

"Good Lord! Absolutely not!" he practically shouted, and his wife woke up. "Some of those taxi drivers are utter knaves!

They'll rip you off at the very least! You may not even get there alive! No, I won't hear of it! Leave it to me. I will sort it out."

So a few hours later, I found myself in the dining room of Mr and Mrs Rajaswamy's enormous house in one of the better parts of Chennai, with their toddler grandson on my lap. Mrs Rajaswamy was serving me a typical Indian breakfast of *idlis* (rice pancakes) and curried vegetables. Mr Rajaswamy was on the phone to one of his friends whose student son, Sanjay, subsidised his income by driving his own taxi.

An hour later, the young man arrived and, in true Indian style, I was kept out of the negotiations while the men, in another room, thrashed out a fair price.

Mrs Rajaswamy insisted that I go upstairs, have a shower and a lie down. So I had a little light sleep as the bargaining continued below. It was almost lunchtime before she put her head around the bedroom door to tell me that the deal had finally been struck. I came downstairs and Mrs Rajaswamy pressed a packed lunch into my hands. Then Sanjay picked up my bags to escort me to his waiting taxi.

The Rajaswamys followed us out of the door, to wave me off. As we walked down the path, I told them about the telepathic conversation with Swami back in England, and that he'd told me to look out for the photo of him.

"Well, we feel extremely honoured to be of service to him, and to one of his devotees," said Mr Rajaswamy. They both looked delighted. "To us, serving you is the same as serving Swami. But why did you not tell us before?"

"I don't know," I replied, shaking them both warmly by hand before getting into the taxi. "It was only just now, when I woke up, that I realised that this was what he meant. Also, in a way, I could hardly believe it! It's been so perfect!"

They stood there, humbly, with their palms folded. Then we all waved to one another as the taxi drove off down the road to start the long journey to Puttaparthi.

CHAPTER 15
MOHINI STARTS HER DANCE

I immediately adopted what was fast becoming my usual position when being driven in India, and lay myself face down on the back seat with the shawl of my *sari* over my head. I didn't want to see what was going on outside. I couldn't bear to be aware of the danger. The criss-crossing honking cars, the gaily-painted trucks, whole families forming pyramid display teams on motorbikes and overflowing motorised rickshaws—not to mention stringy cows walking out in front of us. But I couldn't avoid the sound of the constantly blaring horns and klaxons, the street *wallahs* leaning through the windows with their wares and the overwhelmingly warm and familiar aroma of incense, curry and dung.

Sanjay, however, appeared to be quite confident about negotiating his way through the central Chennai chaos. So by the time we'd left the city, I felt relaxed enough to doze off, albeit with the continual strains of "I drove all ni- y -ght, to get to you," going around in a loop in my head.

I woke up when Sanjay pulled into the gravelled yard of a roadside restaurant for lunch. It turned out to be the same restaurant at which Solomon and I had eaten on our way to Mahabalipuram, the previous year.

"Hello," said our waiter. "How are you? It's good to see you back!"

I was surprised that he remembered me.

After lunch, I resumed my dozing in the back seat and all was well for a while. But several hours later, I was awoken by Sanjay swerving. I spun around to look out of the back window to see that he'd just narrowly missed a young man standing on the side of the road.

We were now going through 'Sai Baba country'. This was still a couple of hours' drive away from Puttaparthi. But I knew that Swami provided these outlying villages with clean water and regular food runs. I leant forward and looked at the speedometer. Young blood Sanjay was doing about 70–80 mph down these narrow country lanes.

"Sanjay," I said, tapping him on the shoulder. "Please go slower. You're going far too fast."

As I said this, we were just entering a tiny village—well, more a sprawling of palm-leaf thatched huts really, which hugged the side of the road. Through the windscreen, I could see, in the middle of the road, an old, raggedy dog slowly coming into view. He looked to be just rousing himself from his afternoon torpor.

"Sanjay!" I yelled, as the dog, suddenly realising that his life was flashing in front of him, shot up and leapt, just in time, to the side of the road. I swear his hair was standing on end as we swept past.

"I'm just trying to get you there in time for the afternoon *darshan*," Sanjay shouted back at me, a little reproachfully.

"Never mind that," I shouted back. "Please go more slowly. I can just imagine what sort of reception we'll get from Swami if we terrorise any more of his villagers or dogs."

"What do you mean 'his villagers or dogs'?" asked Sanjay. "Are you telling me that your guru owns all the land around here?"

"No, Swami doesn't own this land," I replied. "But he takes his responsibilities towards these villagers very seriously. He's spent millions of dollars on providing them with pure drinking water. He's sunk boreholes and wells, built reservoirs and laid hundreds of miles of piping around here."

"Really? I'm impressed," said Sanjay. He was at least impressed enough to slow down a little.

"That's nothing," I continued. "You should see his university students. They give up their free time during the holidays to take food parcels and clothing out to these villages. It's a really heart warming sight to see, when they set off from the ashram. There are hundreds of boys dressed all in white, with white baseball caps, standing among the sacks of food on the backs of the trucks. Sometimes, just as the convoy is about leave, Swami comes out to wave them off and then the boys just erupt with cheers. There is no false reverence or shyness. Just pure exuberance of young men jumping up and down, waving and yelling and exploding with love for him."

By now, Sanjay had slowed right down. Thus it was quite dark when we eventually rolled into Puttaparthi.

My heart was in my mouth as we drove down the long hill towards Prasanthi Nilayam. I could hardly believe that I was finally there. I had tears in my eyes as all the familiar sights swept past—the university, the dairy, the hospital ... and finally, the ashram.

I checked into the hotel opposite the ashram. I took my luggage to my room, but didn't wait to unpack. Instead, I went out, crossed the road and practically ran through the ashram gates.

The tears were rolling down my cheeks now. I felt like kissing the ground as I ran up the hill and past the statue of the elephant-headed god Ganesh. Then I ran round the back of the temple and the precious Prayer Hall, the scene of so many wonderful moments with Swami. Then I approached the auditorium, the large assembly hall that contains his living quarters.

Swami had obviously retired for the night. But I stood there in the darkness, crying in full flood now.

Swami, I prayed, looking towards the upper floor windows and wringing my hands. *I'm back! I'm back now! Please don't ever let me go away again. I should never have left you. I know that now. I was a fool to think I could find satisfaction anywhere except with you. Please take me back! I beg you, please take me back!*

Of course, I didn't expect him to appear—and he didn't. So after about ten minutes, I slowly returned to the hotel, unpacked my things and went to bed.

But that night he came in a dream. We were both sitting in chairs, opposite one another, and I was barely managing to pour everything out to him between great wracking sobs and floods of tears. His face was wreathed in lines of deep concern and compassion as he listened carefully, and he leaned forward to rub my forearms.

So the next morning, I awoke with such a wonderful feeling of delight that he'd come to me, given me such a welcoming reception and listened to me with such love. It was barely light as I got ready to see him. I was brimming with anticipation.

The aroma of breakfast *dosas* greeted me as I walked down the street. Several of the shopkeepers were already out on to the pavements.

"Hello, it's good to see you back!"

"How have you been? We've missed you!"

I couldn't believe they remembered me. Surely, I thought, they must have seen more than a million people since.

I'd noticed the night before that Swami seemed to have the builders in. When I got to the bench in the Prayer Hall, I couldn't take my place on it because it was covered in scaffolding. I wondered if it was symbolic. But it turned out that Swami was extending the hall and redecorating it, in time for his 75th birthday celebrations to which millions were expected a few months hence.

This meant that I had to queue up with everyone else to sit on the floor. My line was one of the last to be led into the back of the hall. So when Swami arrived, I could barely see him.

Never mind, I thought to myself. *There will be plenty of other opportunities.*

After *darshan,* I went to the shoe shop to buy some sandals.

"It's so good to see you again!" beamed the owner. "How long are you staying? Let's hope it's for a long time!"

I didn't remember him and I was sure that I'd never bought any shoes there.

My next stop was the orphanage. I'd brought with me some useful items: a few educational toys, boxes of pens and pencils, and several huge bottles of vitamin pills. So I put them into a bag and I must confess, I felt a little nervous as I walked down Samadhi Lane to the school. Even though the children had written to me regularly, I wasn't sure if my memory had played tricks on me, and whether I'd exaggerated our importance to one another.

When I got to the school, Max came out and gave me a big hug. But it seemed suspiciously quiet.

"The children have been taken for a walk," he said. "They're down by the Chitravathi river."

"Oh," I replied, disappointed. "Well, in that case, I'll come back later."

"No, please go to them now!" he replied, firmly. "They've already heard on the grapevine you're here and can talk of nothing else. We won't be able to settle them down for lessons if they don't see you soon."

So I walked back to the main street, and then turned into Chitravathi Lane. As usual, the market (or the 'bazaar', as Swami calls it) was in full swing. Several of the stallholders did a double take when they saw me, and called out their greetings. The old *dhobi* woman, who always used to do my washing, looked up from her sorting of laundry, recognised me and waved. I had tears in my eyes. I was so moved that these people remembered me.

I carried on down the lane, past my old apartment, until I came to the sandy bank of the river. I could see some children, further on, who were running around and yelling and playing. But they were too far away for me to be absolutely sure that it was them.

I started walking in their direction. As I got closer, I gradually began to make out Devahuti, and then Sita, and then Sukadeva. Then gradually, they all turned and recognised me. One by one, they stopped playing and stood stock still, watching me walk towards them. By the time I'd caught up with them, they were all facing me, absolutely silent. Some of them were holding a hand to their heart area. Others had tears in their eyes.

Some of the newer ones looked on questioningly. So then a whispering went through the ranks.

"It's Ishtar madam. It's Ishtar."

I don't remember much of what happened next. The emotion of the moment was too overpowering. I do, however, remember walking back with them to the school, with Sukadeva holding one hand and Sita the other. But most of the others were too overcome to speak to me. There also seemed to be a deep sadness among them. Instead of it being a joyous homecoming parade, it was more like a funeral march.

As we approached the school, Max came out again.

"So, are you coming back to take your classes?" he asked.

The children immediately stopped walking, and every ear was instantly cocked for my reply.

"Oh, well, no," I stuttered, surprised by the question. "I don't think so. I'm only here for a month, you see. It wouldn't be worth your while changing the teaching staff around. I'll come and visit, though, as often as I can."

"Please come back," he said. "I don't care about the bother of reorganising things. You can teach whatever you like, whenever you like. We can reschedule their timetables so that you won't have to miss any of Swami's *darshan*. Please! The children need you. We need you."

"Well ...okay, then," I replied, quite stunned at the turn of events. "So ...when do you want me to start?"

"Now?" he said.

Within half-an-hour, my sandals were neatly parked once again outside the door of Class 6 and without being asked, Devahuti immediately went to the cupboard and started giving out the Ramakrishna books. It was as if I'd never been away.

However, by the end of that first morning, I found that that was not quite true. There was a reason for the sadness that I'd noticed on that walk back from the river. The children had been through quite a tough time since I'd last seen them. Money had been scarce and some of their teachers had been cruel and selfish. I soon saw that the children associated their time with me, the previous summer, as a sort of bygone golden age, which was partly why they had been so moved to see me. There had been a number of changes at the orphanage during the past twelve months, and some of them were quite disturbing.

The first one I noticed was that Vasudeva and Murugan weren't there. Devahuti told me:

"Their mother took them away a few months ago. They were last seen, begging with her, at the Hanuman temple. They looked really thin and ill. They were starving."

Another one of my girls was missing, a very pretty little one of about nine years old with shoulder-length dark curls and big brown eyes.

"Her aunt came for her," said Devahuti, sadly. "But we fear the worst. The aunt lives on the street and she's a prostitute."

But worst of all, little Hari seemed to be in quite a bad way. I was shocked and suddenly lanced by guilt when I realised that he was still in the lower class.

I don't know whether I'd grown spiritually in the intervening year. But I had a number of realisations as I walked back to the hotel for lunch. I was beginning to see that my anger at Hari's cheating had been more about a failure to meet my own needs, rather than making his needs the priority. That previous summer, I now saw, I'd been living in a sort of 'King and I' fantasy about my relationship with the children. So when reality hit, I hadn't been able to deal with it correctly. And what had been intended to be a punishment, a short sharp shock, to help Hari to learn to be more truthful, had gone badly wrong. To add insult to injury, I hadn't followed it through and recommended that his situation be reviewed after a certain date. So with all the other problems that Max and the others had had to deal with since I'd left, he'd been left in the lower class and forgotten.

Now I could see that Hari's mental state had very obviously deteriorated. The trauma from seeing his father murder his mother was obviously manifesting itself more. It was as if he was permanently disturbed and distracted by something not quite seen, and his face looked as if it was shrouded in a sort of grey light.

That afternoon, I was placed at the back of the Prayer Hall again. So I still couldn't see Swami very well. But I was too absorbed in worrying about Hari's state, and feeling bad about it, to notice it much.

The next morning, after assembly, I went straight to Max.

"You've more or less given me a blank cheque," I said.

He nodded.

"I want Hari back in my class," I replied.

"But he's really been playing up lately," said Max. "Frankly, we haven't known what to do with him."

"Just give him to me," I pleaded, and after only a little hesitation, Max agreed, saying that he would sort out the matter by the end of the day.

Later that morning, as I walked past Hari's classroom, I could hear his class teacher, an old woman with a screechy voice, and she was haranguing him.

"You're a bad boy, Hari! You're a very bad boy! You never concentrate, you're lazy, you don't do your homework and what's more, you're a liar! You hear what I say, boy! You're a liar!"

I couldn't help myself. I walked straight into the classroom. The teacher looked quite surprised. I smiled at her and said,

"Oh no, I'm sure that's not true. Perhaps you don't know Hari very well yet, but I can assure you, he's not a liar. He's a very good boy, these days. He always speaks the truth."

I looked down in time to see Hari's face light up with an enormous smile. Then it slowly spread across his face, and it was as if the grey cobwebs just fell away.

I put my hand out to him and said,

"Come on."

Then I turned my face towards the teacher so that the other children couldn't see it, and I winked at her and said,

"Hari's been promoted to my class now. I'm only having the best boys in my class and so, of course, I must have Hari."

The teacher looked uncertain at first, but then she smiled in acquiescence. Hari grabbed hold of my hand, and stood up straight. Then he raised his head high as we walked together, out of the room.

As soon as we were out of the classroom, and alone in the white-washed corridor, I picked him up and carried him towards Class 6's room, squeezing and kissing him all the while and whispering in his ear:

"Now we're going to have some fun! You'll see!"

He just grinned from ear to ear, and the children cheered as I carried him in through the door.

The next morning, I set off to see Swami once again with high hopes. But, like the days before, I was placed in the back row. That afternoon, I was also put in the back. I was in the back again, too, the next day—and the next day, and the next day, and the day after that. It got to the point where, when we were queuing, I would warn others not to join my line or they would be sure to end up at the back.

But, one day, finally, I was placed about four rows from the front. This was at least near enough to Swami for him to be able to see me and smile at me.

So imagine my disappointment when he swept straight past and totally ignored me. The pain was unbearable.

That night, I went to a local restaurant with Max, and we got to chatting with some German devotees. One of them asked me why I seemed so down.

"Swami didn't look at me in *darshan*," I said, morosely.

They burst out laughing. But one of them seemed quite annoyed.

"I've been coming here every year, for eight years," she said, "and Swami has never once looked at me. I don't expect him to, either. Among all these thousands of people, who am I to think that I'm so special and unique that he should look at me?"

"Yes," agreed another. "It's just your ego that wants Swami to look at you. When you are more developed in your spirituality, you will be more humble about it."

As I walked back to my hotel afterwards, I was sure those devotees were all quite right. My ego was enormous, and they all had a much greater understanding of spirituality than myself. Most people I met there, in fact, were much more spiritual than me. I was just an ordinary woman who'd happened to fall in love with Sai Baba. It was most unfortunate. But there was another factor, too—something that I couldn't quite put my finger on.

Then as I got ready for bed, I began to realise what this was. It was because Swami had looked at me so lovingly, and so often, the summer before. Since then, too, he had given me hundreds of wonderful experiences of his infinite nature, either in dream or in his astral form. So it wasn't a question of whether I was good enough or not, to be noticed by him. It was more that I was finding it practically impossible to buy into this idea about him being limited to that one physical body and therefore far too busy with all these thousands of other people to possibly spare any time for me.

In the past year, Swami had been in every second of my life. He had become the person who was closest to my heart. He had appeared to me in my home on two occasions. He had directed my dreams. He had organised my safe passage through India. I had never looked to fall in love with him. But it had happened, despite the yawning chasm between us in terms of spiritual realisation. I wasn't even sure that we were the same species. But now I totally relied on him, as a wife relies on her husband. So to go to see him and have him walk straight past me as if he'd never seen me before ... Well, it definitely *felt* at least, as if he was deliberately ignoring me. It also felt very personal.

I had heard that Swami would sometimes ignore a devotee if he was displeased with them. So that night, as I lay in bed, I thought hard about what I could have done to incur his disapproval. Of course, I wasn't short of ideas on how often I'd acted in a way contrary to his teachings. It soon became abundantly clear that the list was going to be endless. But I tried to be as honest and thorough as I could. I went through and sincerely repented each tiny transgression. There were a couple, too, for which I could have easily found some really good excuses. But I was still apologetic.

So the next morning, I felt so well and truly purged that I inwardly thanked Swami for the wonderful lesson and went off to see him with a spring in my step. I felt fully confident that I would now, finally, be seated in the front row and all would be forgiven in a blaze of loving smiles and *vibhuuthi*.

I *was* seated in the front row.

After a while, the music started up and Swami entered the Prayer Hall. As he walked along, his face was turned towards our row and he appeared to be scanning it for someone. He was looking intently at every single face and he carried on like this until he got to me. Then his gaze leap-frogged over me to the person sitting just the other side of me. Then he carried on his way, still scanning every face.

I suppose I should feel flattered that he's making so much effort to ignore me, I tried to console myself afterwards.

But I didn't feel flattered, or pleased, or in any way happy about it. I felt bitterly hurt, devastated and very, very angry.

That evening, I came to a resolution.

"If he isn't going to look at me," I decided, "well, guess what? I'm not going to look at him either!"

There was no rule that if you went for his *darshan,* you had to look at him, I reasoned with myself. And anyway, I was fed up with sitting there like a wet weekend, feeling so dependent on every flicker of his eye. Of course, I didn't know how on earth I was going to be able to resist looking at his beautiful face. I was almost hoping that I'd be placed in the back, the next day, to make it easier.

But no—the next morning, I was seated right in the front row again.

After about ten minutes of waiting, there was a disturbance. One of the women, who'd been placed at the back, was insisting on sitting in the front row. When the ushers refused, she sat

MOHINI STARTS HER DANCE

herself bang in the middle of the path that Swami was due to be walking down any minute, and she wouldn't move.

She was shouting and pleading with the ushers:

"Look, you don't understand! I'm special to Swami! Swami loves me! I know Swami loves me! He'll want to see me! He won't want me to be at the back of the hall!"

The ushers tried to politely reason with her. But, probably worried that it was getting close to Swami's arrival in the Prayer Hall, they gently lifted her up between them to move her. She then went completely berserk, screaming and screaming:

"Swami! Swami! Please save me! Please save me!" as they carried her out of the hall.

Sheepishly thinking that "there but for the grace of the British stiff upper lip go I", I felt overcome with sympathy for her. So I started to pray,

Dear Swami, I feel as if you've just played out my own ego's proud and selfish desires right in front of me. Was this a show to demonstrate to me how I am? It feels like it. So please Swami, please help this woman. She loves you so much, she doesn't know what to do and I know how that feels. Please help her, because now she's been taken off the premises, she will be more desperate than ever, and goodness knows what she might do!

The irony of praying to someone that I was refusing to look at passed me by at that point. And because I was usually far more intent on praying for myself than another person, a new but quite pleasant feeling was slowly enveloping me. It felt quite wonderful, and it soon became so irresistible that I found myself closing my eyes and merging into it. So when Swami entered the hall that morning, it was easy not to look at his limited physical form because I was lost in his infinite one.

I remained in this wonderful beatific state for the whole two hours of the *darshan*. So by the time the session was nearing its end, and Swami was leaving the temple and walking towards us, I was still so absorbed in these blissful waves of love that I must have been practically egoless. I say 'practically' because still a small proud piece was clinging on and it was saying,

"Okay, he's coming now. So whatever you do, remember. Don't look at him. Don't look at his face."

In order not to look at Swami's face in such close quarters, I had to look down at the floor. So as I watched Swami's small, brown feet tenderly approaching, I briefly felt the loving concern of his eyes on the back of my head. Then a mega shot of nectar-laden bliss came straight up through his feet and, like a heat-seeking missile, rushed straight into my heart and exploded into a million pieces.

CHAPTER 16
THE THOUSAND NAMES OF GOD

After being kicked into touch by Swami's divine footwork, I floated back to my hotel in a dream-like state. Luckily, it was a Sunday. So I didn't have to go to the school. I could just lie on my bed in a cloud of bliss all day, if I chose. And I did choose it. In reality, though, I had little choice. I could barely move. But later on, I began to realise that something was wrong. I was starting to feel quite ill.

There are some who believe that very pure spiritual experiences can cause the physical body to detoxify itself and that what it actually feels like is the flu. I didn't know if that was true or not. However, during that night, I awoke in a cold sweat. My muscles ached and my head felt as if there was a little man sitting on top of it, whacking it with a sledgehammer.

As if that wasn't bad enough, all the divine, blissful feelings had completely drained away. By morning, I was in so much pain and discomfort, I could barely move. I was also having to face the dire reality that I probably wasn't going to be well enough to see Swami for several days.

Within seconds of this realisation, my ego woke up to the fact that it had me at its mercy. It instantly started planning its next assault with almost military precision and soon came up with this brilliant plan:

There is a book called *Shri Sai Satcharitra,* ('shree-saye-sat-charitra'). It's about the life and teachings of an early 20th century saint called Sai Baba of Shirdi, or Shirdi Sai as he's known. Swami had said that he was the reincarnation of this Shirdi Sai, although I couldn't quite reconcile that with Sai Baba also being the tenth avatar of Vishnu, because this would make him the eleventh. Anyway, I was beginning to learn not to look for rational explanations in India. And I was all the more willing to ignore the inconsistency because I'd heard that Swami had promised to grant a boon to anyone who managed to read the entire *Shri Sai Satcharitra* in ten days.

"This'll be a cinch," I almost chuckled to myself, especially as it now looked as if I was going to have some time on my hands—at least, until I got over the bug.

The book had exactly two hundred and sixty pages. Getting through a mere twenty-six pages a day was no problem for such a voracious reader as myself. I'd been known to devour whole books in one sitting.

So this is how my ego set out to try and outwit Swami. Not only would I read the book well within the required time, but I would also use my wordsmith skills to forge what were really several separate requests into one boon. I'd learned that one of the qualities of Vishnu was that he never failed in his promises. So I knew he wouldn't be able to get out of it.

After only a few minutes, I came up with this:

> "Dear Swami, many obeisances at your Holy Lotus Feet. Thank you for all the wonderful experiences you are giving me. I understand that you promised to grant a boon to anyone who reads the *Shri Sai Satcharitra* within ten days. So when I fulfil this requirement, please would you kindly grant me the following boon? I wish you to place one hand on my head, the other on my arm, all the while looking deeply into my eyes and saying to me 'I love you and you are my devotee.' Thank you."

I put this request on my dressing table, on which I'd created a small makeshift altar, and then settled down into the book.

It turned out to be a really interesting read. It was written by a devotee of Shirdi Sai Baba, who had spent a lot of time with the sage. Hearing about some of the things that Shirdi Sai used to say and do, it was almost like reading about Swami. Even some of his sayings could easily have come out of Swami's mouth. So by the time I was halfway through the book, I'd forgotten that I was reading about Shirdi Sai, and was thinking only of my own Sathya Sai.

I spent the next few days sleeping and reading this book. Occasionally, though, it was difficult to continue because the pain was so bad. I'd try to sleep at such times. But once, during the night, my head was hurting so much that it was keeping me awake. I felt terrible. I couldn't find a way to escape the pain. But then I felt a light, loving touch on my crown. It sent tingling showers of soothing energy through my head, the knot of pain unravelled, and I quickly dropped into a blissful unconsciousness.

The following day, I was in a similar agonised state. But the loving touch came again, this time on my arm, and again, I felt the same energy showers. Then all the pain fell away, and I drifted once more into sleep.

But four days and 141 pages later, disaster struck. The next two pages were completely blank, and when the text resumed at page 144, it was obvious that a whole chunk was missing. It was just a printing error. But I knew that it was going to cost me my boon.

However, not to be outdone, I hauled myself out of bed, stood under the shower and then got myself dressed. Then I rang down to room service for some buttered toast and tea. This perked me up a little more—at least enough, anyway, to go out and trawl around all the bookshops.

First I tried the bookshop where I'd originally bought my copy of *Shri Sai* Satcharitra. They hadn't any more, they said. Then I tried two further bookshops. But neither of them had it in, and one of the booksellers told me that he thought it was out of print. There was just one bookshop left to try. It was up the hill, near Sai Baba's dairy. I staggered up the hill with the midday sun beating down on my head. When I got there, it looked as if I'd struck gold. There was a copy of *Shri Sai Satcharitra* sitting on the shelves. When I explained about the printing error, the young boy shopkeeper grinned. He took it off the shelf and then flicked through it, to show me that it contained pages 142 and pages 143. Yes, they were there. But oh dear—pages 144 and 145 were blank.

At that moment, a group of the children from the orphanage appeared. They'd been out for a walk with one of their teachers. They were delighted to see me back on my feet again. So I walked back with them to the school. Then I went to tell Max that I would be able to resume teaching the following day.

Thus, the following morning, I found myself standing at the blackboard in Class 6 with a big piece of chalk, and writing across it, in big bold letters:

SHRI SAI SATCHARITA

All the children obediently copied this into their English grammar exercise books. Then I turned to face the class.

"This is a book about the life of Shirdi Sai," I explained, "and there will be a reward for anyone who can find me a copy of it."

Then I set about putting into place the other ruse that my ego had dreamt up to get to Swami, which was really the second prong of a sort of pincer movement.

Class 6 had been nagging me, ever since I'd arrived back in India, about putting on a play. Then, just before I'd fallen ill, I'd come across a particularly apt story about a devotee of Vishnu. I thought that if we put on this play, it would allow me to send a very pointed message to the other Mr Vishnu down the road.

I decided that I should first read it to them. So they all proceeded to make themselves comfortable by bunching up into groups and draping themselves over one another.

"Okay, then?" I said. "If you're all comfortable, I shall begin." And I told them the following story:

> Once upon a time, there was a certain chap named Prakash. Now, despite the fact that Prakash was a poor man, he was completely, one hundred per cent, devoted to Lord Vishnu. He would sit by the river Ganges all day, singing his praises. Often, there would be nothing to eat in his house. But he wouldn't care. He would still spend his whole day glorifying his Lord by chanting the *Thousand Names of Vishnu* by the side of the river Ganges.
>
> His life proceeded in this way for many years, and he was quite happy with it. He was so devoted to Vishnu, he didn't care about much else. But one morning, just as he was about to leave for the Ganges, his wife came running out after him.
>
> "Prakash!" she called. "Never mind all that useless chanting to your Lord! Does he care that there is nothing to eat in this house?"
>
> Prakash stopped and turned back.
>
> "What do you mean?" he asked.
>
> "Surely you can see, the children are crying out for food!" cried Mrs Prakash. "So please forget about chanting to your

THE THOUSAND NAMES OF GOD

Lord Vishnu! You would be better off going to the main street and begging for some flour."

As she said this, a verse from the *Thousand Names of Vishnu* flashed through Prakash's mind. It was the one where Vishnu's name appears as 'Feeder of the Entire Universe'. And then he thought to himself,

Ah...so, no! It's not true! Vishnu is not the 'Feeder of the Entire Universe'. In fact, he shirks his responsibility of feeding his beings.

So he immediately pulled out his copy of the *Thousand Names of Vishnu* from his pocket and flicked through it until he found the page that he was looking for. Then he picked up a piece of charcoal and used it to cross out the following words: 'Feeder of the Entire Universe'. Then he announced,

"From today, I shall chant only nine-hundred-and-ninety-nine names, instead of the full thousand."

Then Prakash carried on down to the Ganges.

Now, at this very same time, Vishnu was seated on a pink lotus flower on the planet of Vaikuntha. Beside him, on one of the petals, sat his wife Lakshmi, who was also the Goddess of Wealth. Suddenly, Lakshmi looked at Vishnu and laughed. Vishnu was perplexed at her odd behaviour.

"Why are you laughing?" he asked her. But she just cracked up into further peals of mirth. Vishnu didn't get the joke. So he continued to look at her in a puzzled way until, finally, she managed to pull herself together. Then she said:

"My Lord, as it is, you are fair. But today you're looking fairer still!"

Lakshmi could hardly contain herself over her own joke, and exploded once more into fits of giggles.

Realising that something must have gone wrong with his appearance, Vishnu quickly stood up and went to look in the mirror. He saw a smudge of charcoal on his face. But Lakshmi wouldn't let up.

"So, is that some new sort of sandal paste that your devotee has offered you today?" she carried on, mercilessly.

"He is very poor," replied Vishnu, taking a tissue and trying to wipe off the smudge. "He cannot even afford to feed his family."

"Then why do you not give him wealth and abundance?" she asked him swiftly.

Vishnu gave up trying to wipe off the smudge. He looked thoughtful. Then he said,

"Goddess of wealth, I know your motive. If I shower him with riches, he will shift his devotion to you!"

"Poor chap," said Lakshmi, refusing to let it go. "He has been suffering in poverty for a long time now. Enough is enough! I'm going to nag you and nag you until you do something about it."

So, like any husband who would do anything for a quiet life, Vishnu decided that he must act.

Later that day, Prakash's wife was putting out her washing when she noticed a man with a long train of mules behind him. He was coming along the lane towards her house. The mules seemed to be laden down with goods. The man eventually drew level with her. Then he stopped and asked:

"Madam, are you the wife of Prakash?"

"Yes," she replied, wondering who he was and how he knew her husband's name.

"Then, good woman, please accept all these gifts."

"But how? Why? I don't understand…" replied Prakash's wife.

"I met your husband on the banks of the Ganges and lost a bet with him," he replied.

The poor woman was quite bewildered. She asked him to come in and wait for her husband's return. But the man replied:

"I have no time now. I must be on my way. But I have something to do before I go."

He waved his hand and in less than a flash, a huge palace appeared in the place of the hut. It was surrounded by beautiful flower gardens and fountains, and servants were busily running back and forth, preparing a rich feast for Prakash's wife and children. Then the family looked down at themselves and saw that they'd been dressed in rich silks and embroidered brocades.

As the man prepared to leave, the dazed wife said to him:

"I don't understand all this. A moment ago, we were as poor as church mice. Now, all this wealth is ours! Will you not wait for my husband?"

The man shook his head.

"Well, do you at least have a message for him?"

"Yes," replied the man. "Just one," and he whispered something in her ear.

Soon evening came, and Prakash returned to his house. But when he saw the huge palace and courtyards and flowerbeds, he thought that he must have missed his way and come to the wrong place. So he turned to retrace his steps. But just then, his wife saw him and came running out.

Prakash stared at her new silks and jewels. He rubbed his eyes. He thought he must be dreaming. But she took him inside, and made him sit down. Then she gave him some nice cooling mango juice. After he'd calmed down a little, she began to tell him all about the mysterious man and how he brought about this change in their circumstances. Then finally, she told him:

"He said it was all because you beat him in a bet today."

"But I didn't have a bet with anyone today," replied Prakash. "In fact, I don't believe in gambling. It's against Vedic principles."

So now they were even more confused.

"Well, did he leave any message?" Prakash finally asked.

"Yes," replied his wife. "He said 'please ask your husband to clean off the special sandalwood paste he so lavishly applied to my face this morning.' What do you think he meant by that? Can you make anything of it?"

Prakash suddenly understood all too well who her mysterious visitor had been. He realised that the Lord himself had visited his humble abode—but in his absence!

So he leapt up and ran out of the house, crying in agony.

"Oh Lord! You gave her your *darshan*! She who would always scorn your blessed name! But not me! Why did you avoid giving me your *darshan*? How could you? O, how could you?" and he ran off into the jungle, crying:

"Lord Vishnu! Lord Vishnu!"

After several hours of running around and wailing, poor Prakash felt quite exhausted. So he sat down to rest. But suddenly, there was a dazzling light, and Lord Vishnu was standing in front of him. This time, though, he didn't look like the man who'd visited his wife. Instead, Vishnu appeared in his true blue radiant form. In his four arms, he was holding the disc weapon, the conch shell, the golden mace and the pink lotus flower—and he was smiling down at his devotee in such loving kindness.

But Prakash felt too offended to enjoy this divine vision. He was so bitterly hurt by his Lord's behaviour. So he turned his head away, and refused to look at him.

Vishnu spoke kindly to him:

"I don't know why you are angry with me. I only appeared to your wife as an ordinary man. To you, I reveal my true, divine form."

Prakash at once realised that Vishnu was right. He clasped the Lord's feet, and tears of love rolled down his cheeks. Then in a choked voice, he said,

"Lord, do not forsake me now. Take me back to Vaikuntha with you. Do not send me back into this world of illusion!"

Vishnu lovingly placed his hand on Prakash's head and said:

"Always remember my form, as you have seen it now. Go, my son, and live the life of ease and comfort you so richly deserve. Remembering me always, do your work in the world. My illusion will not touch you."

And then he disappeared.

Eventually, Prakash picked himself up, pulled himself together and went home to Mrs Prakash. And as the days, weeks, months and years went on, he gradually settled into his new life, and he was ever drunk with the bliss of the Lord's divine vision. For now that he was so well provided for, his wife never nagged him again about going to beg for flour, or get new clothes for the children. So Prakash could happily spend the rest of his days on earth in blissful contemplation upon the true form of Lord Vishnu, the Preserver of the Universe. And they all lived happily ever after.

I finished reading, and put down the book. There was silence in the classroom. Then all the children jumped up and started clapping.

"Can we do this play, then, please Madam Ishtar?" Devahuti yelled above the excitement.

"I want to be Prakash," shouted Vijaya.

It's probably obvious. But perhaps I should point out that the only reason that I wanted to do this play was because of this bit:

> But Prakash felt too offended to enjoy this divine vision. He was so bitterly hurt by his Lord's behaviour. So he turned his head away, and refused to look at him.

I'm sure that I don't have to explain why.

I stayed up late that night, turning it into a script. Then, on the way into school the next morning, I stopped off at the photocopy shop. So when I arrived to take Class 6's lesson, I had several scripts to hand out.

We first of all had to sort out the characters. Devahuti was chosen to be the narrator, as it was the weightiest part. Little Narayana would be Lord Vishnu, Vijaya would be Prakash, Radha would be Prakash's wife, Sita, the goddess Lakshmi, and Sukadeva would be the prompter.

The children's homework, from then on, was to learn their lines. But we had varying degrees of success in this. I would often come in to rehearse them to find that they were no further forward in learning their parts and Sukadeva, as the prompter, was having to work overtime.

The head had suggested that we put on the play for an especially invited audience, on the evening of Krishna's birthday. So this added on more pressure to make the play as good as possible.

I was getting plenty of help with costumes and scenery from the other staff. But I really wanted to find a good Vishnu costume. At least, I thought, I wanted Narayana to have the four arms with the disc weapon, the conch shell, the golden mace and pink lotus. These are very important symbolic accessories, as I explained to them one day by chalking up the following verses from *The Thousand Names of Vishnu* on the blackboard:

> Your one hand wields the beautiful conch shell, of which only true fortunates are privileged to hear the divine sound.
>
> You have radiance like the sun, a discus called Sudarshan in the other hand, which can slay the wicked and the demons in a trice.
>
> Your third hand holds a heavy mace, which is ever ready to end the afflictions caused by physical, spiritual and mental afflictions.
>
> And your fourth wields a lotus flower, which is capable of granting all the four kinds of rewards and material riches.

These would normally be strange items to be looking for in a regular high street parade of shops. But it didn't seem such an out-of-place quest in a place where the oddest things regularly occurred. So I spent all my spare time rummaging around the local shops and stalls, not only searching for these arcane ornaments, but also for another complete version of the *Shri Sai Satcharitra*.

When walking through the village, I would also be constantly on the lookout for Vasudeva and Murugan, and the pretty little nine-year-old girl.

I would wander around the well-known beggar haunts, like the steps leading up to the Wish Fulfilment Tree and the Hanuman Temple. In the evenings, I would order two meals in the south Indian canteen. After I'd eaten mine, I'd take the remaining one and give it to the first beggar I came across. Perhaps it was a sort of offering, to appease the god of the beggars. But I felt sure that, if only I could find the children, I could persuade them to return.

There was one woman that I would often go to see, by the dairy farm. She had to lie there in all weathers, on the side of the road, because her body was too withered down one side for her to be able to stand. On one side of her face, she was extremely beautiful and she would always give me the softest, most loving look. But, when she turned her head slightly, I could see that the other side of her face was completely destroyed, and I knew only too well which side the men would concentrate on when they visited her in the night.

One day, somebody told me that they thought they'd seen the nine-year-old girl at a Christian orphanage school in the next village. So I went there, and knocked on the door. I asked to speak to the head, pretending to be a potential donor. One of the teachers was asked to show me around the classrooms. The children all stood up as we entered each room and my eyes scoured around, looking intently at every little girl. But she wasn't there.

Another day, I saw a young beggar woman lying on the pavement of Samadhi Lane. She couldn't have been older than her early thirties. As I approached, I saw a group of about eight people surrounding her.

"What's going on?" I asked.

"She's dying," said one of them, "for lack of food."

"Well, for goodness sake," I cried, wringing my hands. "I'll go and get her some."

They looked at my pityingly.

"No, it's too late for that. It would be detrimental to her, at this stage."

But there was something else that he didn't say. I felt that the crowd was also there to help this soul make this all-important transition in peace and dignity, without being disturbed by a Western, liberal do-gooder like myself.

I suppose it was strange to find so much human suffering and hunger in the place that was said to be the home of the physical body of the all-compassionate Lord Vishnu, the Feeder of the Universe. I'd heard there were some travel writers, notably Mick Brown in his book *The Spiritual Tourist*, who had been put off by what he described as this "rich man in his castle, poor men at the gates" sort of paradigm.

The extent of the poverty, the begging and the degradation in India is shocking, at first. It makes it hard to believe that such a country could have produced such sublime scriptures and powerful spiritual teachings. But if you scratch the surface, it's not difficult to see the truth. This is a culture that has been dispossessed to the point where dependency has become firmly engrained in its psyche. Until relatively recently, these people had been living under foreign invaders for more than a thousand years. They'd been abused by them, in every sense of the word, and robbed of their spiritual and cultural identity. So it seemed to me that it was going to take a lot longer than fifty years—which is how long it had been since Indian independence—to sort out all the social and economic problems.

I was constantly reminded of the views of Rumi, the Sufi poet. He visited India in the 13th century in his search for the 'pearl of great price', or divine enlightenment. But he ended up leaving empty-handed, and said in disgust:

"Yes, priceless pearls of true wisdom do exist in India. But they are scattered among the dung. So if these people are so spiritually enlightened, why don't they clean it up?"

But I'd never before been in a place where the pearls existed, and I was so desperate now that I didn't mind getting down on my hands and knees to extract them. On top of that, I felt that

Rumi, for all his wonderful poetry, had no right to criticise when he was part of the religion, Islam, that had invaded India in the eighth century and which had destroyed so much of the Indian culture and religion.

My impression was that this was a nation of people who had been damaged on a very deep level by having their spiritual roots ripped from under them. At the orphanage school, as in every school in India, the history textbooks were still full of stories about an alien Aryan or Indo-European culture that had invaded India around 1200 BC, bringing with it the spiritual basis of the Indian civilisation, the Vedas. This myth had been invented and promoted by the British colonialists, the Raj, even though there had never been any evidence for an Aryan invasion, let alone that these invaders wrote the indigenous peoples' sacred lore, the Vedas. And now, in fact, archaeological and genealogical research is showing that the evidence is to the contrary. But the Western historical establishment still clings to this ridiculous idea—that Krishna was really a European, or a Turk, or even a Russian—because a whole academic industry is founded upon it.

So these were some of the thoughts that went through my head as I tried to reconcile some of the paradoxes that I was faced with. As I roamed these streets, I felt that what was needed was a total cultural regeneration of a whole nation. As I understood it, that was Swami's main aim and he was mixing in some pretty high circles to achieve this.

One wet evening, I went out of the ashram gates with the offertory meal to find that there were no beggars to be seen. I walked all around the village, in the rain, and I still couldn't find a single one.

I eventually gave up and decided to go back to my hotel. But as I made my way back, I bumped into Ila, one of my fellow teachers. She told me that the Prime Minister of India, Atal Bihari Vajpayee, was coming to visit Swami the following day. She thought it quite likely that the police had moved all the beggars off the streets.

I was intrigued that the Prime Minister of India should visit Swami. I wondered if he was a devotee.

"He often visits Swami," said Ila, "sometimes several times a year. I'm not sure if he is actually his devotee. But judging by what we hear of Vajpayee's character, it wouldn't be surprising."

I pressed Ila for further details.

"Vajpayee is one of India's great visionary poets," she said. "He always supports the side of the lower castes and the Untouchables, and his declared aim is to help India return to her noble Vedic roots."

That night, as I lay in my bed and listened to the monsoon rain beating on the roof, I prayed that the beggars had been given some clean, dry cells and a good meal.

I awoke the next morning, and looked out of my window to find the village in a state of high excitement, with police and army types everywhere. But later on, when I went over to the ashram, I could see that everyone seemed to be much more impressed by this upcoming visit than Swami himself, who just carried on with his usual schedule.

My ego was still running rampant, though. Devahuti, bless her, had found me a new copy of the *Shri Sai Satcharitra* with none of the pages missing. It was only a few days to go before the deadline. So I would put it underneath my *darshan* cushion and whenever Swami left the Prayer Hall, pull it out and fervently read it. However, there was an extremely blissful feeling in the hall that day that even managed to permeate through to me.

When the end of the session arrived, Swami stayed in the temple. So we just sat there, and sat there, and sat there. It must have been a full twenty minutes that we continued to sit there, and with every minute, the spiritual ambience rose higher and higher. It was incredible. I'd never known such a feeling in the Prayer Hall before. It was as if all the devotees were one living, breathing sea of still, pure love. There were no egos, no pushing for position, no devotees more important than the others—even on the ladies' side. There was just a brilliant sea of pure shimmering beings that had at its pulsating heart the beautiful Sathya Sai Baba.

Then, just like an enormous rock falling into the sea, the screeching of tyres and the slamming of car doors announced Vajpayee's arrival. Vajpayee walked into the Prayer Hall and then his entourage of BJP cronies, police, army types, security men and journalists all came tumbling after him, jockeying for position and practically tripping over the seated devotees on the floor in their haste to be the nearest to him as he entered the temple.

They all stayed sequestered with Swami for about half-an-hour. Then they came out again. This time, they looked calmer and some of them had serene smiles on their faces. Then there was a further slamming of doors and screeching of tyres, and they were gone, leaving us still sitting there in our now placid again, blissful sea, and quietly waiting for Swami.

Five minutes later, Swami came out of the temple. Then he stopped dead in his tracks. His face was registering a look of surprise. Then it turned into one of pure pleasure. He seemed pleased that we'd quietly remained and waited for him to complete his business. It was a wonderful look, and a very special moment and, for the first time, I felt what it really meant to be his true devotee.

Unfortunately, though, it still wasn't enough for my ego, as the events of the following days were to prove.

CHAPTER 17
THE LAST DANCE

That night, Swami came to me in a dream. I was living in a house under the Meditation Tree, and he came up to visit me. Then he took me in his arms to teach me to dance. His movements were flowing and effortless and I tried to follow his liquid style. But I was bumbling, clumsy and stiff. On the one occasion that I did manage to surrender to his flow, it felt so ecstatic that I had an uncomfortable feeling that it must be wrong, even erotically sinful, and immediately froze and pulled back from it.

However, this dream just served to increase my desperation for his personal attention. So the next morning, I set off for the school with a determined step.

It was now only a few days before my departure for England. Swami still hadn't looked at me, or given me the smallest flicker of attention. You might wonder how I knew that, given that I wasn't looking at him either. But when Swami looks at you, believe me, you know it. The whole universe knows it too. So I'd finally got the hint. He didn't want me.

There had been nights when I'd been in so much agony over it that I'd considered leaving early. I would lie there in the muggy heat with the mosquitoes zooming in to take chunks out of me and wonder why I didn't just pack up and go to a Club Med. I'd have visions of myself all tanned and manicured, lying on a sun lounger and sipping chilled Camparis. One night, I actually made up my mind to go. But then, I suddenly remembered the children. I realised then that I couldn't possibly leave early. They would be devastated. And so, in the end, it was only the children—and their play—that were keeping me there.

As I walked towards the school that day, I wracked my brains, trying to work out why Swami was treating me so differently from the previous year. Over the past few days, the beginnings of a theory had been beginning to form. But it seemed too incredible. Still, I couldn't think of any other reason. Could it really be, I asked myself, that it wasn't that he didn't love me enough. Instead, it was because he loved me far more than I could conceive of, and so wanted the very best for me? Was his physical form ignoring me so that I would be forced to go within myself and find his true nature, his infinite, eternal form—the one that he showed to Prakash? It sounded a bit Hollywood. But it was beginning to be the only storyline that was making any sense.

On top of that, if this was true, I thought, then there would have to be some changes in my life. I would have become much more humble and receptive in my attitude for this miraculous transfiguration to occur. It wasn't a comfortable idea. I would have to practice the antithesis of what I'd understood, so far, to be the best way to get on in life. Instead of pushing for what I wanted, I'd have to just quietly wait my turn and put others' needs before my own.

I'd once heard his translator, Professor Sri Anil Kumar, comment that it was ironic that while everyone is fighting to get into the front row, Swami's attention is always on the back one. He told us about a time that Swami gave him a bag of some food, money and clothing and wrote down the name of the devotee he wished to receive it. So Professor Kumar went round all the accommodation blocks, hostels and hotels, looking for this devotee. But he could find no one of that name. That night, Professor Kumar returned to Swami and said:

"I'm sorry, I've failed. I have to return this bag to you. I've searched all day, everywhere, but I've been unable to find your devotee."

And Swami replied:

"Of course you didn't, because you were looking in all the wrong places. Now, I will tell you where he is. Go down the main street, take the first turning on the right and then follow the road

THE LAST DANCE

until you come to a ditch. There, sleeping on a blanket under a tree, you will find my devotee."

This meant, I reasoned with myself, that in order to get under this shower of grace, I was going to have to duck down into quite a lowly, humble position, even a ditch if necessary, metaphorically-speaking. If I stood up, I might miss it.

So this realisation was gradually beginning to take shape as I approached the school. But it was forming in a part of my being with which I was, as yet, unfamiliar. It was generating from the soul, or what is known in the Vedas as the *atma*, and this automatically gave rise to another problem. My ego couldn't identify much of a role for itself in this brave new Divine Plan. So it was fervently pacing, primping and preening, and plotting its last ditch stand. Like Shiva's demon, it had absolutely no desire to make itself so small that it would dissolve into an infinite sea, blissful or otherwise. It just wanted to grab all the beauty and love that was being radiated by this Lord of the Dance and keep it all for itself. So it was planning a sort of double whammy.

"Ha, ha!" it was cackling, like a pantomime villain, rubbing its hands in glee. "Just wait until the sweet little orphans put on the play about Prakash feeling so hurt by Vishnu's behaviour that he refuses to look at him. It will make Sai Baba feel so guilty! Then that will soften him up for the *coup de grace*, the boon, which, now that I've finished reading *Shri Sai Satcharita*, he cannot possibly refuse me!

"He will have no choice but to come up to me. Then, in front of everyone, he will look me lovingly in the eyes, and put one of his hands on my head, the other on my arm and say 'I love you and you are my devotee.' Hah!"

By now, I had reached the door of the school. So I went straight up to the roof where the rehearsal was just getting underway. As usual, half of them were stumbling over their lines. So I thought it was time for a bit of an inspirational speech and I gathered them all together on the stage.

"Listen up!" I said. "You've had two weeks to learn these lines, and you still haven't done it. Tomorrow night, you're going to be putting on this play to a big audience and I'm not going to be up there, on the stage, with you. So it'll all be down to you—and how's it going to look if you're still then stumbling over your lines? How do you think people will then view this school…?"

It was the standard guilt-inducing speech, designed to strike terror in the heart ... and I was just hoping that it had worked when I left later to take my lunch.

It was the first day of the Krishna festival and that afternoon, Swami gave a discourse. The hall was completely full up when I got there. But I managed to find a place to sit on the grass behind the temple. A loudspeaker had been mounted on the temple wall.

As usual, though, it was quite difficult to hear what Swami was saying, what with his usual trick of drowning out the English translation at the vital point in the sentence, and the sound reverberating around. This time, though, after a while, one sentence managed to disentangle itself from the brouhaha and it suddenly came ringing clearly through.

Swami, for some unknown reason, switched from Telegu and in English, shouted:

"I love you and you are my devotee!" and then he immediately resumed his discourse in his native language.

Really? I thought to myself. *But ...surely? He's said it!*

I was amazed that Swami should suddenly shout out the words of part of my requested boon, in English. Convinced that it was a message for me, I practically floated back to my hotel afterwards.

I returned that evening, though, because Swami had arranged an entertainment in the auditorium in honour of Krishna's birthday. It was quite a treat as a group of the famous Kathakali dancers had come from Kerala.

I settled back to watch with anticipation. I was amazed at how surreal they looked with their vivid, mask-like make-up. They were all men. But they wore huge headdresses and voluminous bell skirts as they performed their jerky ritual movements and hand gestures to the sound of drums, cymbals and chanting.

The story they enacted was the one about Krishna and his devotee, Sudama, and as I watched incredulously, the following story unravelled:

> Sudama was a very poor man, but he didn't care because he was such a great devotee of the Lord. However, he and his wife were so hungry, they were on the brink of starvation. So his wife asked him to go and visit his old school friend

THE LAST DANCE

Krishna, who was now a wealthy king, to beg him for some help. However, all his wife could find in the house, to take as an offering, were just a few flattened rice grains. So she put these into a packet and gave it to her husband.

Sudama pocketed the packet, and then he set off. He walked for days until, eventually, he came upon the golden, jewel-encrusted domes of Krishna's grand palace. He felt too shy to enter such a glorious residence. But reminding himself of his family's hunger, he screwed up his courage, and went in.

Sudama wandered around the marble-floored corridors lined with golden statues and crystal fountains, until he found the throne room. He entered, and found Krishna sitting on a golden peacock throne. Then when he saw how beautiful Krishna was, all he could do was to fall on his knees and praise him. And he was far too embarrassed to ask for help of a material nature, or to offer the packet of flattened rice grains. So he hid them in his pocket.

Krishna was so pleased with his dearest devotee that he sat him on the throne. Then he fed Sudama sumptuous delicacies with his own delicate hands, and even fanned him, himself, with his peacock fan. Then Krishna offered him his own silken bed to lie on, to recover from the journey, and he continued to praise his devotee in the highest terms.

However, Krishna knew the secrets of his Sudama's heart, as he does with all true devotees. So while Sudama was sleeping, Krishna quickly snatched the parcel of the rice grains from his pocket. The next day, when Sudama awoke, he didn't check his pockets. So he knew nothing about it. And, after breakfast, the two old school friends affectionately took their leave of one another and Sudama set off on his way home.

But on the way back, he started to feel guilty. He tried to brush it away. But the nearer he got to his home, the more it would come into his mind that he was supposed to have given the rice offering to Krishna, and asked for his help. So he was just beginning to wonder how he would explain to his wife that he had failed in his mission, when he rounded the corner to his house and stopped in amazement. What had been a rude hut was now a glittering palace with fountains and servants running everywhere...

And, dear reader, as I'm sure you've guessed, the story continued suspiciously like the one we were rehearsing over the road!

LORD OF THE DANCE

By now, I was beginning to realise that something was up.

The next morning, I awoke with an uneasy feeling. The euphoria produced by Swami's sudden announcement of the day before was already starting to wear off. I began to wonder if he really had fulfilled part of my boon in his speech, or whether I'd imagined it. So on the way to school, I picked up a transcribed copy of his discourse and read his actual words in context. It went as follows:

> "[In Telegu] You should realise my infinite form. Then there will be no need for me to come to you, in my physical form, and say [in English], 'I love you and you are my devotee!'"

I had just finished reading this when I arrived at the school. So I didn't have time to register its full import. Radha, who was playing Prakash's wife, was waiting at the main door, and she greeted me with a big smile and handed me a note. I opened it to find she'd written, in her lovely childish scrawl, "My dear teacher, I love you so much."

The children would often hand me these little love notes and I always appreciated them. But today, I had other things on my mind, not least the play that we were due to perform that evening with nobody knowing their lines. So I just quickly thanked her and put it in my pocket.

The other children were already on the stage when I arrived on the roof. So we began the dress rehearsal and went straight into the scene where Prakash is leaving for the river Ganges and his wife has to call him back with:

"Prakash! Never mind all that useless chanting to your Lord! Does he care that there is nothing to eat in this house?"

When it came to her line, though, Radha just stood there transfixed, fingering the pocket in her skirt and grinning inanely at me.

I could hear Sukadeva from the wings:

"Psst! 'Prakash! Never mind...' ...psst ..."

Still no sound issued from Radha's lips, and she just continued to stand there, smiling at me.

I exploded.

THE LAST DANCE

"Do you mean to tell me that it's the day of the performance, and you still haven't learned your lines?"

She just continued to smile mutely at me.

"Because," I continued, gradually building up to a crescendo, "if that's the case, let me tell you something! I don't want letters from you saying 'I love you'! I don't want smiles from you! I just want you to learn what I'm trying to teach you! If you really loved me, you'd do that!"

And as those words rang through the air, they bounced off the back of the stage. Then they echoed back to me. As they hit me, so did the sudden realisation, and I found myself murmuring "Oh!" quietly to myself as I finally saw my own lesson that Swami was trying to teach me in all of this.

I felt so humbled, and so awful for having shouted at Radha in that way. I quickly ran up on to the stage and hugged her.

"I'm so sorry," I said. "I'm so sorry. Please forgive me."

Of course, Radha being Radha just sweetly smiled and hugged me back, and the rest of the rehearsal continued without a hitch.

The costumes were looking great. Some of my fellow teachers had worked very hard on them. Despite my best efforts, though, we'd been unable to come up with a Vishnu costume with the four blue arms each holding a discus, conch, mace and lotus. But we'd managed to knock up quite a good cardboard crown for Narayana as Vishnu, and another for Sita as Lakshmi. The scenery, too, which Hari had helped to paint, was going to work just fine.

Little Hari, in fact, had become a whole new person in the preceding few weeks. His face had brightened, he'd become more talkative and lively and he positively relished the opportunity for responsibility with the scenery. Whenever I would appear, he would run up, sit on my feet and wrap his legs around mine. Then he would gradually shuffle up the length of my body until he was sitting on my head. It was an arrangement that suited both of us.

So, finally content that all was going well, I left for lunch and I was quite relaxed that afternoon when I went to see Swami.

It being Krishna's birthday, there were thousands and thousands of devotees in the Prayer Hall—almost as many as there were for Guru Poornima. Even so, by some divine decree, I ended up being placed in the second row from the front. But when Swami came in, I was so busy thinking about some last minute bits and pieces to do with the play that I forgot that I was not supposed to look at him. Anyway, just as I was trying to make up my mind where I should buy some candles for the stage, he came walking along into my line of sight. Then he must have decided to transfer his gaze from where it was, somewhere to my right, to some devotees sitting on my left. So he casually swivelled his eyes and, for less than a nanosecond, they inadvertently grazed over mine. It was enough.

As his eyes briefly touched my own, it was like a laser striking deep into my being. I felt as if I'd been fed, and that all my hunger, on any level, was completely satisfied. Just in that one tiny glance, which didn't even appear to be deliberate, my ego, with all his petty desires and dastardly plots, was immediately burnt to a cinder. I suddenly felt totally fulfilled by him, totally satisfied and wanted nothing more than to be allowed to be just his humble devotee.

Swami carried on in his usual casual, nonchalant way. Then after he'd walked around the men's side, he got into his red BMW and was driven out of the hall to, I was told, a meeting at the university.

As soon as he left, I returned to my hotel room, grabbed the scrap of paper containing my boon request off the dressing table and tore it up into lots of tiny pieces. Then I burnt them and flushed the residue down the loo. Afterwards, I sat on my bed, in utter bliss, and prayed in gratitude for a long time.

An hour or so later, there was a knock on the door. I slowly got up and opened it. It was the boy who usually cleaned my room. He was hopping from one foot to the other.

"Quick, quick!" he said. "Swami's just come back from the university and he's in the hall giving extra *darshan!* All the devotees are there! You must go now!"

"No, that's okay," I replied, softly. "Thanks for letting me know. But I'm always with Swami. I don't have to go and see his physical body."

He looked surprised. So did I. I hadn't realised, until I said it, that that was the truth. But it was.

Later, I had a quiet and thoughtful lunch in the hotel's restaurant. Then I went back to my room and took a long afternoon nap. So I felt quite refreshed, when I woke later, and fairly buoyed up as I set out for the orphanage to help the children get into their costumes and make-up.

As it turned out, they were in no need of such help. They'd been dressed up and made-up and thoroughly hyped up for hours. Narayana was grinning fit to bust under his magnificent crown and Sita looked gorgeous as Lakshmi.

All the children who weren't in the play were in their best whites and already seated where the audience would be, watching some local young men who were helping to set up the sound system and the lighting.

Eventually, it was time, and as the people from the village began to arrive to take their places, they came in to a tape of Swami singing the Gayathri Mantra. So a very special atmosphere was created.

Backstage—in other words, behind a sheet draped over a washing line—the tiny actors and actresses were almost exploding with nerves and excitement. But finally the audience's lights dimmed and a spotlight lit the stage as Devahuti stood and took a deep breath in order to project her voice, and started the narration:

"Once upon a time, there was a certain chap named Prakash. Now, despite the fact that Prakash was a poor man, he was completely, one hundred per cent, devoted to Lord Vishnu. So although there would often be nothing to eat in the house, he wouldn't care a jot about it. He would just continue to spend his whole day chanting *The Thousand Names of God* by the side of the river Ganges. But one morning, just as he was about to leave for the Ganges, his wife came running out after him."

Enter Radha, bang on time, stage left.

"Prakash! Prakash! Never mind all that useless chanting to your Lord! Does he care that there is nothing to eat in this house? The children are crying out for food! So please forget about chanting to your Lord Vishnu! You'd be better off going to the main street and begging for some flour."

She was word perfect! And so the play began.

The audience was rapt, and the rest of the children had great fun picking out their various chums who were now in the guise of characters from ancient Vedic times. A great roar of recognition went up when little Vishnu entered in his enormous golden crown.

Of course, in all good school plays there is always one hilarious moment and ours was no exception. In fact, we had two.

For obvious reasons, we'd been unable to hire any mules. We'd dressed Jaya up as best we could as a mule. So when he came crawling on behind Vishnu, the whole audience cracked up.

I'd also asked a couple of the very young girls to be flower fairy attendants to Vishnu and Lakshmi. I gave them bowls of jasmine petals. However, I'd failed to explain to them the finer points of being a flower fairy. I'd assumed that they would know that they were expected to gently flutter the petals on to Vishnu's and Lakshmi's feet. So there were howls of delighted laughter from the audience when they just proceeded to turn their bowls upside down and dump all the petals, at once, on to Lakshmi's head.

But, despite these comic interludes, the rest of the play went very smoothly. Despite my threats that I wouldn't be backstage to help them, I was. As each child went on, I encouraged them with a good slap on the back and a big smile. I was expecting at least a couple of lines to be fluffed, and that was the optimistic forecast. But I am delighted to report that the children did not forget a single word. So when the play finished, there were rousing cheers and applause from the audience. The children had to take several bows. It was wonderful to see. Their tiny faces were shining and sweating under the lights, and their eyes were also alight and on fire with the feeling of accomplishment.

I rushed up and started hugging them all.

"Well done! It was excellent! Poor Sukadeva was out of a job. You didn't miss a single line."

Then I stood back and watched them, with the greatest of pleasure, get mobbed by their schoolmates. The guests from the village went up to each of them, and shook their hands, shouting "Brilliant!" and "Encore!" The other teachers, like me, stood round the edges of the crowd, and hugged themselves with delight.

But my own feelings of joy at the children's excellent work were tinged with sadness at the thought of leaving the next day. This time, I knew that I was really leaving for good. I tried to

THE LAST DANCE

hide my feelings, so as not to spoil the evening's triumph for the children. But not much would get past Max, and he came over to me.

"I can see you're sad," he said kindly.

"Yes," I replied. "I never expected all this to happen, this visit, and to get so close to the children again."

"There'll always be a place for you here," he replied. "You know that, don't you?"

"Yes, I do," I replied. "But I don't think that I will ever come back again."

"Come every year," said Max. "That's what the other devotees do."

"Hmmm ... I don't think that's Swami's plan for me," I replied.

I had realised, finally, that Swami wasn't interested in having any kind of physical relationship with me. My own play had taught me that lesson, as well as the one that the Kathakali dancers had performed the previous evening. I had been like Prakash's wife, not being able to see any further than grabbing some food for my clamouring children, my desires. But when I'd shouted at poor sweet little Radha, I'd realised the truth of the matter. Swami wanted me to learn the lessons that he was setting for me, and not the ones my ego wanted to learn. Those lessons, too, hadn't changed from when I'd picked up that first book about him in Goa, and thrown it across the veranda. Now I knew that I needed to go back to my life in England and make some drastic changes. I would have to learn to be far more humble, more giving and much less selfish, if Swami was ever going to reveal to me his divine form.

I tried to hide my heavy heart and started to work my way round to all of the children. I gave each one a special hug, and a promise to write as often as I could. It must have taken an hour or so to complete all my goodbyes. Then they all came out to wave me off as I walked for the last time up Samadhi Lane.

There had been a power cut, and the whole village was plunged in darkness. As I walked, I kept looking down to make sure that I didn't stumble into any potholes. So it wasn't until I got to my hotel that I happened to look up. Over the road and through the ashram gates, I could see thousands of devotees leaving the auditorium where they'd been celebrating Krishna's birthday with Swami, and pouring down the drive.

I decided to say one last goodbye to Swami. So I walked through the gates and headed towards his living quarters in the auditorium. My plan was to stand outside, as I had at my arrival, and quietly bid him goodbye.

But as I walked, I began to notice that there was a huge milling crowd of about a hundred small beings, like imps, tripping towards me. They were all chattering and laughing as they danced along. As they got nearer, I began to notice that they all had blue skins. Then I saw that they were all wearing golden crowns and, amazingly, each had four arms in which they held the discus, the conch shell, the mace and the lotus. Then they surrounded me on all sides and suddenly, I was swallowed up in a sea of laughing and dancing Vishnus.

CHAPTER 18
POSTSCRIPT – CHRISTMAS DAY, 2005

As I sit here at my writing desk today, people throughout the Christian world are opening their presents, roasting their birds and toasting in a happy Christmas and another New Year. Not me, though. If there's one thing that I learned from Swami, it's that religious festival days are sacred. In the hurly-burly of my busy life, these are the only times when everything stops. So it's solely on these days that I get the space and time to show my appreciation of my loving Lord. Besides, I have my labour of love to finish, my love letter to Swami. You know how it is when you're so in love? You just want to shout it from the rooftops. So I'm hoping that this book will do that for me.

Seven years later, I look back with vast amusement and awe at what an incredible dance Swami led me on. How gently and sweetly he had played with me, like a lion toying affectionately with one of his precocious cubs. One ill-considered swipe of his paw, and that cub would have been dead. But this Narasimha lion was an avatar of Vishnu, and Vishnu never does anything in an ill-considered way.

At the time, though, as my last day dawned, it was as much as I could do to get out of bed without collapsing into tears. Luckily, it was big, kind Solomon who arrived at the hotel after breakfast to drive me to Chennai. Then, during the nine-hour flight back to England, I had plenty of time to think over the events of the past month and not least, the previous night's experience.

Of course there was a rational explanation for the sea of dancing Vishnus, as there always is for this sort of thing. It turned out that the blue-skinned imps were children from a school in

Southall, West London, which has a large Indian community. They had just come from putting on a play about Vishnu in the auditorium, and their parents had obviously found no difficulty in renting Vishnu costumes, complete with discuses, conch shells, maces and lotuses, from a costume hire shop in Southall high street.

But because there was a rational explanation, I'd come to learn, it didn't necessarily mean that there wasn't also a divine one. They were just two sides of the same coin. For, of course, Swami had to have the last dance, and the last laugh, in the wonderful *rasa lila* that he'd been playing with me.

As I settled more into the flight back home, a stream of realisations began to unfold like a lotus flower. I began to see that I'd been so intent on the part in the play where Prakash turned his face away from his Lord that I hadn't paid much attention to what followed. But now the words began to resound in my head.

> Vishnu lovingly placed his hand on Prakash's head and said:
> "Always remember my form, as you have seen it now. Remembering me always, do your work in the world. My illusion will not touch you."
> And Prakash spent the rest of his days on earth in blissful contemplation upon the true form of Lord Vishnu, the Preserver of the Universe.

As I sat dozing in my seat, I remembered another time that I'd been slipping into sleep and 'someone' had touched me lovingly on the head and then, the next day, on the arm. Then I remembered that Swami had also looked into my eyes and that, shortly before that, he'd shouted in English, during his discourse, "you are my devotee and I love you."

Then I realised with a start that Swami *had* fulfilled my boon—and half of it before I'd even completed my end of the bargain. But, typically, he'd met my ego's desires in such a way as to destroy it. It was then that I began to understand that only Lord Vishnu has that kind of brilliant genius and, by no means least, that amount of love.

When he'd shouted, "I love you and you are my devotee", it was presented in the context of the truth. He was telling me that his form was infinite and would always be with me. If only, he said, I would realise that, then I wouldn't need to hanker any more after his physical form. But because he said that part in Telegu, I'd had to wait until the next day before I could read the full quote. This meant that, for a full twelve hours, my bloated ego had believed that it had got what it wanted. And it had turned out to be the hearty breakfast of the condemned man.

Now that I was nearing the end of my journey, I could see that it had been a success. I had found what I'd been looking for, the path to divine love. But would I now have the courage and the perseverance to walk this narrow path, to reach the final goal? As we began the descent into London's Heathrow airport, the full enormity of what work Swami was expecting of me began to dawn. I knew that merging with his infinite form was going to be plain impossible unless he was going to be holding my hand, metaphorically speaking, every step of the way. It was all very well, I thought, wafting around and having spiritual thoughts when you're in the special atmosphere that he produces at Prasanthi Nilayam. But how would I be back home?

It was true that, during the past year, I had often sensed, and even seen, Swami's spirit form around me. But there had also been times when I'd gone for days and weeks without feeling his presence. So I was wondering, nervously: would an ordinary woman like myself, brought up in and now surrounded again by all the temptations that the Western world has to offer, have enough faith and the strength of her convictions to stick to his teachings?

Would I be able to be more humble and giving? Would I continue to try to see the best in people, instead of the worst? Would I manage to overcome all the fear, envy and jealousy that made my life, and that of others, such a misery? I knew that if I didn't, all the meditation in the world was not going to help me achieve my goal of merging into divine love.

We finally landed and eventually, I arrived home.

That night, Swami came to me in a dream. He was dressed as a *dhobi* washerwoman. I stared at him in disbelief:

"I just went all the way to India to see you, and you totally ignored me!" I chided him "Now I've just got back and you come in a dream!"

"I had to ignore you," replied Swami. "You understand why. You were a child when you first came to me. I cleaned you up as much as I could. But now you are growing up, and you need to start doing this cleaning work for yourself."

Then he gave me a hug.

"Don't worry, my dear," he said. "You'll be fine."

The next morning, it hardly seemed real when I swarmed out of the Tube at Canary Wharf with all the other worker ants, and crossed the road to the glass-and-steel skyscraper building where I worked. In fact, I was still scratching the mosquito bites on my arm when I walked out of the lift and into my office and saw, for the first time, my desk.

Like Prakash, I thought I'd taken a wrong turn. My desk, and the floor surrounding it, was covered in piles and piles of papers. There must have been thousands of documents. Some were in huge, tottering towers; others were strewn all over the floor.

Just then, my boss arrived, looking distraught.

"I'm so sorry," he said as he took off his coat. "I was hoping to get here before you, to tidy it up a bit before you saw it. But while you were away, I was given a very big project to manage and it meant that I needed all these papers. Then, after I'd finished with them, the temp couldn't file them because she wasn't familiar with your filing system. So I'm really sorry that you've had to come back to such a mess!"

I calmly surveyed the leaning towers of papers, and then thought:

Okay, Swami. Let's get this cleaning underway.

But to my boss, I just smiled and said,

"That's perfectly all right," and I picked up the first piece of paper to file it.

Of course, in the past seven years, I haven't always been so sweet and humble and understanding. Sometimes, Swami has had to give me the same lesson several times before I finally got it. I'm still learning—and often learning by my mistakes.

But what of everybody else—all the other players that appeared in Swami's wonderful *rasa lila* in India? What has happened to them?

Well, Swami himself was 80 years old last month and, despite falling and breaking his hip a few years ago, nothing seems to stop him from soldiering on. He says that he's going to stay in his physical body until he's 96.

CHRISTMAS DAY, 2005

Miranda met her soul mate soon after she returned from India, and quickly settled down to a life of rural domestic bliss in a tiny, off-the-beaten-track village in Cornwall. Two years ago, my granddaughter, Laya, arrived. We feel so privileged that such a beautiful soul has been born into our family.

Becky also got married—to an Indian devotee of Swami, in Bradford. I've just received a Christmas card from them both, containing a photo of their lovely two children, a boy and a girl.

I seem to have lost touch with Ted, and Aggie, and the last I heard from Sophia, she was teaching yoga on a Greek island. But the children from the orphanage school have stayed in touch. A few years ago, Max wrote to tell me that Swami's Educational Trust had taken them over. Now they've been moved to a much bigger and smarter set-up on the outskirts of the village with proper classrooms, textbooks, dormitories and playing fields and everything.

Soon after that, I received an email that brought tears to my eyes. It was from Vasudeva.

"Dear Ishtar Madam," it read. "Please accept my humble respects. I hope that you and your family are in very good health. I am very glad to inform you that Murugan and I are now safely back in the orphanage. Sadly, our dear mother has died. But we are very grateful to have been adopted by Max, and now our aim is to attack our studies with gusto, especially English…"

Vasudeva went on to become top in the whole state of Andhra Pradesh in his exams. Now we are all hoping that he will be offered a place at Swami's university to study engineering. Actually, all the children have done well, in their own ways, although I've yet to hear that any of them have been headhunted by Microsoft.

So that just leaves me. Well, I haven't been back to India. Swami came in a dream several years ago, and told me that I should stay in England. Since then, I haven't taken so much as a day trip to Calais. So, unless he lifts that edict, I'm unlikely to see him in that physical form again.

But it's not been too difficult to remain celibate, as "Nothing Compares"—or should I say, no-one compares—to the Lover that I'm expecting any day now. I live very quietly, at the back of a big, old rambling house that sits among the oak trees in an out-of-the-way part of town. Only the birds know that I'm here, and their melodic chirruping is a reflection of the song of rejoicing that plays constantly in my heart.

The other day, I came across this. It's from a Gnostic text called *Exegesis on the Soul*:

> Her Father promised to send from Heaven his firstborn son, her brother, to be her bridegroom. So she gave up whoring and washed off the foul odours of her former abusers. She prepared herself in the bridal chamber, filling it with sweet perfume, and waited for her true husband. She no longer frequented the marketplace, having liaisons with whomever she fancied. She waited only for him, anxiously asking, "When will he come?"
>
> Sometimes she felt a little frightened because, since she had left her Father's house, she couldn't remember how her brother looked. Yet, like any woman in love, she even dreamt about her lover at night.
>
> Then one day, at last, the wait was over. Her bridegroom came to take her as his bride, just as her Father had said he would.
>
> Gradually she recognised her bridegroom, which filled her with happiness. She wept and wept when she remembered her former life. She made every effort to make herself beautiful, so that he would be pleased to stay with her. She knew that she must forget all her false lovers and devote herself to her true king.
>
> Their marriage was not an earthly type in which, after sexual relations, the man and woman behave as if some irritating burden has been relieved and turn over without looking at each other. In this marriage, the two united share a single life.
>
> And so they both enjoyed each other. And when they made love, she received his seed and bore good children.

So I don't know when He will come, as only He holds Time in his hands. It may be in a week or so, or a month from now. It may even be a year or a decade away. Or He may not come until I'm old and toothless, or possibly even on my deathbed. But I know that one day, my Redeemer, my Lord of the Dance, my true husband will draw up at my door in his shiny red BMW. And so I continue to prepare our bridal chamber.

The End

ADDENDUM

As this is the third edition of "Lord of the Dance", I thought it might be a good idea to bring us up to date, as so much has happened since first publishing it.

But at the beginning of the book, there is a dedication, which is taken from a Bengali hymn addressed to Shiva, and it goes as follows:

*Because You love the Burning-ground,
I have made a Burning-ground of my heart.
Day and night blazes the funeral pyre
That You, Dark One, hunter of the Burning-ground,
May Dance Your eternal Dance.*

I have lived this poem the last ten years — but now the fire in my heart has also entered my head.

'Fire in the head' is a term first used by WB Yeats in "The Song of the Wandering Aengus" to characterise the visionary experience of the shaman.

I should have realised that Swami, all those years ago now, put me on the bench with those dear ladies for a good reason - because he wanted me to become a shaman.

I didn't dwell on this aspect too much in that part of the book, because I didn't understand its relevance at the time. But remember the Miss World of Reiki Masters? These veritable ladies were gradually replaced by a Miss World of Shamans. Many of them were from Mesoamerica and were part of the tradition of the nagual, Don Juan, the shaman that was written about by Carlos Castaneda.

But all this is just a long preamble to what I really wanted to tell you – that my work these days is based in the shamanic. I explore with those who have an interest about the mystic

CHRISTMAS DAY, 2005

understanding of our ancestors — the vastness of which is gradually being revealed by work in the fields of archaeology, mythology and anthropology. I work to help uncover the truth about our past, which has been hidden for so long.

We are gradually rediscovering the old shaman trails that existed worldwide during the upper Palaeolithic and Neolithic eras, and coming to understand how much those researching in the new sciences today could learn from what our ancestors knew then about the universe and its workings.

If you think you might find all that of interest too, you'd be welcome to join us. We have our own website and forum called Ishtar's Gate and its address is: http://www.ishtarsgate.com/.

Until then ...

May the road rise up to meet you.
May the wind be always at your back.
May the sun shine warm upon your face;
The rains fall soft upon your fields and until we meet again,
May the Lord lead you gently in the Dance.

Ishtar, 2009

LaVergne, TN USA
31 August 2010
195247LV00001B/284/P